AF513565

VIMARSH

New Frontiers in Public Debate

VIMARSH

New Frontiers in Public Debate

Edited by

C D Sahay

Vivekananda International Foundation
New Delhi

PENTAGON PRESS LLP

VIMARSH: **New Frontiers in Public Debate**

Edited by: C D Sahay

ISBN 978-81-944659-7-3

First Published in 2020

Copyright © Vivekananda International Foundation, New Delhi

All rights reserved. No part of this publication may be reproduced, stored in a retrieval system, or transmitted in any form or by any means, electronic, mechanical, photocopying, recording or otherwise, without the prior written permission of the Publisher.

Disclaimer: The views and opinions expressed in the book are the individual assertion of the Author. The Publisher does not take any responsibility for the same in any manner whatsoever. The same shall solely be the responsibility of the Author.

Published by
PENTAGON PRESS LLP
206, Peacock Lane, Shahpur Jat,
New Delhi-110049
Phones: 011-64706243, 26491568
Telefax: 011-26490600
email: rajan@pentagonpress.in
website: www.pentagonpress.in

Printed at Aegean Offset Printers, Greater Noida, U.P.

CONTENTS

FOREWORD

I am happy to present to the readers Vivekananda International Foundation's latest publication Vimarsh: New frontiers in public debate edited by Sh CD Sahay. The book is a collection of 15 essays based on the lectures delivered by eminent personalities at the VIF in the last ten years.

In India, the discourse of national regional and global issues is often reactive and guided by western concepts, ideas and thinking. The Vivekananda International Foundation (VIF) was set up in 2009 to promote and project Indian nationalist and civilisational perspective in the strategic domains.

The VIF promotes dialogues to seek and establish harmony in diversity. Since its inception, the VIF set up a public forum titled 'Vimarsh' to encourage debates on issues of national importance. Over one hundred Vimarsh lectures, delivered by eminent scholars, experts, thinkers and practitioners of public policy have been held in the last ten years. The subjects cover a wide variety of topics ranging from the study of ancient India to affordable health care and failures, lapses and opportunities in Jammu and Kashmir. A wide variety of thought-provoking ideas and concepts have been put forward in Vimarsh discussions.

It was felt that during the 10th year of VIF's establishment, it may be worthwhile to select some of these talks and collate them in the form of a book which would not only record the evolution of the VIF but also give an indication on how the public debates on important issues have moved over the years.

Sh. CD Sahay, a Distinguished Fellow at the VIF, who has been associated with the institution almost since the beginning, readily agreed to undertake the responsibility of editing a volume on selected Vimarsh talks. As he notes in his preface, the problem was not what to include in the volume but what to exclude because of the constraint of space. Eventually, 15 talks on four key themes, namely, civilization, governance, national security and international relations were selected. The editor had to go through vast material including audio recordings for selecting the 15 essays. It is hoped that the readers will get a flavour of which discussions that have been held in the Vimarsh forum in the last few years. We will be happy to receive feedback from our readers.

New Delhi
December, 2019

Dr. Arvind Gupta
Director, VIF.

*

EDITOR'S NOTE

It is now widely recognised that the two most important functions of any Think-Tank are to create public awareness and to generate informed public debate on issues of critical importance. In a paper authored in 2016 by Pawel Swieboda, Dy. Head, European Political Strategy Centre of the European Union, defined the role of a think-tank as, "play a fundamental role in shaping policy agendas. They mobilise expertise and put forward evidence. They push for innovative changes and they build networks and communities through which they nurture and spread ideas and catalyse action."[1] He went on to suggest, "Finally, on the way to 2030, in an increasingly networked society, think tanks must provide a space between governments, research and academia, and, increasingly, civil society and media, within which ideas can be tested, strategies can be debated, and action for the future can be designed".[2]

Many experts have expressed similar views on the critical role that think tanks must play in today's networked societies, to raise the level of public discourse on an entire gamut of issues that impact efforts towards nation building.

Vivekananda International Foundation (VIF), in its vision statement, also highlights this, and I quote, "It strives to bring together the best minds in India to ideate on key national and international issues; promote initiatives that further the cause of peace and global harmony; monitor social, economic and political trends that have a bearing on India's unity and integrity; analyse the causes for social and ethnic conflicts leading to extremism and offer policy alternatives....".[3]

An important instrument at the VIF for achieving the objective, particularly in the area of generating public awareness and by debating issues of critical national import, has been its monthly public forum debates titled *'VIMARSH'*. In fact, even before the VIF was formally launched, its public outreach programme through *VIMARSH*, had commenced, attracting enthusiastic popular response. It may surprise many that this important forum was initiated even before our headquarter building became fully operational!

As VIF celebrates the completion of ten glorious years of existence this year, we take special pride in bringing out this publication, *VIMARSH-New Frontiers in Public Debate*, putting together a collection of 15 selected issues that were discussed and debated at *VIMARSH* over the years.

As Editor of this exercise, I must admit that it was a challenging assignment to cull out a representative set of discussions from a library containing nearly 100 recorded events under *VIMARSH*, each one of them covering issues of national and international significance. Understandably, the toughest part of the exercise was not what to include but rather, what to exclude.

So we decided to work on thematic parameters to ensure coverage on subjects under four main themes namely; Civilizational issues, Governance, National Security and International Relations. While short listing events under these four heads, we also tried to spread the evolving perceptions over the years to give our readers an idea of how the discourse under *VIMARSH* was gradually covering a growing range of issues.

Keeping these in view, we started our efforts with getting the audio recordings of nearly fifty lectures converted into transcripts. These were then subjected to editing and re-editing to convert the discussions into articles for publication, taking care to ensure that the essential messages of the speakers were not lost. And then, obtaining concurrences of the speakers was not an easy task; in fact very few of them eventually responded. Since all this had to be done within the timelines set for the publication, we had to do without this and as Editor of the project, I owe an apology to the speakers for any inadvertent omissions.

At the end of all this, I am happy to present to the readers, a compilation of articles dealing with three exciting aspects of our civilisational history; the mystery of the Saraswati River; Myth and Reality of Ancient Indian History and the Contemporary Relevance of the thoughts of Swami Vivekananda.

The selection of issues for inclusion in the subsequent chapters also presented a problem of plenty. On each of the subjects of Governance, National Security, and the fast evolving regional and international diplomacy, we had the benefit of a large number of highly placed, well-informed practitioners presenting their perspectives on a range of issues covering different aspects of the challenges faced by policy makers in critical areas of ensuring good governance, water management, dealing with economic slowdown, providing healthcare to all, and need for legal and constitutional reforms.

Similarly, on issues relating to National Security, on account of space-constraint, we could include only three representative items on Kashmir, Left Wing Extremism and Indianising Defence Technologies. In the field of diplomacy and international relations too, we had to settle for only three articles dealing with Climate Change debate, Rise of Islamism and economic transitions in China and the US with their implications for India.

I am conscious of the fact that non-inclusion in this publication of a vast number of important issues that were discussed at over eighty plus sessions of *VIMARSH,* is a major deficiency. Depending on your response, we might soon repeat the exercise by enlarging the canvass of coverage by including in our next issue, some more selected items from our archives and some new events that happen in the coming months.

Before concluding, for this initial effort, I would like to thank members of the VIF Editorial Committee, the administrative setup and the group of transcription professionals for their guidance and overall assistance, without which it would not have been possible to bring out this publication.

New Delhi
December, 2019

C D Sahay
Distinguished Fellow, VIF

*

NOTES

1 *A think piece for the ESPAS 2016 conference by* Pawe³ Œwieboda *(@pswieboda), Deputy Head, European Political Strategy Centre, European Commission*

2 Ibid

3 https://www.vifindia.org/AboutUs1

ABOUT THE CONTRIBUTORS

Prof Michel Danino is an Indian author, originally from France. He is a guest professor at IIT Gandhinagar and has been a member of the Indian Council of Historical Research. Danino has been a major proponent of the Indigenous Aryans hypothesis. On 25 January 2017, the Government of India conferred on him Padma Shri, the fourth highest civilian honor of the country, for his contribution towards Literature and Education.

Dr Dilip K. Chakrabarti is Emeritus Professor of South Asian Archaeology at Cambridge University and Dean, Centre for Historical and Civilizational Studies, VIF. He has a large number of research books and articles to his credit. He was elected member of the Executive Committee of World Archaeological Congress representing South Asia (1986-94) and also Academic Programme Co-ordinator and Treasurer of World Archaeological Congress-3 (1990-94). He is a Senior Fellow at Vivekananda International Foundation.

Ku. Nivedita Raghunath Bhide is the current Vice President of Vivekananda Kendra, Kanyakumari. She has extensively worked on the life and teachings of Swami Vivekananda and has also been engaged in social work for many years. For her contribution to the social work, she has been awarded with the fourth highest civilian award of India, Padma Shri.

Dr Mahesh N. Buch was an Indian civil servant. In 1957, he joined the Indian Administrative Service in the Madhya Pradesh cadre. He was a great urban planner, considered by many as the architect of Modern Bhopal. He held several government positions of authority during his civil service such as the post of the District Collector, District Magistrate, Director, Principal Secretary and the Commissioner of various important departments such as Tribal Welfare, Housing, Forests and Town country planning. The Government of India honored him with the third highest civilian award, Padma Bhushan in 2011 for his meritorious services to the nation. He passed away on 06 June 2015 in Bhopal.

Shri Soli Jehangir Sorabjee is an eminent jurist and former Attorney General of India. He has defended freedom of press in many landmark cases in the Supreme Court of India and has been instrumental in revoking censorship orders and bans on publications. He has also held several offices in organizations of national and international repute, including the Chairmanship of the UN-Sub Commission on the Promotion and Protection of Human Rights from 1998 to 2004 and Membership to the Permanent Court of Arbitration at The Hague from 2000 to 2006. He was honored with the Padma Vibhushan award in March 2002 for his defense of freedom of speech and the protection of human rights.

Dr Bibek Debroy is an Indian economist and author. Debroy has made significant contributions to game theory, economic theory, income and social inequalities, poverty, law reforms, railway reforms and Indology, among others. He is currently serving as the Chairman of the Economic Advisory Council to the Prime Minister.

Shri Suresh Prabhu is an Indian politician and India's Sherpa to the G20. He was formerly a Minister of Civil Aviation, Commerce and Industry, and Railways in the previous NDA government. He is constantly featured in the list of top five ministers in India from 2014 to 2017 in terms of both performance and accessibility in nation-wide surveys conducted by various institutions.

Dr Devi Prasad Shetty is the Founder, Chairman and Executive Director of Narayana Health, a chain of 45 hospitals across India. He is a cardiac surgeon with around 34 years of experience. He initiated the concept of "micro health insurance scheme" in Karnataka, which eventually led to the Karnataka government implementing the Yeshasvini Scheme, a micro health insurance scheme for rural farmers. He has a number of awards and honours to his credit including "Padma Shri" and "Padma Bhushan", conferred by the President of India.

Shri Vishwaranjan, I.P.S. (Retd), a Chhattisgarh cadre IPS, had served in various capacities in the state before he joined the Intelligence Bureau on deputation in 1986. He was Additional Director in the Intelligence Bureau (IB) when he returned to the state as Director General of Police in 2007, an appointment he held till July 2011. As DGP of Chhattisgarh, he led many successful operations against the Left-wing extremists. He is best remembered for successfully cracking down on the Maoists' urban networks.

Dr Vijay Kumar Saraswat stands out as one of India's most gifted scientists, who has more than four decades of experience spanning over several fields and areas in both basic and applied sciences of defence research. Dr Saraswat formerly served as the Director General of the Defence Research and Development Organisation (DRDO) and the Chief Scientific Advisor to the Indian Minister of Defence. Among his other achievements and laurels, he is regarded as the principal architect of India's Ballistic Missile Defence Programme, which included major technology breakthroughs. He is the recipient of many national and international awards, including Padma Bhushan (2013) and Padma Shri (1998). Dr Saraswat is presently the Member NITI Aayog and shouldering many honorary positions in the Government and academic institutions.

Dr Sudhir S. Bloeria began his career in the Indian Army and served with distinction in the J&K Rifles. With experience ranging from NEFA in the East, to Fazilka in the West, Dr. Bloeria saw active service during the 1971 war. Soon after the war, Dr. Bloreria decided to exchange military service with civil service. He was inducted into the Indian Administrative Service in 1972. He held various appointments in the erstwhile state of Jammu and Kashmir, including the post of Chief Secretary. In 2011, he was appointed as the founder Vice Chancellor of the Central University of Jammu for a period of 3 years. He has written extensively on matters related to national security, including the publication of four books.

Ambassador Shyam Saran joined the Indian Foreign Service in 1970 and rose to become the Foreign Secretary to the Government of India. In 2006, Ambassador Saran was appointed as the Prime Minister's Special Envoy for Indo–US civil nuclear issues and later as Special Envoy and Chief Negotiator on Climate Change. In 2011, Saran was awarded the third highest civilian award, Padma Bhushan, by the President of India for his contribution to Civil Services. He speaks and writes regularly on foreign policy, climate change, energy security, and national and international security–related issues.

Ambassador Prabhat P. Shukla I.F.S. (Retd), joined the Indian Foreign Service in 1974. During a career spanning 37 years, he served in Moscow, Brussels, London and Kathmandu, among other places. He served in Delhi twice, including as the Diplomatic Adviser to the Prime Minister from 1996 to 2000. He retired in 2011 as Ambassador of India to Moscow and has settled in New Delhi. He is currently Distinguished Fellow in the Vivekananda International Foundation, New Delhi.

Shri R N Ravi is a 1976 batch IPS officer from Kerala cadre, who retired from service as the Special Director of the Intelligence Bureau in 2012. For his expertise in the north-east affairs, he was appointed as the chairman of Joint Intelligence Committee (JIC), as the interlocutor between the Central government and the Naga armed groups, in August 2014. He is presently serving as the Governor of Nagaland.

Mr Tarek Fatah is a Canada-based author, journalist, broadcaster and liberal activist of Pakistani origin, who appears regularly on TV shows, and speaks freely on issues related to human rights in Islam, Pakistan, among other relevant subjects. He is author of two award-winning books, 'The Tragic Illusion of an Islamic State' and 'The Jew is Not My Enemy'. He is also the founder of the Muslim Canadian Congress, an organization for liberal and secular Muslims who believe in the separation of religion and state and gender equality within Islam. He is recipient of a number of awards and honours including Queen Elizabeth's Golden Jubilee Medal.

*

I. Civilisation

1

SARASWATI: THE LOST RIVER

Prof Michel Danino

I am very happy to be here again, in a slightly better physical environment than what it was nearly two years ago when I was here last. It is a pleasure to see how this institution has been growing with lots of energies working on different fronts.

I think one reason why Indians are always fascinated with their ancient past, something which I am going to talk about today, is because it strikes a deep chord inside. It has lot to do with issues of identity; issues of origin that are debated in the current context in many ways and ultimately issues of what is India, what defines India? Very often, when we try to define India, we have to go back into the past and try to get hold of certain strong anchorage. What I am going to talk about now is something on the same lines. It is part of that great story about what India is; what defines its civilization, how did it evolve, how did it grow, how did it decay at times? And in this, the Saraswati River has its place, and has a very central role to play.

The Saraswati River initially presented itself as a sort of riddle, a mystery for the Indologists of the 19th century. The story was almost of an addictive kind, if I may say so. There was a riddle about it in the *Rig Veda*, which was initially translated into European languages in the 1830s and 1840s; before that, no one knew what this mysterious compilation consisted of.

The Rig Veda describes a certain physical environment, mostly through the rivers; there is not much geographical data for the regions like mountains, just a few stray references. But what is centrally important is the rivers, and for obvious reasons, rivers are the life givers. Without rivers you cannot have a civilization at all.

The broad geography was pretty clear, because the Rig Veda speaks of the *Sapta Sindhavah* (seven rivers). That was fairly obviously the Indus River (*Sindhu*) and its tributaries and, in addition, one river known as the Saraswati, which is in fact the river most highly praised in the Rig Veda. It is more highly praised than the Indus or any other. And the biggest enigma was that whereas the other rivers mentioned, like the Indus and so on, were still on the map, Saraswati was nowhere on the map. So, what did happen to that river, which was praised as a river of mighty waters flowing from the mountains to the sea – '*Giribyat a Samudrat*' – and flowing, with an impetuous flow unbroken? It was also not just a river; it was a goddess; it was a mother. In fact, there is a *sloka* that says, "best of rivers, best of mothers, best of goddesses."

So, there is some peculiar phenomenon that this deified river was actually non-existent when we looked at it. And there was one important element of physical precision that is quite rare in the Rig Veda. Rig Veda is not much concerned about geography; all this information is "just by the way". Rig Veda is concerned with something else which, as you know, is "building bridges with the Gods" and getting those divine powers to come down and to be incarnated in our lives and so on.

There is, however, one hymn in the 10th and last Mandala of the Rig Veda, which is the "*Nadistuti Sukta*". This hymn is in praise of the rivers. If you look at the total hymn, you have more than 30 rivers listed.

But the core part is a hymn that highlights the rivers from east to west, and beginning with Ganga, Ganga, Yamuna, Saraswati, Shutudri, which is the Sutlej, we have the proper etymological connections and it continues with the Ravi, Chenab, Jhelum, and so on. In fact, it goes on to the Indus and Afghan tributaries of the Indus.

If you put this on the map, what you get is, in the order of mention in this hymn, Ganga, Yamuna, and Saraswati; exactly why do I place the Saraswati here, you will know in a moment and it continues. So, you can see that the poet or *rishi* who composed this hymn had this entire map of the northwest of the subcontinent in his mind, and in just two mantras, he correctly listed all the rivers right up to the Afghan tributaries of the Indus. That itself is quite a feat, but then, it again poses the question of where is this Saraswati?

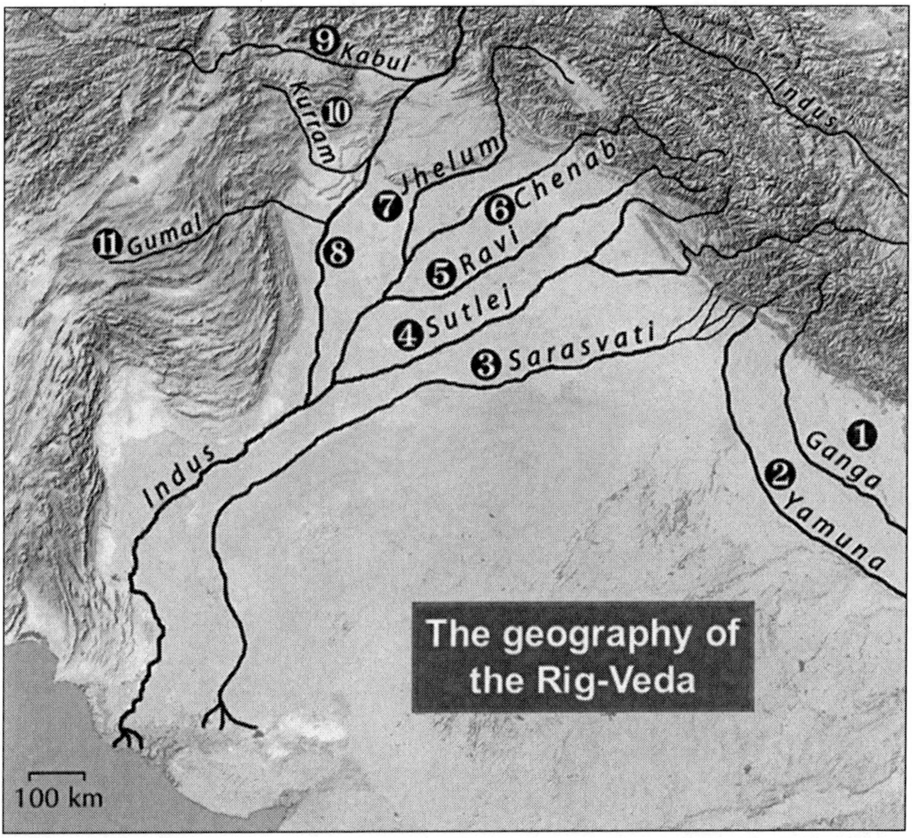

The Geography of the Rig-Veda

The 19th-century Indologists initially did not have such a map with them. What they had was a series of topographic and geographic surveys made by the British in the first half of the 19th century. The British, for all their faults, were great documenters. Devendra Swaroopji would know better than anyone else as to how they scrupulously amassed documents in all areas of Indian life. In the early 19th century, there was a strategic angle to it that they were targeting both Punjab and Sindh that they had not yet conquered.

Maharaja Ranjit Singh was opposing their passage through Punjab to conquer Sindh, and they were looking for a direct route from Delhi to Sindh. They sent some of their topographers and surveyors and found a very convenient route consisting of a huge dry bed of a river, which was locally known as the Ghaggar. Its extension into what is today Pakistan is known as the Hakra River or Hakror. So very often we refer to it as the Ghaggar-Hakra River.

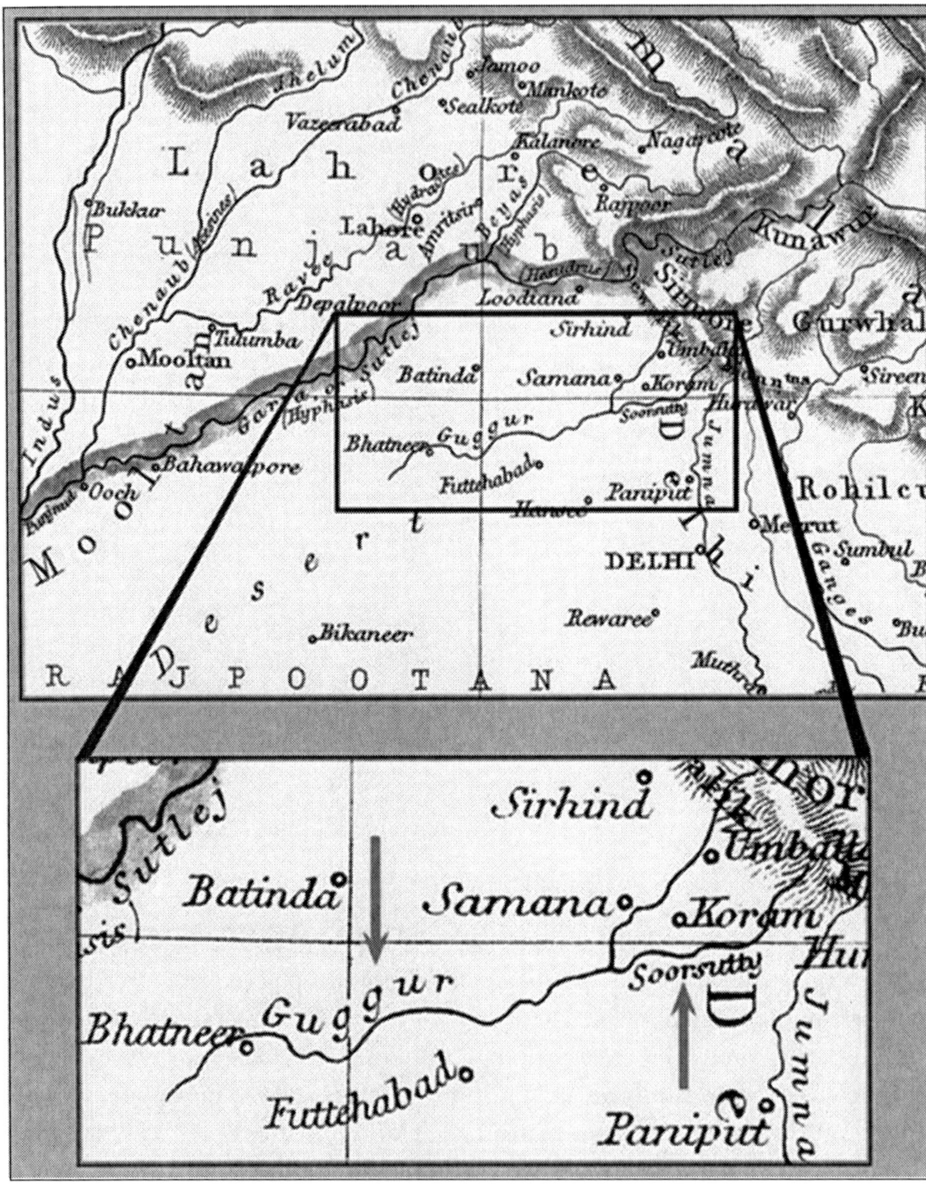

A 1862 British map showing the Sarsuti and the Ghaggar

They found that this huge bed going from Haryana into what is today Indian Punjab and then northern Rajasthan was a very convenient route into Sindh and they therefore documented it. There they found three main features:

- There were lots of ruined sites, settlements, even perhaps cities, all along this bed. This fact was noted from 1820s or so, and in fact the local population had a lot of folklore traditions, songs, regarding what these ruins were;

- The tradition was that a great river was flowing in this dry bed. In fact, the Ghagguar-Hakra was still a seasonal river in the 19th century. During good monsoons, some water would always be carried to what is today the International Border. Tradition has it that this river somehow disappeared and that caused total desolation and destruction of this region. They also took careful note of this local tradition;
- The third thing they noticed was that at the top of this basin, in the upper reaches, as a tributary of the Ghaggar, there was, in what is today's Haryana, a small stream called Sarswati, as addressed in Hindi by the local people. Sarswati was obviously a corruption of Saraswati.

These facts were noted, published and the very first person who put one plus one together was (this I discovered in the course of my researches) a French geographer who, in 1855, published a book, a big volume in fact, called, in English I translate, "*The Geography of North-West India According to the Rig Vedic Hymns*. He was interested in what the Rig Veda had to say about the geography of North West India.

This geographer, Louis Vivien de Saint-Martin, who was one of the most eminent geographers of the 19th century, spent some time and, in the process, encountered the Saraswati riddle. He said that Ghaggar-Hakra River had to be the Vedic Saraswati. He maintained that the Saraswati River was there and Ghaggar-Hakra was the only river located between the Yamuna and the Sutlej, as the Rig Veda was pointing out.

He said the trace of the river bed was recently found; here recently means that it was a reference to the work of the British topographers. This discovery confirmed the correctness of the tradition, the local tradition, that there had been a mighty river there. From that point onward, we get a lot of studies, especially by British officials who were working sometimes with the British Army or with some other department of the empire. They took interest in this question. There are lots of papers and I am not going into the details; C F Oldham is one of them, confirming the thesis of Vivien de Saint-Martin saying that this has to be the only possible solution to this mystery of the vanishing river as you might call it.

Then you begin to find maps published in British documents – you see the area which corresponds roughly to Haryana and Indian Punjab and northern

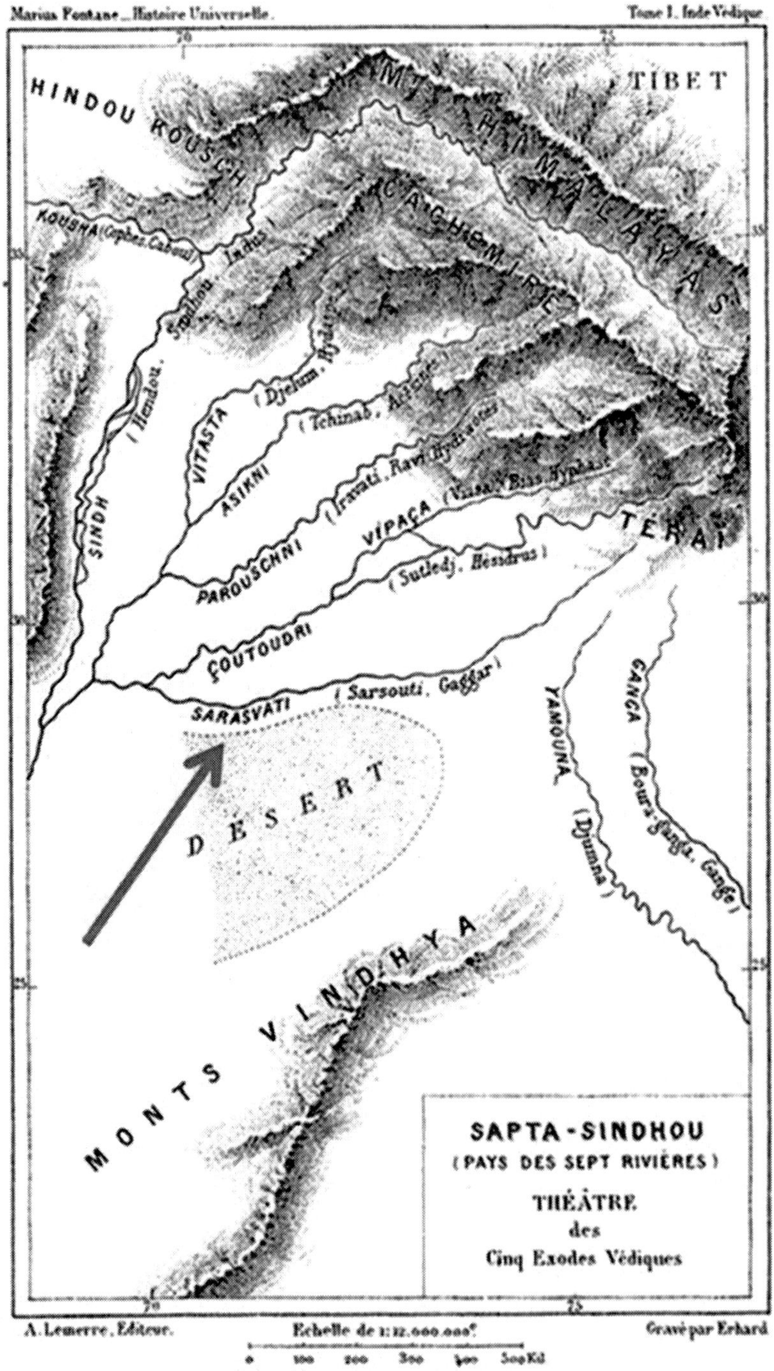

An 1881 map (from a French book) identifies the Sarasvati with the Ghaggar

Rajasthan *(refer to 1862 map. This area is spelt as Sarsuti and this is the Ghaggar River)*. But near it is a place called Hanumangarh. It is in northern Rajasthan, what was previously the Bikaner state.

Then we have more maps. For example, there is one by Alexander Cunningham, who was the founder of the Archaeological Survey of India (ASI), a man of prodigious energy who criss-crossed many parts of India, often on horseback, and who documented all the sites, monuments, heritage sites that needed to be urgently preserved. Whatever his biases, prejudices, we owe a lot to him as some Indian monuments could be saved through his action. He was also fascinated by the problem of ancient Indian geography. His book, which I think

A. Cunningham's map (detail) showing the Sarasvati (1870s)

is called *Ancient Indian Geography*, is still in print. He wanted to know how to match the ancient science mentioned in the ancient literatures like Mahabharata, Ramayana, the Buddhist texts. How do we spot them on the map? This was a virgin field in those days – nobody, hardly anybody, had researched that. He gave a lot of maps. I just want to point out that he also writes Saraswati, quite correctly, as flowing into the Ghaggar and beyond. So, this was based very largely on the work of this French geographer.

- Topographic surveys of the Thar Desert by Lt. Colonel James the region's Tod (1820s), Major Colvin (1833), Major Mackeson (1844):
  1. a wide dry bed called 'Ghaggar' dotted with ancient ruins;
  2. a local tradition that the drying up of the river caused desolation;
  3. a seasonal river called 'Sarsuti' as a tributary to the Ghaggar.
- Louis Vivien de Saint-Martin, 1855: 'The trace of the ancient riverbed was recently found, still quite recognizable, and was followed far to the west. [This discovery] confirmed the correctness of the tradition.'
- C.F. Oldham, 1893: 'Although the river below the confluence [with the Ghaggar] is marked in our maps as Gaggar, it was formerly the Saraswati; that name is still known amongst the people.'

In fact, this is from a French book of 1881, which is simply a kind of summary of what was known in those days about Vedic India. Here you find very clearly, perhaps for the first time, Saraswati, totally associated, identified with the Ghaggar River. You can see Ganga, Yamuna, Saraswati, Shrutidhuri (*he has put this with a French spelling*), Parasuni, Asikni and so on. This is exactly a pictorial representation of the "Nadistuti Sukta". I should add as a side remark that Ganga in the Rig Veda is a totally insignificant river; it has no importance whatsoever. It is mentioned twice, once in this hymn, and otherwise, it does not exist. The Gangetic geography is not part of the Rig Vedic horizon at all. So Ganga has no importance and among all the rivers, as I said, only Saraswati becomes a goddess.

C F Oldham, about whom I have briefly mentioned earlier, produced some wonderful papers on not only where the Saraswati was, but also why did it disappear. He began to enquire into the causes of the disappearance and was one of the first who put forth the theory that it must have been fed (*referring to the map*) and you see here Saraswati and Ghaggar again. It must have been fed by waters flowing from the Sutlej; near Rupar, the Sutlej has a kind of U-turn bend; you see a hairpin bend. He said that the Sutlej must have been flowing directly (and these are the palaeo-channels you see) into the Ghaggar system. Similarly, through the Chautang River – Chautang or Chitrang – the Yamuna must have been also feeding part of its waters to the Saraswati.

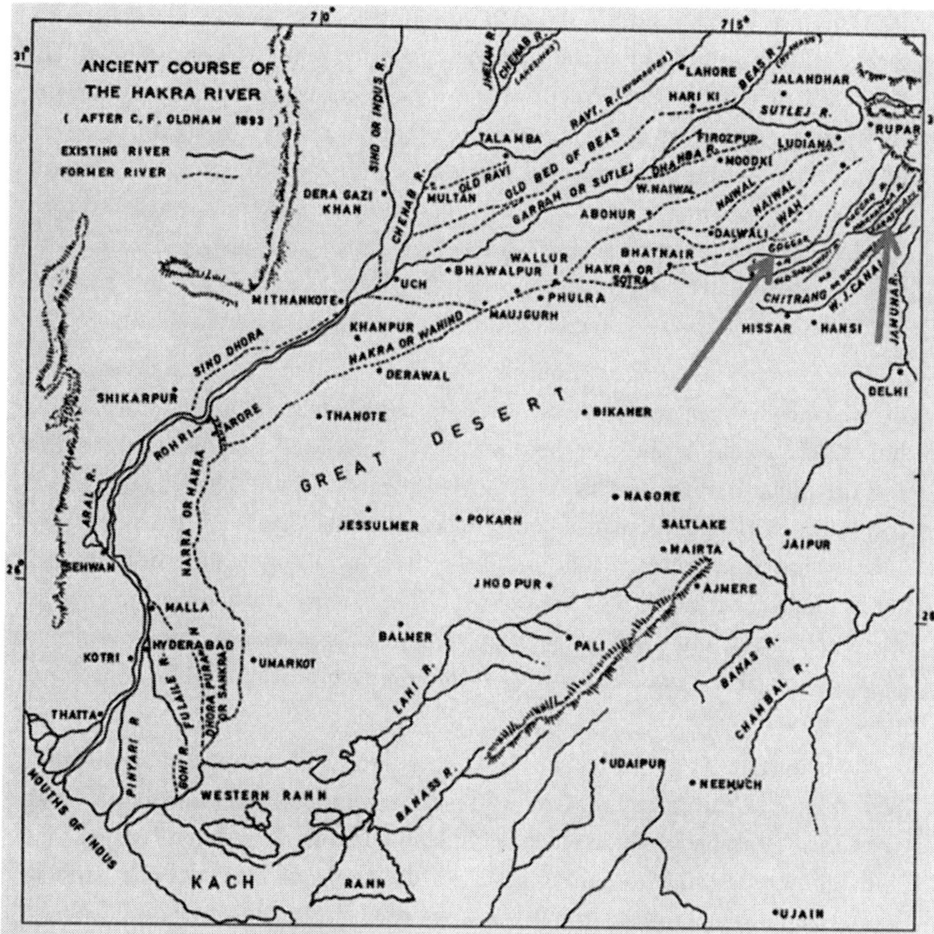

C.F. Oldham's map of the Sarasvati (1883)

So, this is how Oldham explained in the 19th century that the Saraswati had such mighty waters that later disappeared because, through some reason, the waters of the Sutlej and the Yamuna were driven away. The present theory is that there must have been a tectonic uplift of this whole watershed region between Yamuna and Sutlej, which, as most of you would know, is extremely flat. So any small change in the elevation of this would lead to changes in the flow of rivers. The assumption is that some event took place, perhaps a major earthquake, which uplifted this region between the two and by just a few meters of upliftment, the waters of the Yamuna were repelled eastward and those of the Sutlej pushed westward.

This is at least the simple and brief current thinking. So, in the 20th century, the same location and explanation is widely accepted in the Indological world. In fact, barring one or two exceptions, we have complete unanimity among Indologists, even the most conservative ones that this must be where the Saraswati flowed. This is from Rihanu, who was a very eminent Vedic scholar, a French Vedic expert, who had no doubt whatsoever that this was the Saraswati. And then this Chautang River became, and which I mentioned previously, identified with the Dhrishadvati River, which is one of the rivers listed in the Rig Veda and usually in association with the Saraswati. So, it must have been a tributary.

In the later literature, for example, in the *Manu Smriti*, we find descriptions of the land between the Saraswati and the Dhrishadvati. It is described as the holiest land. And it is said that those who lived there, lived as if in heaven. So, this was the strength of the tradition up to Manu Smriti. I should have added that it is not just the Rig Veda that of course talks about the Saraswati; we have a very interesting and consistent evolution of the river, including its progressive drying up in the later literature. For example, the *Brahmanas*, which are commentaries on the Vedas, describe the Saraswati as disappearing at a certain point and that point is named as *Vinashana or Adarshana*; it is a point where the river becomes invisible.

We don't know how, after the Rig Veda and the Mahabharata, there are more texts that very clearly locate the Saraswati in the same region and make the Saraswati cross the Kurukshetra region – for example, the last battle between Duryodhana and Bhima was explicitly taking place on the banks of the Saraswati River in Kurukshetra. Mahabharata knows nothing of the later traditions like the *Triveni Sangam* that is the confluence of the Ganga, Yamuna and Saraswati, at Prayag, which is a Puranic tradition. It does not exist either in the Vedas or even in the Mahabharata.

Then we have more technical researches starting in the 1960s, because a lot of questions were still unanswered. Herbert Wilhelmy, a great German geographer and a very eminent scholar, spent a lot of time studying the problem of the Saraswati and all the stages of its desiccation. One of his many maps is actually the first stage of Vedic time where you can see the Sutlej, instead of flowing as it does today into the Beas, is actually flowing into what he calls "Veda-Sutlej", or into the Ghaggar system. Similarly, Yamuna, instead of flowing into what is today its bed, is actually going into the same, and that is what feeds the Saraswati or the Ghaggar River.

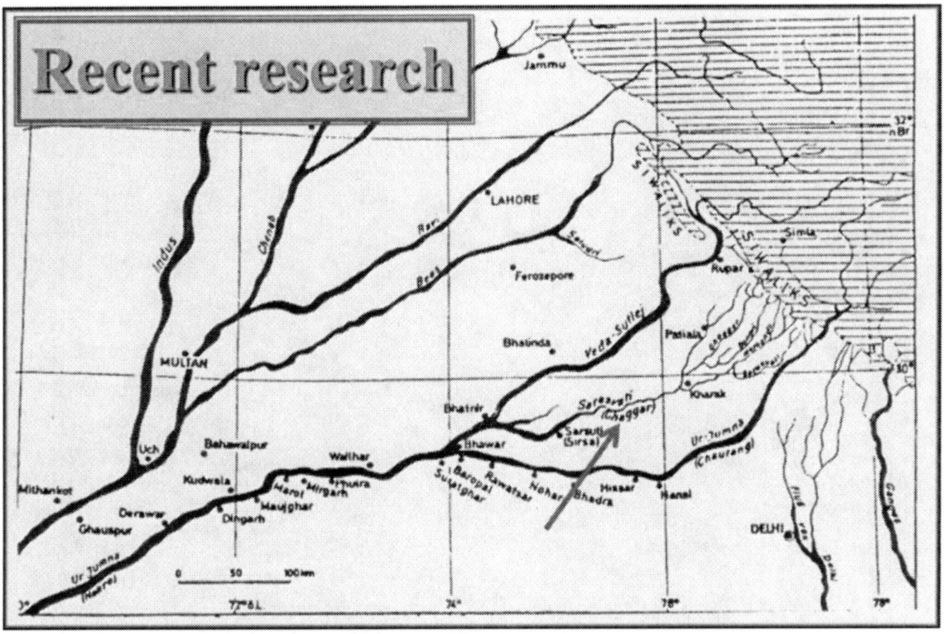

The Sarasvati basin according to Wilhelmy (1969)

I want to show a new stage of research, which is the stage of satellite imagery, but I want to stress at the same time that there is a misconception often propagated by the media that it is satellite imagery that rediscovered the Saraswati. It is not so. It has already been known to a lot of scholars since the early 19th century as I mentioned. But what satellite imagery did was to give a dramatic, a graphic illustration of first of all the bed of the river, because it remains highly visible from a certain altitude. Here you see the Yamuna River, the Sutlej and you see this dark, broad mark crossing the landscape where today, there is no water flowing; especially whatever water was still flowing in the 19th century has been virtually, completely diverted away to agriculture through a dense network of canals in Haryana, in Indian Punjab. So today no water ever reaches so far down as it occasionally used to in the 19th century.

So, why do we have this very marked bed? It is not because of any difference of altitude on the ground – what the satellite imagery picks up is either a difference in humidity in the ground or as is the case here, it picks up a difference in vegetation, because there is still some humidity at the location. Near the location of the bed, the vegetation is different and this is what appears on the satellite imagery.

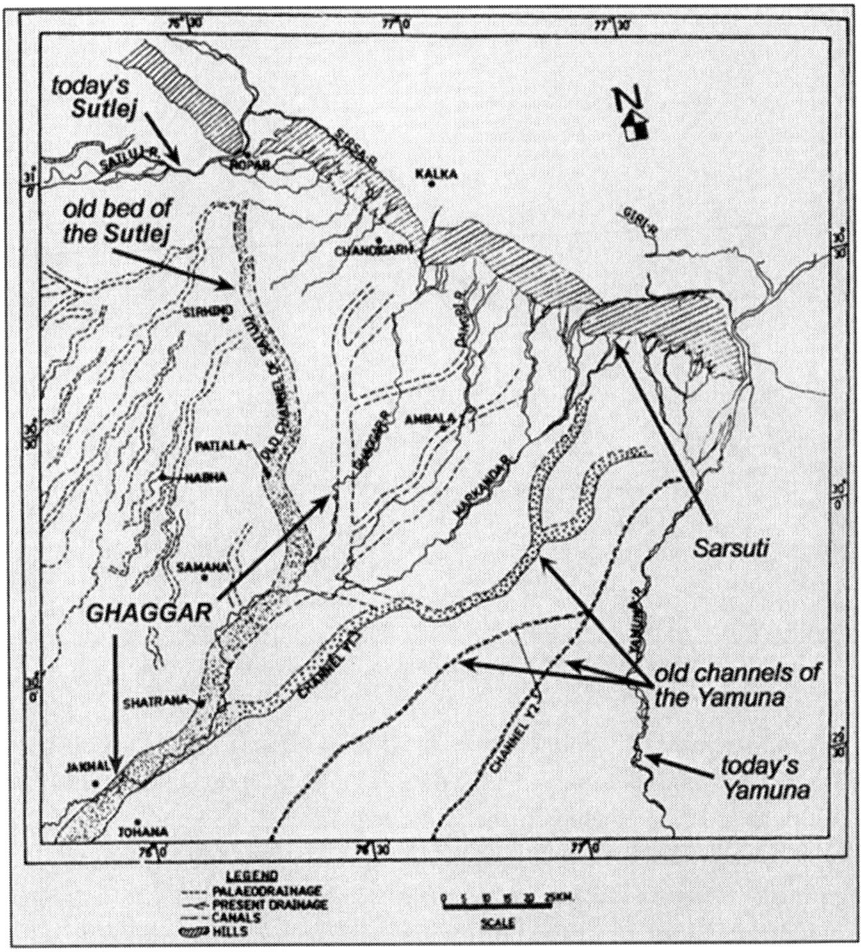

Courses of the Sarasvati determined by satellite imagery, with contributions from the Yamuna and the Sutlej (Yash Pal and others, 1980)

So, following that, we had lots of studies tracing again the paleobeds, the ancient beds, from Rupar, connecting Sutlej to the Ghaggar, and similarly with Yamuna. These are all the paleobeds and the main Ghaggar River and the small Saraswati, the small stream that still bears the name today, are here. And, on a computer, if you open Google Earth, you will see a very dramatic 'bed' of the Saraswati and the Chautang River or Chitrang, joining the Saraswati at a place known as Suratgarh in northern Rajasthan. There is interestingly a major Harappan site just north of the confluence, i.e. Karibanga.

Satellite imagery has become more and more sophisticated especially by exploiting multi-spectral photographs, that is, combining photographs taken at different wavelengths, and digitally enhancing all this together. What you get to see is the western most part of the Rajasthan desert, the Great Indian Desert abutting Pakistan. Here you can see some darker traces pointing to the paleobeds. This was confirmed by Rajasthan Water Board drilling a number of bore wells, tentatively, based on the data the satellite imagery was giving and they found fresh water from these bore wells and at a fairly shallow depth of 30-60 meters in complete desert.

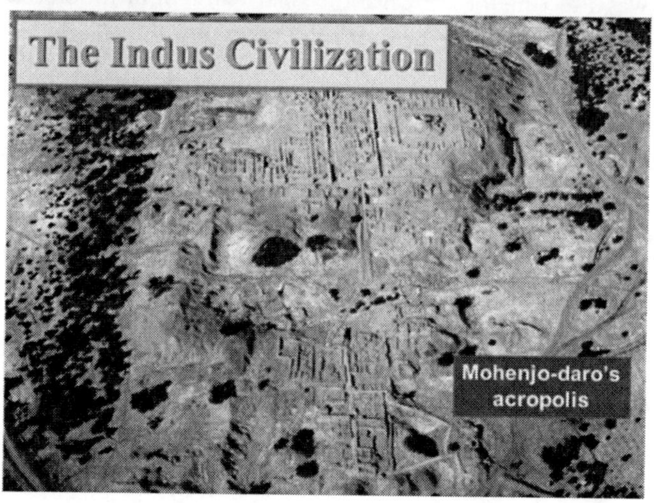

The Remote Sensing Centre of ISRO at Jodhpur spent quite a few years and produced a number of papers compiled together by Dr A K Gupta, Dr J R Sharma and others. They traced the various paleobeds of the Saraswati all the way down to the Rann of Kutch. You see a wide expanse of how the Saraswati was flowing into the Rann of Kutch. This was actually the estuary and the delta of the Saraswati, and the Rann of Kutch in those days was navigable. It remained navigable all the way to the campaign of Alexander the Great.

What you can see immediately is that Saraswati did not have a single course through the entire period. It had multiple courses; it shifted its bed and the exact sequence of history; all these shifting remains to be worked out. It is not as if we know everything about the evolution of the river. The Indus River also used to shift its bed sometimes in a dramatic brutal fashion, obliterating hundreds of villages because all this region is extremely flat. So, any change by accumulation of sediment that all those rivers are depositing, will eventually cause obstacles to the flow of the rivers and force them to flow in another direction.

These were briefly the latest findings just depicting raw, physical data. But there is another context which came to light in the 1920s and which was quite unexpected. This relates to the Indus civilization, initially located in the Indus Valley. Harappa and Mohenjo Daro were the first two sites. The aerial view of Mohenjo Daro shows wonderful town planning, meticulous geometric alignments of the buildings in the upper city of Mohenjo Daro. This was initially thought to be confined to the Indus valley which was why it was called the Indus Valley civilization. Although John Marshall, the Director General of the Archaeological Survey, who was directing these excavations, had a kind of intuition that it had to somehow be extending beyond, he didn't have a chance to explore.

Let me now briefly show you the map. These are the initial sites: Mohenjo Daro, Chanhu Daro, Amri and so on; Harappa is on Ravi. During 2600 to 1900 BC – the dates of the civilization – is when you get the cities in full functional order and it was a very vast civilization. And then in 1900 BC, something happened. But before that, let me mention what happened in 1941, for the first-time explorations beyond the Indus Valley.

Sir Mark Orenstein, a British explorer, was a great adventurer, very famous for his explorations of Central Asia; he also worked in Balochistan. He loved tough landscapes, very desolate regions, which were challenging. The forbidden parts of Central Asia attracted him tremendously. When he was 78, he conceived of an expedition into this region that identified explicitly with the Saraswati. He

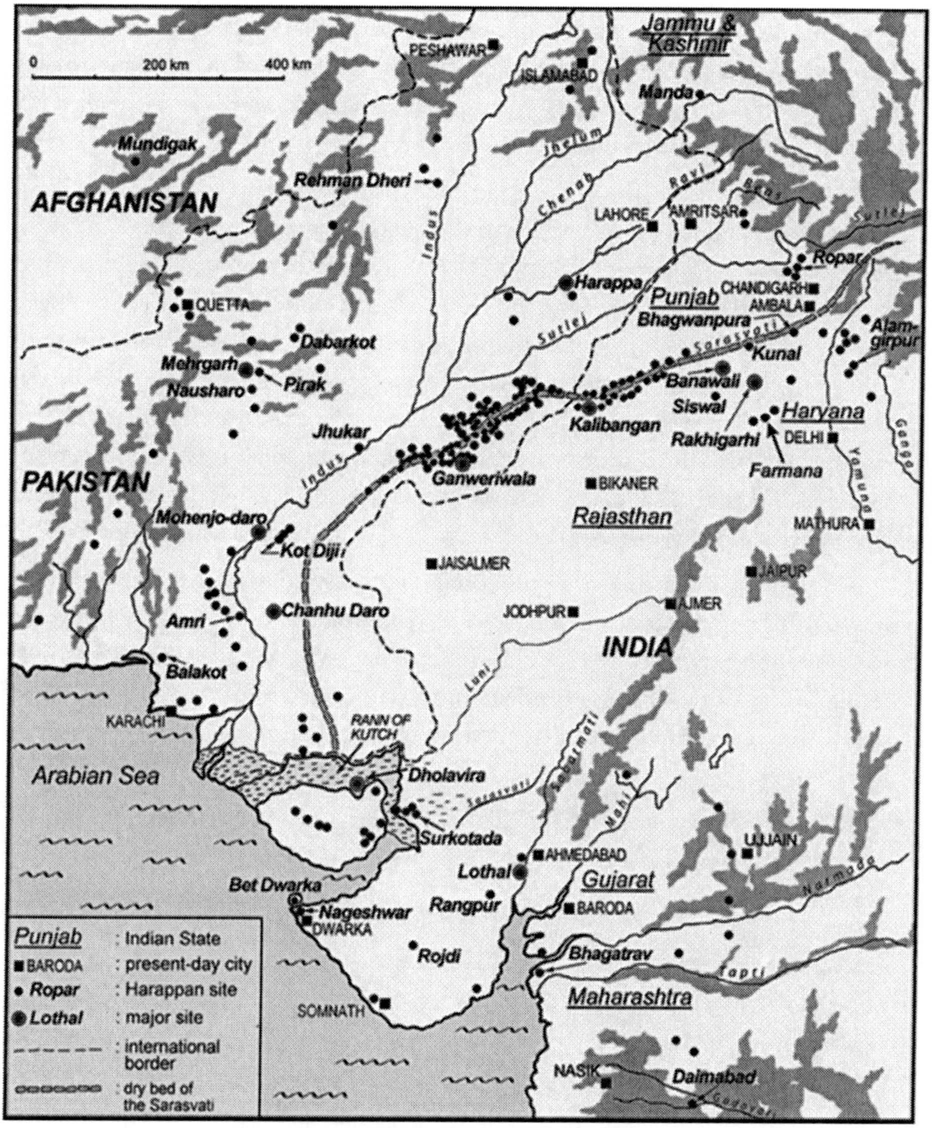

2600-1900 BCE (Mature phase), 1 million km^2

was also a great Sanskrit scholar and had published some papers on the location of the Saraswati and other Vedic rivers; he accepted what was then the consensus. He wanted to test the physical cultures available in this region and started from Bikaner. He couldn't find much in Bikaner, but in a complete desert called Cholistan, he very soon found and identified quite a few sites that were of Harappan culture. He knew the Harappan pottery and other Harappan artifacts and by the simple process of surface collection, without excavating anything really, he just took one trial trench to establish the chronology and showed that there were sites of Harappan culture in this region, which was the Saraswati. This happened for the first time ever in 1941.

After the partition, this became the International Border and therefore, Indian archaeologists no longer had access to the major Harappan sites where they had been working – Harappa, Mohenjo Daro and so on. Therefore, they wanted to do whatever they could to explore the limited parts in India. Noted archaeologist A Ghosh began exploring Bikaner and upstream. The Archaeological Survey of India in fact received a grant of Rs. 10,000 specifically sanctioned by Jawaharlal Nehru to explore what was called by K M Panikkar, "Saraswati Civilization". He was the Dewan of the Bikaner state and said that the region was even more ancient than the Indus civilization, which was not quite correct, but then he wrote to Jawaharlal Nehru saying that this "Saraswati Civilization" must be explored.

In contrast, today there is a major project of Saraswati River that Mr. Jagmohan was piloting to explore again, but more systematically and in greater depth at the site along the Saraswati River within India. That project was considered as "un-secular" when the UPA government came to power and it was shelved. They forgot that it was Nehru who had started the whole thing. There is a bit of an irony there.

So anyway, A Ghosh identified Kalibangan and lots of other sites closely following the bed of the river. Therefore, there is no doubt that there had to be water available in this bed of Ghaggar-Hakra when the Harappan civilization was in full bloom.

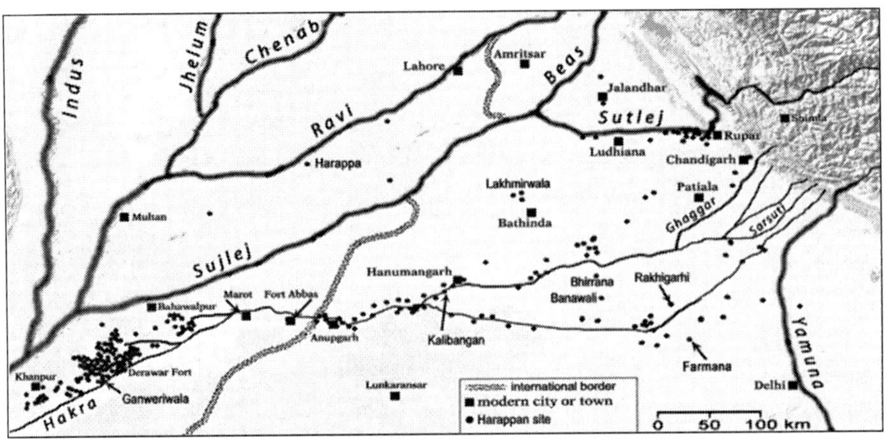

Settlement pattern in the Sarasvati basin in the Mature Harappan phase (2600-1900 BCE): the river breaks up as it enters Cholistan

Now if we plot the sites today of the mature Harappan sites i.e. during the height of the civilisation, this is what we get; these sites were either identified by Oreinstein or by Pakistani archaeologist Rafiq Mughal who did a lot of grueling exploration in this desert and these are all the sites we get in India. And you can see that again that the bed of the Ghaggar is fairly well followed. There is also interestingly another bed that is one of the paleobeds connecting the Sutlej to the Ghaggar. This is additional evidence that the Sutlej was contributing waters to the Ghaggar system, and then along the Dhrishadvati, quite a few sites.

Table 1: Overall Distribution of Harappan Sites (based on S.P. Gupta & Possehl)

Regions of the subcontinent	*Early Harappan*	*Mature Harappan*	*Late Harappan*	*Total*
Sarasvati Valley	640	360	1378	2378
Uttar Pradesh	2	32	10	44
Himachal, Jammu & Delhi	1	-	4	5
Gujarat	11	310	198	519
Pakistan's Indus Basin & Western Regions	367	416	12	795
Total	1021	1118	1602	3741

These are the figures that were kindly given to me by the Late S P Gupta, one of our finest archaeologists, and also compiled with other figures given by the American archaeologist Gregory Possehl. What you can see here is that it is not going to other, i.e. pre-urban and post-urban phases – let us not go into that. But you can see that out of 1,100-odd mature Harappan sites, which have been explored through this entire north-west region of India, we find 360 in the Saraswati Valley alone, including the Pakistani side of the Saraswati Valley, including the Cholistan region.

Then another major heartland, and that was a big surprise, is Gujarat – Gujarat 310 – a very big chunk, and a very important area for the development of the Harappan civilization. The rest of Pakistan has 416 minus the Saraswati region. The Indus Valley alone has about 130 or 140. So, you can see that the Saraswati region was the dominant region in terms of number of sites, which is why certain scholars, including S P Gupta, proposed a few years ago that this civilization should be renamed as "Indus-Saraswati Civilization" and some scholars also call it "Sindhu-Saraswati". This terminology has not been adopted by all scholars, especially Western scholars who have been a little scared of the prospect because too much controversy has been raised in recent times about the Saraswati issue. I'll come to the reasons for this controversy right at the end.

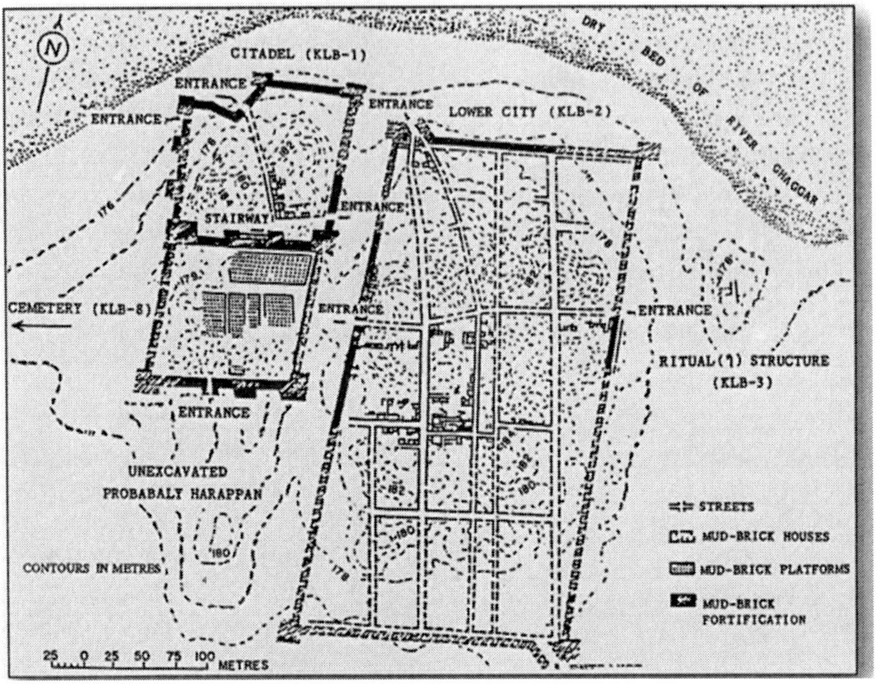

Kalibangan (in Rajasthan, on the Sarasvati)

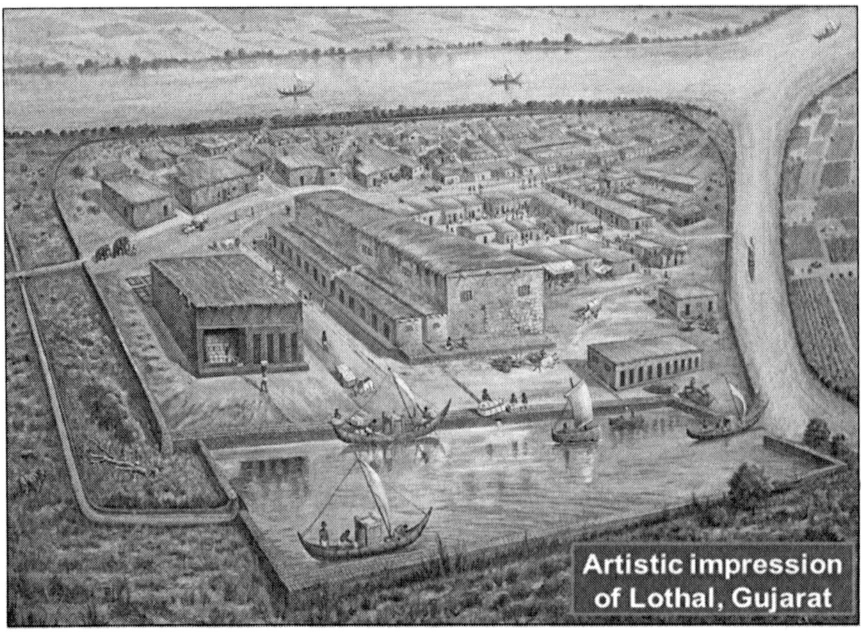

This outlay shows meticulous planning of Kalibangan in Rajasthan. This is a view of Lothal, an artistic view/reconstitution of Lothal in Gujarat, which was a small port town but important from the point of export of goods. This is the plan of Dholavira located in the southern part of the Rann of Kutch; Saraswati was flowing from the northern end. Town planning was done on a grand scale; there were massive monuments in stones and colossal reservoirs. One reservoir was in the southern side of the castle of Dholavira, which measured 33 meters in length and all cut in the sheer rock. And they had around 17 hectares of reservoirs, simply for the preservation of water. The biggest of them all was 70 meters in length and nearly 30 meters in width, much larger than an Olympic swimming pool.

So these were people who were able to adapt to the forbidding conditions of the Rann of Kutch and plan rainwater harvesting on such a scale that the city would be able to survive throughout the year, with the rainfall happening during a brief time in the monsoons.

Ship making, export of goods are well documented in the Harappan world. We know the Harappans were trading with the Gulf region; two civilisations, Dev Magan and Dilmun; and with Iran. These sites are being excavated today in Iran near Jiroft, where Harappan goods, seals and jewelry are coming to light. The same was found in Ilum and Mesopotamia and finally in Central Asia – Bactria and Mahjana – the Harappan presence is found all over the place, even though, very strangely, the reverse is not true. We have no Mesopotamian presence in the Harappan civilization: no presence in the Gulf, no presence in Mahjana, Iran; no artifacts whatsoever, just a few from Bactria visible on the western fringes of the Indus civilization.

So, what is it that the Harappans imported as a result of their trade? We just do not know, perhaps some recyclable material like gold or silver or some perishable goods? These are typical Harappan beads found in the royal graves of Mesopotamia. They were very highly praised because they were technological feats. The fact of drilling such long beads, up to three or four inches in length, was actually a secret of the Harappans and it was recently rediscovered. But let's come back to the Saraswati and what role the Saraswati River played as a bridge between the Harappan Civilization and the later Classical Civilization of India that started in the Gangetic Region in the First Millennium BC.

The gap between the two – the Harappan Civilization collapsing around 2000 BC and the Gangetic Civilization starting around 800 BC – is of more than

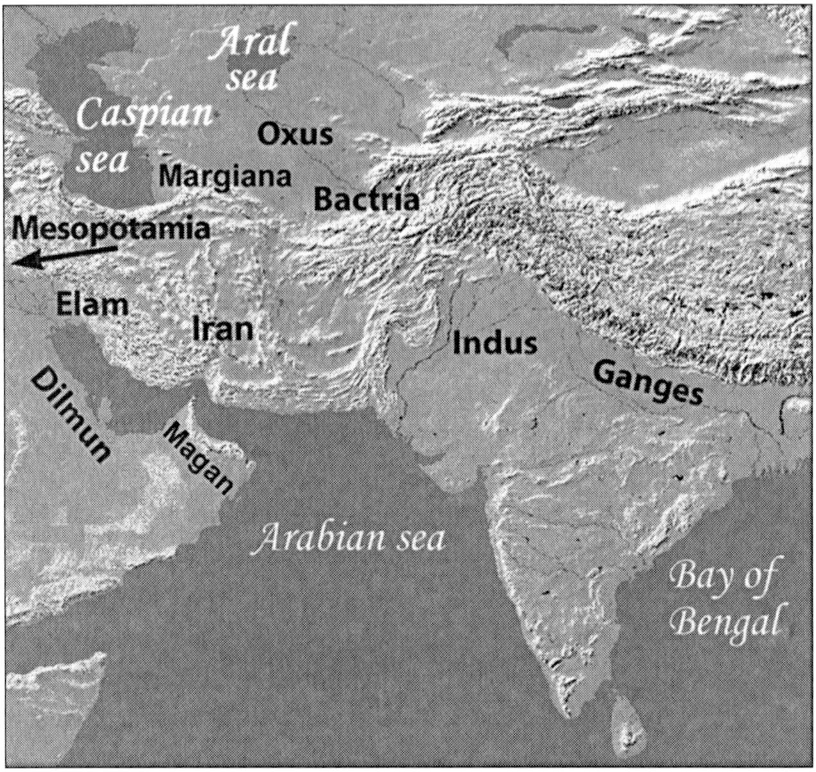

Drilled Harappan Carnelian Beads from the Royal Graves at Ur (Mesopotamia)

a millennium. Roughly till the Second Millennium BC, we really don't know what happened on the ground. There were many cultures evolving fast, changing fast, but the exact evolution is still to be traced. This is a grey area in Indian archaeology.

But what we do know is that, somehow or the other, despite the collapse of the cities, the Harappan culture survived and was transmitted to the Gangetic region. This is something that is more and more accepted by not only archaeologists, but other scholars as well. I am just giving very briefly some examples of how the origin of chess maybe traceable to the Harappan culture. This is from Lothal on the left; on the right is another game, typical dice that you might take to be modern dice.

A lot of symbols survived – on the left is a typical Harappan symbol known as the "Endless Knot" and you find the same in historical inscriptions. This is from Gujarat in the 9th century AD. So the survival of symbols is very important; the most dramatic of it is Swastika that is represented on hundreds of terracotta tablets in Harappan culture and of course is a very sacred Hindu, Buddhist and Jain symbol also.

Then, lots of modes of worship were noted by the archaeologists and have been very reminiscent of what is still prevalent in India; for example, purification through water, testified here by the Great Bath of Mohenjo Daro, which was not something for daily washing up, because people had individual bathrooms in their houses. This is one hallmark of Indus Civilization, sanitation and amenities. This must have been a place of worship through water and this typical of what we find in temple tanks of modern India still today. Tree worship was very prevalent and nature was worshipped through other modes, like the worship of animals that are visible on the seals.

Fire worship at Lothal and other sites can be established by the structures found in streets, which were full of ash, but without any bones whatsoever. So these places must have been used for fire worship. At Banawali, which was also excavated by R S Bisht in Haryana, you find such a structure where there is a semi-circular altar enclosed within a semi-circular structure and nothing was found within this alter except again ash and a little bit of charcoal. This points to fire worship highly reminiscent of Vedic ritual.

Then, certain traditions like a figurine of Nausharu, which is in Baluchistan, from 2800 AD was unearthed by a French team of archaeologists. They found several of them having traces of red pigment at the parting of the hair. This is obviously the origin of the Hindu tradition of applying *Sindoor* by females. Then there are all kinds of figures on the seals that cannot be easily identified but present iconographic features with which we are very familiar, for example, the three faces of this figure seated in a yogic posture on a raised platform with two antelopes or deer beneath it. These are classical iconographic features that can be found easily in the later Classical Civilizations.

There is presence of *Linga*, not in many sites, with just two of them with the platform, but there could be other objects also that were used as Lingas, and not only Linga but Trishula is in evidence as well. So, there might be some kind of Shiva-like cult in the Indus Civilization, but that is to be researched further. We have evidence of *asanas* in various postures.

And finally, meditation – this is the famous priest-king who probably was neither a priest nor a king, these are arbitrary designations. You find him in deep contemplation. So, it goes fairly well with the asanas. Therefore, the assumption, rather the agreement amongst most archaeologists, is that there was some tradition of yoga in the Harappan culture.

The conclusion drawn by John Marshall in 1931 in his report stated that "the Harappan religion is so characteristically Indian as hardly to be distinguished from still living Hinduism." This is a very strong statement. If I were to make it today, I would be instantly attacked – for saying something communal or chauvinistic. Since this was by John Marshall, who had served as the Director-General of the Archaeological Survey of India, nobody can object, and what remains in front of us is to understand the mechanism of this transmission.

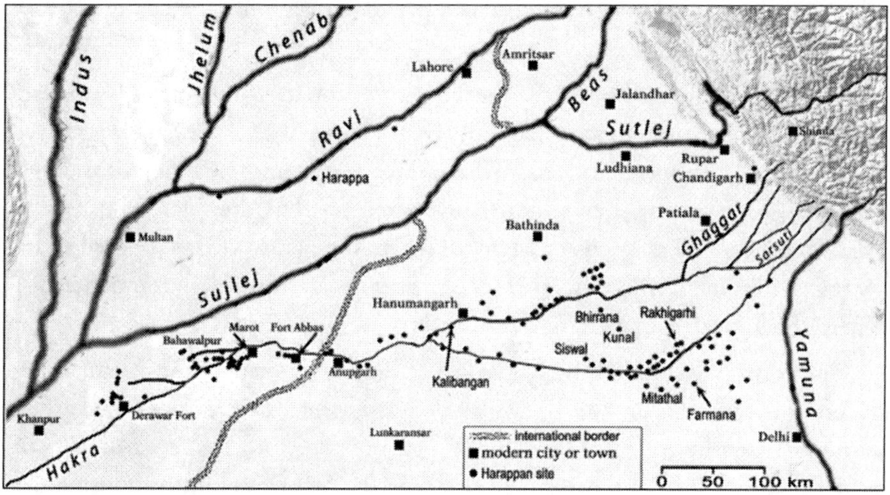

Settlement pattern in the Sarasvati basin in the Early Harappan phase (3500-2800 BCE): the river's flow is "unbroken"

Let me show you the map of the early Harappan sites; here again, the Saraswati comes into play. Before the urban phase comes into view, you have a continuous sequence of sites along the Ghaggar-Hakra system. Then around 2700 BC or so, something happens where we have a break of about 200 kilometers, where there are no mature Harappan sites at all. This seems to point to a breakup of the Saraswati around 2700 BC which is what is documented in the Brahmanas; the Saraswati disappears, becomes invisible at a certain point, which interestingly would coincide very precisely with the Indo-Pakistan border of today. So, the Saraswati disappears there. This means that the sites downstream probably were fed by a deviation in a paleochannel from the Sutlej.

Again, something even more dramatic takes place around 1900 BC, where one can see that suddenly we don't have any Harappan site in the central basin of the Saraswati. It's all *abandoned. Kalibangan which was here, is abandoned almost* overnight; within a generation or two, the city is just abandoned; there is no later development, there is no late Harappan phase in those mature sites of the central basin. But one finds a lot of late Harappan sites hugging the Shivalik Hills and whatever little streams that were still flowing downstream and then crossing the Yamuna and even Ganga eastward. Now this eastward movement was first written about probably by Jagatpati Joshi in 1984. We see a partial eastward migration, what is now rural settlements. There are no longer cities, merging into the Gangetic plains whatever communities that were living there. This movement and this fusion are what would give rise to the Gangetic Civilization a few hundred years later.

So what we can see now is the mechanism of the transmission of Harappan culture to the Gangetic regions. Not only that, you see that while Saraswati River disappeared, the people who migrated kept her as a memory as they considered her sacred. That is why they relocated the Saraswati, but the river being totally invisible, they made the Triveni Sangam, where the Saraswati is supposed to be flowing, a holy spot. Of course, there is no Saraswati at this spot, but the memory is there. That is what matters in the Indian mind.

Now I may conclude how the Saraswati got embroiled in the Aryan issue. The point is very crucial that the *Nadistuti Sukta*, which I have mentioned at the beginning, lists the river not from west to east as you would expect from Aryan invaders coming into India and then reaching the Saraswati and composing the Rig Vedic hymns. The rivers are listed from east to west. This is itself a contradiction of the Aryan invasion or migration theory. And then the biggest contradiction is the chronological data that this evolution in the patterns of Harappan science brought to light sometime in the 1980s.

The chronological clash is this that we are told according to most of our text books and the proponents of the Aryan invasion or migration theory that the Aryans entered India; whether they clashed or not with the Harappans, but they somehow migrated eastward toward the Gangetic plains and on the way they stopped for a while along the Saraswati. That is obviously compulsory because the Saraswati is very highly praised in the Rig Veda as a mighty river flowing from the mountains to the sea. The problem here is that the Aryan invasion or migration takes place about 1500 BC and they would have reached the Saraswati even much later than this. But there was no Saraswati anymore in this region. There was at best a stream flowing from the Shivalik and stopping somewhere in Haryana or Punjab. It was a seasonal stream, not a perennial stream anymore. So how could have they praised the Saraswati as a mighty river flowing from the mountain to the sea? That could have happened when the river was in full flow. One of the Harappan sites has demonstrated that this was during the mature phase or even before 2700 BC; before that break of 200 kilometers that took place beyond the International Border.

This is the major contradiction, and once in the 1980s the contradiction was understood and came to light, then only did the controversy start and then only did a number of scholars declare that this cannot be the Saraswati because they would like to retain the Aryan invasion or migration at any cost.

So, this is what I call an a posteriori controversy. If they had this viewpoint that this cannot be the Saraswati, right from the 19th century, we would have understood and we could have discussed. But here, there can't be any possible discussion because this is not a dogma. This is where the issue becomes a bit complex. And there is another perennial question; accepting that this is Sapta Sindhavah, this becomes the location of the Rig Vedic culture which nobody will deny. Then, how many cultures do we find there? Basically, we find only one – the Harappan culture – we don't find a Vedic, identifiable non-Harappan culture covering the same region. There are a few local cultures; for example, along the Aravallis, there are a few local cultures of the Bronze Age, but they are very limited, geographically speaking.

So, to summarise, this great river had a very strange destiny. It is the only river that disappeared, the others are still there with us today. Yet it was regarded as a goddess for mysterious reasons. Perhaps because there was a big concentration of rishis composing the Rig Veda living along its banks. For example, the Mahabharata locates the ashram of Vashishtha specifically on the Saraswati. Perhaps for this reason, they regarded this river as more sacred than the others. This is a hypothesis; we don't know for sure, but whatever it may be, the goddess was portrayed in the Rig Veda as a Goddess of Intuition, Illumination; the prayers to her were usually to impel, to purify our thoughts.

This is the role of the goddess in the Rig Veda. In the *Yajur Veda*, she goes one step further and she becomes explicitly the Goddess of Speech. Of course, speech is the vehicle of knowledge. Later on, in the late Vedic literature, she becomes the Goddess of Knowledge and then still a little later, the Goddess of Arts as we usually worship her. You can see the representation of the classical Saraswati in the Thanjavur temple of Tamil Nadu. But this is still a memory symbolized by this *Kamandalu*; it's still a memory that she was once a river.

I have earlier explained about the Triveni Sangam at Allahabad, and therefore, the river very interestingly, as it vanishes, takes a greater and greater stature as a goddess and plays a more important role in the transmission of the culture.

In fact, there have been very interesting studies that show how many features of the Saraswati were transferred to Ganga, which must have been the time when the Harappans entered the Gangetic plains and then Ganga took the sanctity that we usually associate with her today. But the Ganga to my mind, culturally speaking, is nothing but an avatar of the Saraswati. This is how I look at it in the entire chronological perspective.

The river Saraswati, therefore, I would not say, is the origin of the Indian civilization. Nobody really knows what the origin is, but Saraswati is certainly a powerful symbol of the flow of civilization. Even when the river "dies", the memory remains alive and all the cultural features get carefully transmitted. This a mechanism that has happened at other stages of Indian culture and this is how the Hindu mind works: to preserve the memory; to preserve the worship; to preserve the culture, even though the physical features may at times disappear.

That is in a nutshell the story of the Saraswati – the river and the goddess – and this is something we learn at many levels, ecologically speaking as well, because we still don't fully understand how the Saraswati disappears, and now some people are saying that even Ganga may sometime in the 21st century become a seasonal river as the Saraswati eventually became. So perhaps there are many lessons to be drawn from the Saraswati River.

(*Ed:* Not all the slides mentioned in the text are included due to space contraint.)

(This talk was delivered by Prof Michel Danino on April 30, 2010 at the VIF)

*

2

STUDY OF ANCIENT INDIA: ERRONEOUS PERCEPTIONS AND THE REALITY

Dr Dilip K. Chakrabarti

The ancient past of India came in for modern scrutiny in the middle of the 18th century. The most important preliminary concern was to identify the Graeco-Roman references to some ancient Indian cities and other geographical features in terms of modern Indian geography. For instance, what was the location of Pataliputra, a city, for which Megasthenes, the Greek ambassador in the court of Chandragupta, left behind an elaborate description? It was identified as Patna in the late 18th century by the English geographer James Rennel. In the field of working out the basic ancient historical frame of India, an important initial step was taken by William Jones, who identified Sandrocottus of the Greek sources with Chandragupta Maurya. As the date of Sandrocottus was known to be in the late 4th century BC from his association in the Greek context, the date of Chandragupta also fell in place.

With these two starting points, the study of ancient India began in the modern sense. Among the intellectual contexts in which it began, the first concern was to relate India to the scheme of world history as it was then understood. Please note that before Darwin published his ideas in the mid-19th century, the scheme of world history had been Biblical. If one accepts the scheme of the world being created by God on a particular date, one has to accept that all human beings and civilisations are related in origin to one of the three sons of Noah – Ham, Shem and Japheth. William Jones emphasised this point in various ways, including his championing of the belief that Sanskrit, Greek and Latin were linguistically related. This was hardly a novel matter, because having descended from the God's word, all ancient languages had at some point been related. In fact, in one of his early discourses, Jones puts Sanskrit at par not merely with Greek and Latin, but also with Peruvian and Japanese. It is indeed curious that only the Greek and Latin parts of the conclusion are now remembered.

The second intellectual context is no less interesting. The 18th century was the age of enlightenment in Europe, especially France. This was an age when there was a conscious movement to break away from the Judaic and Christian orthodoxy, and seek the origins of culture and civilisation outside it. Initially, China was the most favoured area from this point of view, but soon India came into the picture. Some people, including the French philosopher Voltaire, believed that India and/or Central Asia was the centre from which civilisation got disseminated elsewhere. Some interesting writings, all championing the cause of India as the centre of culture and civilisation, and invoking migrations of learned Brahmins and Buddhists to areas as far West as Scotland, were published in the first half of the 19th century and the last part of the 18th. One may note that all the writings of the Asiatic society scholars codifying Sanskrit and its literature belonged to this period. There was no intellectual compulsion to mention ancient India and its language and institutions in derogatory ways.

However, the idea of India as the origin or centre of culture and civilisation in the encyclopaedists' thoughts, or the people trying to relate India to the Biblical scheme of the world origin, came to an end around the middle of the 19th century. In fact, the end of this idea tallies well with the date of the revolution of 1857. This is one of the clear proofs in the Indian contexts that academic ideas in the humanities or social sciences are intimately related to the contemporary power structure. The second half of the 19th century witnessed a number of inter-related things in the field of ancient India. There was steady progress in the understanding of the ancient literary sources and associated dynastic chronologies, partly on the basis of the English translations of the accounts of Chinese pilgrims Huen Shang and Fa Hian, and also on the basis of the translations of the Sinhalese texts – the *Mahavamsa* and *Deepavamsa*. It was also during this period that Cunningham undertook his archaeological surveys, mapping out the historical potential of various sites around the country.

Secondly, different linguistic hypotheses gained ground during this period, the Aryan concept being the most important of them. The concept gained respectability in the voluminous writings of F. Max Mueller – a German Sanskritist who never visited India and whose opinion of anything Indian, except spirituality, was very low. The point is that Max Mueller was widely read by Indians, and the idea that the rulers of India of that period – the British and the higher classes among the subject people of India – belonged to the same racial stock held great appeal for many Indians, especially those of the upper order. The urgency with which even people like R.C. Dutt accepted this idea and described the age of establishment of the Aryan rule in India as among its most glorious periods must have sounded fairly distressing to those outside the Aryan pale.

In fact, this is precisely what happened. Reactions against the idea had emerged from the Dravidian Tamil Nadu and came also from the social reformer Jyotiba Phule and Constitutional expert and social reformer, B.R. Ambedkar. A few comments may perhaps be made here on Dutt who was one of the earliest members of the Indian Civil Service. Later in life, he was a nationalist who theorised about the drain of wealth from India. He also wrote two inspiring novels in Bengali, with clear nationalist undertones: *Maharashtra Jiban Prabhat* and *Rajput Jiban Sandhya*. He also translated the Rig Veda into Bengali. However, he could not go against the established scholarship of the time and had no difficulty in accepting the Aryan hypothesis. The inability or refusal to question the basic structure of the study of ancient India has possibly been the weakest point of nationalist Indian scholarship.

Thirdly, hard racist ideas had come to rule academia in the name of science by the middle of the 19th century. The correlation and timing between the development of comparative philology or historical linguistics (as it is called nowadays) and the consolidation of racist ideas is striking. J.F. Blumenberg, who first divided human groups into a few racial types, wrote towards the end of the 18th century and so did William Jones, the so-called father of comparative philological studies. The racial classifications of India took concrete shape with the publication of 'Risley's Scheme' during the Census operation of 1901. It is indeed interesting to point out that the complete acceptance of the idea of Aryan invasion of India and the associated language schemes and the first major publication of the racial scheme of India took place in about the same period, thus highlighting the close relationship between the postulated language history and history of the country. In the case of India, further consolidation of this idea took place in the 1931 Census, when J.H. Hutton, later professor of Social Anthropology in Cambridge and B.S. Guha, later Director of Anthropological Survey of India, amplified the earlier scheme of Risley. These racial schemes of Indian culture and history were accepted without question by scholars like

S.K. Chatterjee and others in the first volume of the series on the History and Culture of the Indian People.

Once again, this trend of development highlights the premise that even nationalist scholars and historians could not challenge some of the fundamental colonial speculations about ancient Indian studies. Before turning to the story of further development, one has to point out that the Aryan language concept went hand in hand with the concept of race. The reason for its persistence even today is closely linked with the Western scholar's quest to discover a past situation in which the supremacy of the Western powers and their language in the world stage would be adequately reflected in the ancient contexts. If one is asked why many non-Western scholars also are equally interested in keeping alive the myth of the Aryan language and its dissemination, the answer can be found in the socio-politics of the historical studies of the countries to which these non-Western scholars belong. I shall come back to the problem in the context of Indian scholarship later.

There are two important developments in the field of ancient Indian studies in the early part of the 20th century: the publication of the text of *Arthashastra* in 1905 and the discovery of the Indus civilisation in the 1920s. The publication of the text of Kautilya's Arthashastra may be less momentous than the discovery of the Indus civilisation, but it was very significant in its own right. It showed at a stroke that there was an organised study of the various aspects of statecraft in ancient India. The fact that it belonged, by and large, to the Mauryan times showed that the development of a pan-Indian state was associated with and possibly depended on the ideas of organised administration. Furthermore, this text showed that ancient India was concerned not only with matters of mind but also with many mundane matters including espionage and warfare. The date of the Arthashastra has been discussed many times, but without specific results. On the whole, the overall image of a highly centralised administration, keeping all spheres of life under supervision, is likely to tally more with the powerful pan-Indian Mauryan state than with any later development.

The discovery of the Indus civilisation caught the scholars of ancient India completely unawares. The only thing that excited them was whether it was Vedic or post-Vedic. S.K. Chatterjee, a professor of comparative philology in Calcutta University, expressed (1924) his belief, for no particular reason, that the people of this civilisation were likely to have spoken a language belonging to the Dravidian family. The alacrity with which this opinion, although based on nothing very profound or viable, was accepted in Tamil Nadu, is well known. The publication in 1931 of John Marshall's three-volume report on the Mohenjo Daro excavations was a very important event. This is because it brought out the true outline of the different aspects of the life of Mohenjo Daro including religion, and emphasised Marshall's belief that civilisation was deeply rooted in Indian soil. If Marshall believed that the civilisation was post and non-Vedic, there were other scholars who believed many Vedic elements could be seen in the civilisation.

On the whole, this is where the study of ancient India stood in 1947. By this time, it had about 200 years of research in the background with the following achievements to its credit: ancient places identified with archaeological sites and mapped, the ancient texts translated into English and examined for historical context, the laying down of the basic framework of ancient Indian dynastic and other aspects of historical chronology, and finally, the discovery of the Indus civilisation and its Indian roots. The Aryan and other associated linguistic ideas were accepted as facts along with the theoretical premise of race-language-culture correlation. Expression of Indian nationalism did not find its representation in anything more serious than the idea of republican institutions in ancient India. There were also perfectly logical attempts to put back the dates of some texts by one or two centuries and deny that the Greeks, Romans and other external forces had exerted particularly powerful influences on different technological and cultural aspects of India's ancient development.

In fact, the national historians of India stated nothing startling. They very much conformed to the ruling scholarship of the day and tried to modify things here and there in bits. The post-Independence study of ancient India may best be seen in its initial phase, through the relevant volumes of the *History and Culture of the Indian People* series. Its first volume, *The Vedic Age*, was a summary of the generally accepted scholarly ideas about the ancient texts and the Aryan hypothesis. There was also an analysis of the results and pictures of the traditional and legendary view of the first phase of Indian political history. From the second volume onward, there was a routine synthesis of what was known of the various phases of ancient India. With some of the analysis, one could disagree on technical grounds, but such methods of discourse had long been known, and nowhere in the text of these volumes can one find any unnecessary glorification of ancient India.

Soon after Independence, any expression of nationalism in writings on ancient India came under attack from historians who later on became institutionally powerful. For instance, in 1959 in the first edition of his book *Aspects of Political Ideas and Institutions in Ancient India*, author Sharma dwelt at length on the historiography of the ancient Indian state. When he considers the merits and limitations of 'the nationalist and revivalist approach' to the study of the past Indian polity, one wonders why it is to be called revivalist simply because most of the historians, who wrote on ancient Indian political institutions, were writing in the context of the nationalist movement and made clear comments on the merits of these institutions. Among the further limitations of this approach, he states that by their fulsome adoration of ancient Hindu institutions they tended to antagonise the Muslims, although it was not done deliberately. Sharma has not cited any detailed Muslim responses. The whole thing is possibly a concoction on his part, because why should any community take umbrage, if a different community's institutions long before its own time in the land were praised. In short, Sharma calls the nation's historians revivalist and then calls them responsible for adding fuel to the Hindu-Muslim sense of separation and jealousy. It may be noted that Sharma was closely associated with the Communist Party of India and is not reputed to have command over the primary sources of ancient Indian history.

By the time Romila Thapar, who added Sharma's antipathy to what they called 'nationalist historians' to an adulation for Western anthropological writings and like Sharma had little command over the primary sources of ancient Indian history, wrote an article on 'Interpretations of Ancient Indian History: History and Theory' in 1968, the tone of criticism became more strident. In Thapar's language, "nationalism was replaced by former militant Hinduism and earlier attempts at proving the indigenous origins of all things Indian were accentuated". If Sharma and Thapar had undertaken detailed empirical research showing that professional historians of ancient India were all communalists and believers in militant Hinduism, we would have had the opportunity of critically analysing the data cited by them. As they have not done so, we cannot give a moment's credence to their opinions. In their professional writings, our nationalist historians are not known to wilfully distort data. On the other hand, I find Thapar's opinion, 'earlier attempts at proving the indigenous origins of all things Indian were accentuated' a wilful distortion of the truth. Which nationalist historian did Thapar have in mind? As far as I know, the professional study of ancient Indian history and archaeology had been out and out diffusionist till recently. Not long after Thapar, H.D. Sankalia of the Deccan College wrote, 'for India the sun of culture and civilisation always rose in the West'. His was not a lone opinion of the period. Whatever shortcomings one may lay at the door of the post-Independent Deccan College, glorification of ancient India cannot be one of them.

Such opinions are still held by many scholars both inside and outside the Deccan College. My contention is that Sharma, Thapar and people who belong to that group wanted to justify their own position in the community of ancient Indian historians by raising the bogey of communalism and militant Hinduism among the professional historians before them. I have another contention: declaring India from time to time as an ageless colony of foreign powers has been a pastime of our ancient historians and archaeologists. Why was the voice of historical materialists represented by people like Sharma never raised against this? Which principle of historical materialism says that the cultural development of any place has to be conditioned primarily by foreign influences? In which national area of archaeological scholarship, does the find of three copper arrowheads make you undertake a long journey outside India in search of their parallels and origin? This is an allusion to the discovery of three small copper arrowheads in a site near Bagor in Rajasthan. After these arrowheads were discovered and later found to be identical with some arrowheads found in North East Rajasthan, the man who excavated the site, V.N. Mishra of the Deccan College, went out of his way to seek their parallels all over western Asia and the Mediterranean. In this he was following the scholarly tradition set up by his predecessors H.D. Sankalia and M.K. Dhavalikar.

Post-Independence ancient Indian historical scholarship of the professional variety is not known to believe in nationalism. A few people before Independence tried to show that there were a few good things in India, including political institutions; we should respect them instead of calling them militant Hindus or Hindu revivalists. I do repeat that post-Independence ancient Indian historical scholarship of the professional variety is not known to have believed in nationalism. I have taught for many years in Delhi University and I can tell you that nationalism was the last thing to be considered in the history department of that university. In the book which I have cited, Sharma calls himself a historical materialist just as Henry Morgan, the author of *Modern and Ancient Society* and Friedrich Engels, the author of *The Origin of the Family, Private Property and the State* describe themselves.

The problem doesn't lie in what one believes in; it lies in how you try to build your case and how logical you are in putting forward your structure. It is time that Sharma, Thapar and their fellow travellers' writings are critically analysed from the point of view of logical academic arguments and in the light of the primary historical data. In any case, the tendency we have seen in Sharma and Thapar's writings soon led to the political creation of the Indian Council for

Historical Research (ICHR) in the early 1970s. It is not for me to go into the roots or justification for setting up this government-sponsored institution. However, I believe that the total concentration of power for historical research in the hands of a single government-sponsored organisation, which in turn has been controlled by government-nominated members of various political orientations, has led to unprecedented politicisation and consequent criminalisation of the Indian historical field since the early 1970s, irrespective of the parties the historian politicians in control bore their allegiance to.

I am aware that virtually anybody retired from Indian historical academia could secure for himself an ICHR fellowship to do research. In most cases, no research testified by major publications was done by these retired academics. As long as one was of the right political view and had friends in ICHR administration or other sectors, there was no problem in getting money for research. I gather that Arun Shourie has discussed aspects of this in his book *Eminent Historians*, but the rot is not limited merely to the eminent ones. It is far more widespread than that. In fact, I doubt very much whether any other country in the world possesses a government-sponsored organisation such as the ICHR, to control and criminalise historical studies in the country. I use the term criminalisation quite deliberately.

What are the major grounds of dispute in the study of ancient India today? The first of these disputes is about the continuity of the Indian civilisation and Hinduism. This is more visible in archaeological studies than in the traditional literary framework. It is in archaeology that the problem has sharply emerged in recent years. It has also got a lot to do with the problem of religion in the Indus civilisation. To many archaeological scholars, including the editor of the first report on Mohenjo Daro, there are unmistakable shadows of latter-day Hinduism in what has been excavated at the site such as the *yagna* practice, *Shiva Pashupati* cult, representation of the *Sapta Matrikas*, sacredness of *peepal* tree, the ritualistic characteristics of mother goddess figurines, ritual use of water and so on. The presence of Shiva has been categorically demonstrated with the find of a terracotta *shiv linga* set in *yoni patta* in a later Harappan dig at Kalibangan.

I am not suggesting for a moment that Hinduism in all its varieties and complexities as we find it today was present in that civilisation, as modern Hinduism is as much as product of its historical evolution as any other religious or cultural phenomenon. All that I am suggesting is that many traits of latter-day Hinduism can be traced back to the Indus civilisation. In fact, the continuity of the mother goddess worship tradition has been traced back to circa 9000 BC in a Stone Age context in Madhya Pradesh. However, the continuity of Hinduism or

Hindu ritualistic belief is something that is unacceptable to a significant number of scholars. How many books on ancient Indian history discuss these aspects of continuity? One of the reasons why this is so is due to our ingrained belief in the theory of Aryan migration, and the consequent belief in the origin of Hinduism in the Vedas.

All that I would say is that the linguistic premise of a common Aryan language or a common Aryan homeland may all be true, but strictly in the context of historical language studies alone. Like all linguistic premises of its kind, it is unverifiable and cannot be dated on its own term. This has got nothing to do with archaeology or history. Whether there is archaeological continuity from the Indus civilisation or not can be debated and discussed. However, there is no scope for debate regarding the archaeological or historical presence of any particular group of people called the Aryans. The Vedas no doubt exist, but they exist as a category of the Indian literature, without the vast Indo-European constructs behind it. The sooner we get used to the idea of the history of ancient India without the Aryans, or any other linguistically constructed category such as the Dravidians or the Austrics, the better.

I am not one of those who fall over backwards in the name of multidisciplinary research. You do research in your own field and take the help of other disciplines, as far as they help you realise your own research goals. You do not take the help of any approach that makes you flounder helplessly in mud, which is exactly what the so-called historical linguistics do to archaeology. My own department that is Cambridge Department of Archaeology is a great place where scholars debate all the time about the relationships between historical linguistics and archaeology. I prefer to view this as a completely unverifiable academic exercise.

From the India nationalist point of view, belief in fanciful linguistic constructions can be very damaging. Because in the long run, they planted the seed of implacable differences in identity between different language speaking groups. Rajeev Malhotra and Arvind Neelakandan highlight some of these dangers in their book *Breaking India*. The dangers are very real as ethnic strife based precisely on imagined differences in the historical trajectories of various ethnic groups shows. What I fail to understand is why ancient historians like Sharma and Thapar have always been ardent believers in the Aryan idea. It is possible that the idea of continuity of Hinduism is anathema to them. To them, there does not seem to be much difference between belief in this idea and Hindu fundamentalism.

How is it that a large percentage of foreign archaeologists working in India are believers in the Aryan hypothesis? The only explanation is that they like to view the Indian past as a disjointed series of interactions between different groups of people. Furthermore, the idea of the coming of the Aryans satisfies the notion of a superior group of people taking over India. On the national level, India has every reason to be wary of foreign archaeological presence, because many of their ideas can plant the seeds of difference among Indians regarding their identities. The leader of a particular foreign archaeological group interested in working on the Indus Civilisation did not hesitate to poke fun at the Hindu deity Hanuman and also made unsupportable statements about Hindu religion. Recently, another member of this group has published a general study of the Indus Civilisation, without even raising the issue of the massive continuity of the civilisation. This type of attitude which I see here among the foreign archaeologists working in India has been discussed well in *Invading the Sacred: Analysis of Hinduism Studies in America* by Ramaswamy, Nicholas and Banerjee.

I may also point out, that the study of ancient India suffers from two serious limitations in modern India. First, it is marginalised in the Indian university framework. The main emphasis of most History Departments is Modern India, the history of the last 200 years. In fact, professional Indian historians are interested generally in the 20th century and later India. In Delhi University, for instance, ancient India is taught in the first year's honours, and by the time the students come up to their MA and are supposed to select their MA options, they've forgotten what they've studied about ancient India in their first year. Most of them opt for Modern India.

The second danger lies in the fact that in the modern Indian academic world, the difference between those taught in English medium and those who have been taught in the vernacular languages is huge. It is incredible, but the fact remains that the intellectual roots of vernacular medium students are deep in the soil. It is they who can read vernacular literature in its original form. It is they who are in a position to raise original questions about the ancient history of the land. As far as my experience goes, the furthest the English medium students of history and the teachers can go is to faithfully show their familiarity with the current and fashionable academic theories. There may be exceptions, but they are rather rare.

The danger lies in the fact that the vernacular medium students are almost invariably neglected in the teaching schedules and very few of them want to do research later on. This is also one of the reasons why research rooted in our land is hard to come by in the context of Ancient India. Apart from the socio-political factors I pointed out, the study of ancient India has a few inherent limitations of its own. The main thing is the paucity of sources and K.N. Sastri in his famous study of the Cholas wrote, 'of the utter impossibility of basing any part of the ancient history of India solely or even primarily on literary evidence'. There is no way we can get out of these and other limitations. Whichever sociology or anthropology we may swear by, this will not illuminate our ancient historical scene. Archaeology has enormously helped in expanding the character of ancient historical sources, but let us remember that about 85 per cent of the excavations conducted since Independence have remained unpublished. While advertising for the position of Director of Archaeological Survey of India sometime back, the Ministry of Culture and Government of India found it completely unnecessary to emphasise that they needed an archaeologist first and foremost, and a good one at that. This is one of the most curious archaeological advertisements that I have read.

According to the relevant advertisement, the only firm requirement was that the aspiring candidate had served three years on a specified senior salary scale. Otherwise, the net was thrown very wide – a postgraduate qualification without the subject being specified and without any emphasis on the applicant's academic performance and 15 years of experience in any of the following subjects, archaeology, architecture, conservation, history and anthropology. Furthermore, they had to have 5 or 6 years of experience in administration matters. A Bachelor's degree of Management was considered desirable. Apparently, the Ministry was not looking specifically for a field archaeologist with proven brilliance to run its Archaeological Survey, which incidentally is possibly, the largest organisation of its kind in the world.

What about the Archaeological Survey of India's professed commitment to archaeological research? I shall base myself again on the website of the Ministry of Culture. The Mission Statement of the Ministry refers to only the maintenance and conservation of heritage of historic sites and ancient monuments. Following this, the Archaeological Survey in its own website announces that the maintenance of ancient monuments and archaeological sites and remains of national importance is its primary concern. From this official point of view, the Archaeological Survey of India is not a research or academic body. It is essentially a maintenance organisation modelled on the PWD. I am using only their website information and my source is what they state there. So yes, they are reduced to the level of the PWD.

Whereas the PWD is concerned only with the construction and maintenance of modern structures, the Archaeological Survey of India's focus is on the maintenance and preservation of historic sites and monuments. We should soon get rid of the notion that the Archaeological Survey and its state-level counterparts are supported by the Government to advance academic purpose of archaeology. On a different level, let me point out that the study of inscriptions has always been one of the basic strengths of the Survey. Today a visit to the headquarter of their branch in Mysore is likely to be distressing, because of the lack of morale among the Survey epigraphers, if not for anything else.

The study of epigraphy and palaeography has to be raised to a higher level in the universities too. The Survey's conservation policy needs a close examination. I do not understand how the Ajanta paintings have been allowed to lose the warmth of their colours and how some portions have been allowed to be completely obliterated in one lifetime. I also do not understand why modern constructions are the rule of the day at conserved sites, basically changing their ancient character and ambience. It is indeed saddening that here is such a vast gap between idea and reality in Indian archaeology. However, behind all this litany of sorrows, still lies the basic task of researching ancient India.

About 200 years of research has built tapestries of various kinds in this field. One major tapestry is missing and that is history in relation to the present landscape of the country. People were moving about in the ancient context as they do now. They carved out kingdoms, cities and villages. They prospected and mined for resources, conducted trade and battles. They crossed rivers, passed through jungles, high mountain passes and deserts. How do they all relate to the land that we see, the land which still survives? If at all these different aspects of studies can be translated, in terms of the actual grounds that you can identify, the ancient history of the country is likely to be far more meaningful to us, than it is now.

I have attempted to achieve some of this in my own way, and my experience is that the ground that the ancients trod is still here before us. We know that Ashok, the prince, found the remaining relics of Buddha, but assuming that he travelled to Lumbini from his capital Pataliputra, can we trace his footsteps today, more than 2,000 years later? Can we know where he is likely to have crossed the Ganga, having set out from Pataliputra for Lumbini early one morning? Where could he have spent the night and where could he have crossed the Ghaghra? It is certainly possible to know all these things, provided you care for this kind of history – history that takes you to the past of this ancient land. In England, the study of this kind of topographical history goes back to the 17th century, providing the very important arc of reality to the historical knowledge of the country. It is still a neglected field in India, but is likely to lead to a fresh understanding between us and this land. We'd also realise that what happened in the ancient past has still not gone out of the landscape.

Finally, I would say, that the relationship between ancient Indian studies and the modern socio-politics of India as a country is more important than you realise. Many of our old premises regarding ancient India are academically wrong – its race-language-culture framework, the way its sources have been looked at, the ideas related to the origin of its various cultural elements, the way the different sections of the country have interacted and more. Each of these has bearing on how we think of our country as an ancient land and each of these is in need of careful scrutiny. It is unlikely that this established framework of studies, as sanctioned by the dominant groups of power in the Indian and foreign academia, will yield its place to the on-rush of new thoughts and approaches, quietly or peacefully. If a very senior Deccan College archaeologist can write that for India, the sun of culture and civilisation always rose in the West, and if challenging opinions such as these would be considered an act of Hindu fundamentalism by some of the established historians of the country, we must realise that we are in for sharp battles. Such battles can only be fought by well-trained, nationally committed historians and archaeologists. Leading the way with woolly ideas is no answer.

(This talk was delivered by Dr Chakrabarti at the VIF on August 31, 2011)

*

3

SWAMI VIVEKANANDA AND HIS CONTEMPORARY RELEVANCE

Ku. Nivedita Bhide

All those who are present here, my *namaskars* to you all. As it has been suggested by some in the audience here, I would speak more in Hindi and may be less in English.

You know when we speak about the relevance of Swami Vivekananda, अर्थात स्वामी विवेकानंद की प्रासंगिकता आज के काल में क्या है, अगर हम, वाह्य रूप से देखते हैं तो शायद स्वामी विवेकानंद एक ऐसे व्यक्ति हैं, जिनका जन्म, भारत भ्रमण, भाषण, भारत में पुनरागमन, जिनकी इन सारी घटनाओं का चाहें सौ वर्ष हो जायें या एक सौ पच्चीसवाँ हो यह उत्सव तो हम मनाते ही रहेंगे। It is not only his birth, but every landmark in his life is being celebrated in our country. This year we are celebrating the 125th anniversary of his speech at Chicago.

शायद ही ऐसा कोई व्यक्ति है जिनके जीवन की हर मुख्य घटनायें, जब सौ वर्ष होते हैं, एक सौ पचीस या एक सौ पचास वर्ष होते हैं, तो वो हम मना रहे हैं। हम देखते हैं कि स्वामी विवेकानन्द में ऐसी सकारात्मकता थी, और है, कि आज भी उनका नाम लेकर हम जहाँ भी जाते हैं, स्वागत ही होता है अर्थात, no one says I have nothing to do with Swami Vivekananda or I don't want Vivekananda or I don't accept Vivekananda. इसका एक बहुत उत्तम उदहारण है कि जब विवेकानंद शिला स्मारक बनाया जा रहा था और उसके लिए अनुमति की आवश्यकता थी, तो उस समय सांसदों के हस्ताक्षर लिए गए, उसमें सभी पार्टियों के सभी सांसदों ने हस्ताक्षर किया। अर्थात उस समय दिल्ली में उपस्थित 323 सांसदों ने उसके लिए स्वीकृति दी। उसके बाद भी स्मारक बनते समय जिस भी पक्ष की राज्य सरकारें थीं, सभी राज्य सरकारों ने उसके लिए लगभग एक-एक लाख रूपये दिए।

इस सन्दर्भ में एक घटना याद आती है कि when someone went to Rabindranath Tagore and said, 'I want to know India, so what should I do?' He said, 'Read Vivekananda. In him everything is positive, nothing negative.'

जब हम सब, स्वामी विवेकानन्द की एक सौ पचासवीं जयंती मना रहे थे, उस समय भी ऐसा अनुभव सबको हुआ था। जो स्वामी विवेकानंद सार्ध शती समारोह समिति बनाई गई थी, जहाँ भी गए स्वामी विवेकानंद का सब जगह स्वागत हुआ था।

तो सारी सकारात्मकता उनमें है। हम देखते हैं, आज भी उनसे प्रेरणा लेकर अनेक रचनात्मक विधायक कार्य करने वाले लोग, पूरे देश भर में, आप कहीं भी जाइए, उपस्थित हैं। अभी हम उत्तरकाशी में थे। उत्तरकाशी से गंगोत्री जाने के मार्ग में भी स्वामी विवेकानंद के नाम से एक विद्यालय देखा गया है, कन्याकुमारी के बहुत छोटे–छोटे गांवों में जाते समय स्वामी विवेकानंद के नाम से सेवा कार्य करने वाले नाना प्रकार के सेवा मंडल मिलेंगे। आप देश में और कहीं जाइए, असम से लेकर कन्याकुमारी तक में भी आपको मिलेंगे, स्वामी विवेकानंद सेवा मंडल इत्यादि। उत्तर हो या दक्षिण, पूरब हो या पश्चिम, स्वामी विवेकानंद से प्रेरणा लेकर समाज में सकारात्मक कार्य करने वाले अनेक लोग हैं। हम वाह्य स्तर से देखते हैं तो ये तीन बातें दिखती हैं, इसका मतलब निश्चित ही स्वामी विवेकानंद ने भारतवासियों के हृदय को छुआ है, स्पर्श किया है और आज भी वो उन्हें प्रेरणा देते हैं।

So, definitely he is very relevant. However, we are not going to take only what is evident, but we shall also see at the thought level, what is the relevance of Swami Vivekananda, even today. There are many dimensions, as Arvind Gupta ji was mentioning – youth, women and so on, but I am not going to touch on these topics today though these are also very important, or even the personality development or personal enrichment for which Swami Vivekananda inspires whosoever reads his works. (May be we can address them during the question and answers.) We are not going to dwell on those dimensions now in the given time, but we shall try to see 3 important dimensions at the national level in the context of nation-rebuilding.

जब स्वामी विवेकानंद शिकागो जाने से पहले परिभ्रमण में गए तो उन्होंने भारत का जो चित्र देखा, वह वेदना देने वाला चित्र था। जो राष्ट्र, इस विश्व में सबसे ज्यादा काल के लिए धनी रहा है, स्वर्ण भूमि रहा है, ऐसा देश दारिद्र्य में घिरा हुआ था। ऐसा देश जिसमें ज्ञान की साधना होती थी, उपासना होती थी, दूर-दूर देश से लोग, यहाँ आकर सीखते थे, वह देश अज्ञानता में घिरा हुआ था। लेकिन उसी समय स्वामी जी ने यह भी देखा कि ऐसे भी लोग थे, जो एक–एक दर्शन के अध्ययन के लिए अपना पूरा जीवन लगा दिए थे। जिस दर्शन की चर्चा विद्वान करते थे वह सहजता से अपनी जीवन की भाषा में बोलने वाले, जिनको हम अशिक्षित या निरक्षर कहते है, उनको भी स्वामीजी ने देखा। ऐसे लोग जो आसानी से बोल देते थे कि 'ठीक है मेरा तो यही कर्म है, ये सारी भगवान की लीला है', अर्थात जीवन का दुख सहन करने की ताकत भी उन्होंने गाँव–गाँव में भ्रमण करते हुए गरीबों में, किसानों में देखी। जिसकी आध्यात्मिकता गहरी होती है, वही जीवन की चुनौतियों को आसानी से झेल सकता हैं – हँसते हुए, सहजता से। As we say in English, he flows with the tide, he flows as a river. He doesn't get stuck or get stagnated with misfortunes. He doesn't keep crying.

स्वामी विवेकानन्द ने देखा कि दारिद्र्य, अज्ञानता और अवनति के बावजूद कुछ शक्ति भारत में निहित है। उसी समय उन्होंने जो अवनति हुई थी, वो भी देखी। इसीलिए बहुत दुख से वो कन्याकुमारी गए और वहाँ समुद्र में स्थित शिला पर बैठकर, he meditated for three days and three nights to find out what he should do to raise his people, his country. Sitting there on the last bit of Indian Rock, he took the decision to go to America and to participate in the Parliament of Religions to represent the eternal principles of Hindu Dharma. उसके बाद वे अमेरिका गए, शिकागो में उन्होंने हिन्दू धर्म का प्रतिनिधित्व किया। लेकिन उस इतिहास में हम जाने वाले नहीं है।

स्वामी विवेकानंद ने राष्ट्रीय पुनरुत्थान के लिए हमें क्या दिया, जो आज भी हम अपने कर्म से, कार्य से साकार कर रहे हैं और पूरा नहीं करे हैं। एक तो उन्होंने देखा कि सतत आक्रमणों के कारण हम स्वसंरक्षण के मोड में चले गए थे। हर आक्रमण में जो भी थे, स्वयं का, स्वयं के परिवार का, ज्यादा से ज्यादा गाँव के संरक्षण का ही विचार कर रहे थे। अनेक वर्ष ऐसा करते-करते हमारे राष्ट्र का परिप्रेक्ष्य छूट गया था। Somewhere we lost our national consciousness, जो पहले कभी था।

वेदों में हम राष्ट्र की धारणा करते हैं, राष्ट्र सूक्त है, अश्वमेध यज्ञ पूरे भारत में होता था। हमारे चार धाम और बारह ज्योतिर्लिंग हैं और भी ऐसी अनेक बातें हैं। हम उनकी चर्चा नहीं कर रहे हैं, लेकिन वह राष्ट्रीय चेतना जो थी, वह हमने खो दी है। We were, so to say, caught in our own family or at most, community web and were not going beyond that.

Swamiji Aroused National Consciousness

Therefore, the first work that Swami Vivekananda did was to rouse the national consciousness. Swami Vivekananda acknowledged this in an interview to the representative of the '*Prabuddha Bharata*' (*Prabuddha Bharata*, Vol. V, p. 225, September 1898). He asked Swamiji, "And what do you consider to be the function of your movement as regards India?" Swamiji replied, "To find the common bases of Hinduism and awaken the national consciousness in them."

How did Swamiji do it? We will take a look at two or three points. We see how Swami Vivekananda always stood for the whole nation. Each one of us has to take birth in some region or the other. Because of that we belong to certain region. We are born into certain traditions; therefore, may be we have a certain *ishta devata* and one *sampradaya*. But when one is in society or when one stands for the nation, he or she should work only from a national perspective and not from any of the smaller perspectives. मुझे पूरे राष्ट्र का, राष्ट्रहित का विचार करते हुए ही, राष्ट्र का प्रतिनिधित्व करते हुए ही, मैं जहाँ भी हूँ, मैंने कार्य करना है।

हम देखते हैं स्वामी विवेकानंद स्वयं ऐसे थे कल्पना कीजिये जो स्वामी विवेकानंद कहते थे कि, 'मेरे गुरु, श्री रामकृष्ण परमहंस एक मिट्टी के ढेले से हजारों विवेकानंद बना सकते थे, मै क्या हूँ। मै कुछ भी नहीं हूँ'। ऐसा कहने वाले स्वामी विवेकानंद जब शिकागो में गए और धर्म संसद में उन्होंने जो भी भाषण दिये (11 सितंबरसे 27 सितंबर तक) उन किसी भी भाषण में श्री रामकृष्ण परमहंस का उल्लेख उन्होंने नहीं किया। इससे उनके कुछ गुरुभाई नाराज़ हुए और कुछ लोग भी नाराज़ हुए। उन्हीनें प्रश्न पूछा कि 'आपने गुरु रामकृष्ण परमहंस की बात क्यों नहीं की?'

तब उन्होंने जवाब दिया कि 'मैं जो भी बोला हूँ, वह सब मैं रामकृष्ण परमहंस से, ठाकुर से ही सीखा हूँ। लेकिन, यदि उनका नाम लेकर बोलता तो मैं सारे हिन्दुओं का प्रतिनिधित्व नहीं करता', यह जो मोह होता है कि मै कहाँ से हूँ उसको लेते हुए ही बात करना उस मोह के कारण पूरे हिन्दू समाज का प्रतिनिधित्व करना हम भूल जाते हैं।

यहाँ विविधता होने के कारण कभी-कभी तो ऐसे प्रश्न पूछें जातें हैं की क्या सच में यह राष्ट्र एक हैं? यहाँ इतनी विविधता हैं, क्या कोई समानता भी हैं? ये जो सारी विविधता है, उसके परे जाते हुए हम सबको जोड़ने वाले समान सूत्र क्या है ? उन सूत्रों पर हमारा ध्यान आकर्षित करना आवश्यक था और उन्होंने यह कार्य किया। We have to focus our attention on the commonalities, on the common basis of our Hindu society.

ये क्या सूत्र है ? स्वामी विवेकानंद ने बताया कि हम सभी इस सृष्टि को एकात्म भाव से ही देखते हैं, यानी यह जो पूरी सृष्टि है, ये परस्पर जुड़ी हुई है, परस्पर संबंधित और परस्परावलंबी है। एक ही अनेक रूप से प्रगटित हुआ है। यदि हमें ईश्वर की भाषा में बोलना है तो ईश्वर ही इन सभी रुपों में व्याप्त है। चाहें द्वैत दर्शन हो, अद्वैत हो, विशिष्टाद्वैत हो, मधुराद्वैत हो लेकिन ईश्वर सर्वत्र है। इसे सब मानते हैं। एक ही अनेक रूपों से प्रगटित होने के कारण पूरी सृष्टि परस्पर जुड़ी हुई है, परस्पर संबंधित और परस्परावलंबी है। स्वामी विवेकानंद बार–बार कहते थे, 'This vision of oneness is going to be India's greatest contribution to the world.'

यह एकात्मता हमारे परिवार का आधार था, हमारी सामाजिक व्यवस्था का आधार था, हमारे ग्राम्य व्यवस्था का आधार था और हमारी शिक्षा व्यवस्था का आधार था। स्वामी विवेकानंद कहते हैं कि इस एकात्मता को यदि हम खो देते हैं, तो हमारी विविधता इतनी है कि हम एक दूसरे से जुड़े नहीं रह सकते। इसलिए यह एकात्म जीवन दर्शन हमारी राष्ट्रीयता का आधार है। उन्होंने जो दूसरा महत्वपूर्ण सूत्र बताया, वह था कि हम मनुष्य को पापी नहीं समझते हैं, उसका बेकार का जन्म नहीं हुआ है। मनुष्य तो ईश्वर स्वरूप है।

Swami Vivekananda used to say, 'Each soul is potentially divine. The goal of life is to manifest that divinity, by controlling the nature external and internal. Do this by work or worship, by psychic control or knowledge, by one or more or all and be free.' यह प्राथमिक महत्व का है बाकी देवता, पुस्तक, उपासना की पद्धती सारे उस ईश्वरत्व के प्रगटीकरण के केवल माध्यम मात्र है।

कोई भी सम्प्रदाय हम लेते हैं, तो उसका मुख्य उद्देश्य क्या है? मनुष्य को अपने ईश्वर स्वरूप को समझना है, उसकी अनूभूति करनी है। Swami ji puts it still better. He called, 'To manifest the divinity.' Therefore, whatever we do, it should have excellence, oneness and compassion in that. But unfortunately, for centuries as we were concerned only about our self-defence. The focus on this was lost. We have to manifest that excellence, that divinity, that feeling of oneness. यह मनुष्य जीवन का परमोच्च ध्येय है और यह हम सब मानते हैं। मनुष्य की आत्मा ईश्वर स्वरूप है, इसलिए हम मनुष्य को पापी नहीं कहते हैं।

तीसरा सूत्र यह है कि हमारे लिए समय अर्थात काल चक्रीय है। Time is cyclic. It is not linear in which it is said that the world started on such and such date and will permemnantly end on one day. Today, in scientific circles also it is realized that time is not absolute and it is not linear. कर्म, पुनर्जन्म बहुत है लेकिन उसमें ना जाते हुए

एक और समान सूत्र जो वे कहते हैं, वह है धर्म, जिसका जिक्र श्री अरविन्द जी ने भी किया था। Swami Vivekananda says, 'It is not in believing but it is in being and becoming. It is in practising.' जैसे कोई कहता हैं 'हाँ, मै भगवान श्री कृष्ण में बहुत विश्वास करता हूँ' लेकिन उसके व्यवहार में आत्मीयता और नैतिकता शून्य हैं, तो भगवान श्री कृष्ण उसे बचाने वाले नहीं हैं – केवल विश्वास नही, व्यवहार क्या है इस पर जोर दिया जाता हैं। Therefore, dharma is in being and becoming, not in believing.

स्वामी विवेकानंद 'मैं' की परिभाषा देते हैं। जब मैं 'मैं' कहता हूँ, वह मैं क्या है? एक व्यक्ति तो हूँ ही लेकिन मै किसी परिवार का भी अंग हूँ या गाँव का अंग हूँ, किसी शहर का भी अंग हूँ, 'मैं' इस राष्ट्र का अंग हूँ, 'मैं' इस मानव समाज का अंग हूँ, 'मैं' इस पूरी सृष्टि का अंग हूँ, इन सब समष्टियों का अंग होने के नाते, I have a certain duty towards each collective.

हर समष्टि के प्रति मेरा कोई कर्तव्य है, वह कर्तव्य मेरा धर्म है और उस धर्म की हम बात करते हैं। मै एक परिवार का अंग हूँ तो मेरे कारण परिवार में आनंद रहना है। समरसता रहनी है, 'हार्मोनी' रहनी है। मै एक समाज का अंग हूँ तो वहाँ भी मुझे वैसे ही व्यवहार करना है, मै इस राष्ट्र का अंग हूँ तो इस राष्ट्र के प्रति मेरा जो कर्तव्य है, वो मुझे पूरा करना है और मेरे कारण मेरे राष्ट्र की एकात्मता बढनी है, मेरे राष्ट्र को और आगे जाना है। मैं इस सृष्टि का अंग हूँ तो इस निसर्ग का, इस पर्यावरण का मुझे संरक्षण करना है, क्योंकि 'मैं' इससे अलग नहीं हूँ। यदि हम इसका शोषण करते हैं, तो हमारा शोषण हो जाएगा। इसको नष्ट करते हुए हम नष्ट हो जायेंगे। क्योंकि एकात्मता हमारे अस्तित्व का आधार हैं, हम सब परस्पर जुड़े हुए, परस्पर सम्बन्धित और परस्परावलम्बी हैं।

The understanding and practice of Dharma is related with oneness, all our values come from this vision of oneness. Actually, values are always visional. जीवन दर्शन से ही, उस जीवन मूल्य की व्याप्ति और प्रत्यक्ष में उसकी क्या प्रैक्टिस होती है ये समझ सकते हैं बाकि प्रेम, करुणा, अहिंसा, शांति, इन शब्दों का उपयोग तो दुनिया के सारे लोग करते हैं। परन्तु सच में इन मूल्यों का प्रत्यक्ष में कैसा व्यवहार होगा यह तो उस संस्कृति का जीवन दर्शन क्या है, उससे ही समझते हैं। Therefore, values are always visional. They are not in isolation or with absolute meaning. जैसे भाईचारे के बारे में बात करेंगे, तो हमारा दर्शन जिससे पूरे विश्व को एक ही ईश्वर तत्त्व का प्रगटीकरण देखते हैं तो हमारे लिए भाईचारा का अर्थ सिर्फ मानव के प्रति ही नहीं, सबके प्रति भाइचारे का होगा – सर्वे भवन्तु सुखिनः।

स्वामी विवेकानंद कहते हैं कि हम परिवार, समाज, राष्ट्र, सृष्टि सबके अंग होने के नाते हम जहाँ भी हैं, हमें हमारी भूमिका एक साथ निभानी है, ऐसा नहीं है कि इस जन्म में परिवार का अंग हूँ वह दायित्व निभाऊंगा और अगले जन्म में समाज का देखूंगा। इसलिए ये जीवन सही अर्थसे दूसरों के लिए जीकर ही धन्य होता है। He said, 'The life is short and the vanities of life are many. But they alone live who live for others the rest are more dead than alive.'

A person is part of all these collectives simultaneously and therefore, he or she has a duty towards all these collectives. ऐसे ही भारतियों का जीवन था। जिस भी देश में भारतीय गए उन्होंने वहाँ योगदान ही दिया। वे कभी वहाँ समस्या नहीं बनें। भारतीय लोग प्राचीन काल से, यानी बौद्ध काल के पहले भी जो हिन्दू व्यापारी अलग–अलग देशों में गए, जो

धर्म प्रचारक गए। ब्रिटीश जो बंधुआ मजदूर (bonded labour) लेकर गए, आज जो आईटी प्रोफेशनल्स जाते हैं, हम जिस भी काल में, देश में हों, हम जहाँ–जहाँ गए, वहाँ सर्वथा हमने शांति और समृद्धि ही लाई।

We always contributed to the harmony of the local society. We never destroyed it; we never became a problem there. Generally nobody cherishes the invaders or those who came and occupied their land and brought a foreign culture. But if we look at Cambodia, Thailand and all these countries, they cherish India. Why? Because we did not destroy the local gods and goddesses; because we knew how to integrate without destroying. We only gave them a larger vision.

For example, when we Indians went to Thailand and saw that the local worshiped certain deities, we never said their deities were wrong. We only said, 'she is mother to you, true. But not only to you, she is also Mother of the whole world and by different names she is invoked by others'. We only enlarged their understanding of God. We never destroyed the local deities. That is why even today they cherish us. Wherever Indians went, they brought only harmony there, because of this understanding of dharma that I am part of the *samashti*, therefore, my duty is always to the collective.

आज दुर्दैव से हमने धर्म का अनुवाद 'रिलिजन' कर दिया है। और हमें किसी रिलिजन (That means exclusive religion) के अनुसार राज्य नहीं चलाना है, इसलिए हमने अपने आप को 'धर्म निरपेक्ष' घोषित दिया। स्वामी विवेकानंद कहते हैं, 'भारत का प्राण धर्म है। जिस राष्ट्र का प्राण ही धर्म है, उस प्राण को ही अलग रखते हुए हम राष्ट्र का पुनर्निर्माण करने जा रहे हैं।' प्राण को अलग कर दिया। धर्म हमारी शब्दावली से, अपनी समझ से जा रहा है, भ्रांति निर्माण हो रही है इसलिए स्वामी विवेकानंद ने धर्म पर बहुत जोर दिया।

यदि मै इन सारी समष्टियों का अंग हूँ और मुझे उसके अनुसार व्यवहार करना है तो जीवन में एक महत्वपूर्ण आयाम जुड़ता है, जो अपने भारतीय सम्प्रदायों में, पंथो में महत्वपूर्ण माना जाता है और वह है संयम – आत्मसंयम।

If I am excessively individualistic, I cannot really bring harmony for others. ये जो restraint हैं वह मनुष्य जीवन को उन्नत करने के लिए आवश्यक है। As Swami Vivekananda says, each soul is potentially divine and the goal of life is to manifest that divinity by controlling the nature external and internal. Though there are diverse संप्रदाय, this importance of self-restraint is also common for all. Life of restraint is essential if we want to rebuild our nation. इस प्रकार स्वामी जी ने हम सबके समान सूत्र क्या हैं? यह बताया, कि विविधता होने के बावजूद भी हम एक राष्ट्र हैं, यह उन्होंने हमारे ध्यान में लाया।

Swamiji Emphasized on the Destined Mission of India

उन्होंने यह भी बताया कि भारत की संस्कृति का, इस राष्ट्र का कोई प्रयोजन है। जैसे पूरे विश्व में हर संस्कृति ने कुछ न कुछ मानव विकास के लिए योगदान किया है। He said, 'Each nation has a destiny to fulfil. Each nation has a message to deliver; a mission to accomplish. Therefore, from the very start, we must understand the mission of our own race; the destiny it has to fulfil; the place it has to occupy in the march of the nations, and note which it has to contribute to the harmony of races' (*Complete Works of Swami Vivekananda* [henceforth, *CWSV*], Vol. III, p. 369).

What is the contribution that India has to make for the good of the humanity? Swami Vivekananda explains, 'This is the theme of Indian life-work, the burden of her eternal songs, the backbone of her existence, the foundation of her being, the raison d'être of her very existence the spiritualization of the human race. In this her life-course she has never deviated, whether the Tartar ruled or the Turk, whether the Mogul ruled or the English' (*CWSV*, volume IV, p. 315). But he also warns us, 'we must not forget that what I mean ...by spiritual thought is the sending out of life-giving principles, not the hundreds of superstitions that we have been hugging to our breasts for centuries. These have to be weeded out even on this soil, and thrown aside, so that they may die for ever' (*CWSV*, volume III, pp. 277-278).

This vision of 'Oneness' which India internalised and built her national life on it; the acceptance of diversity; the divinity of man; the understanding of Dharma, are to be the contributions of India. Swamiji explains it beautifully,

> "The other great idea that the world wants from us today, the thinking part of Europe, nay, the whole world ...**is that eternal grand idea of the spiritual oneness of the whole universe.** I need not tell you today, how the modern researches of the West have demonstrated through physical means the oneness and the solidarity of the whole universe; how, physically speaking, you and I, the Sun, moon, and stars are but little waves or wavelets in the midst of an infinite ocean of matter; how Indian psychology demonstratedthat ages ago. Similarly, both body and mind are but mere names or little wavelets in the ocean of matter, the *Samashti*; and how, going one step further, it is also shown in the Vedanta that behind that idea of the unity of the whole show, the real Soul is one. There is but one Soul throughout the universe, all is but One Existence. This great idea of the real and basic solidarity of the whole universe ...is the one great life-giving idea which the world wants from us today, and which the mute masses of India want for their uplifting, for none can regenerate this land of ours without the practical application and effective operation of this ideal of the Oneness of things". (*CWSV*, Vol. III, pp. 188-189)

Whenever the word India is uttered, what comes before our minds is the diversity of colours, forms of Gods and Goddesses, dresses, traditions, festivals etc. And yet this land has been emotionally, culturally one land. Swami

Vivekananda explains, 'Ekam Sat Viprah Bahudha Vadanti' – 'He who exists is One, the sages call it variously'. This is one of the most memorable sentences ever uttered, one of the grandest truths that was ever discovered. And for us Hindus, this truth has been the very backbone of our national existence. Throughout the vistas of the centuries of our national life, this one idea comes down, gaining in volume and in fullness till it has permeated the whole of our national existence, till it has mingled in our blood, and has become one with us. We live that grand truth in every vein, and our country has become the glorious land of religious toleration. It is here and here alone that they build temples and churches for the religions that have come with the objective of condemning our own religion. This is one very great principle that the world is waiting to learn from us. Little do we know how much of intolerance is yet abroad. It struck me more than once that I should have to leave my bones on foreign shores owing to the prevalence of religious intolerance. Killing a man is nothing for religion's sake.

The civilizations, after making contribution to the humanity, disappear in the flow of time. But Indian civilization lives on. क्योंकि भारतीय संस्कृति का एक ऐसा योगदान है, जो सतत चलता रहेगा। यह है ईश्वर स्वरूप का प्रगटीकरण या एकात्म जीवन दर्शनपर आधारित जीवन पद्धति। राष्ट्र के इस नियत कार्य को यदि हम भूलते हैं तो फिर राष्ट्र की अवनति निश्चित है, ऐसा स्वामी जी कहते हैं। We are connected to the whole world, thus we should not be only living for ourselves. That is contraction. Contraction is death. Thus, when we reduced the scope of our actions, when we said that even crossing the sea is a sin, when we stopped working for the good of the humanity, then the degeneration had begun.

इस राष्ट्र का प्रयोजन है, पूरे विश्व का आध्यात्म में मार्गदर्शन करना, उसी को हमने छोड़ दिया। इस प्रयोजन को ध्यान में लिए बिना, इस राष्ट्र का पुनरुत्थान नहीं हो सकता। राष्ट्र का पुनरुत्थान यानी बहुत अच्छी सड़कें बन गयीं, बहुत अच्छे infrastructure हो गए, हमारी इकॉनोमी सुधर गई, इतने से नहीं होगा। ये सभी चीजें बहुत आवश्यक हैं, लेकिन राष्ट्र की आत्मा को यदि प्रगटित होना है, इस राष्ट्र के प्रयोजन को यदि सफल करना है तो हमें अपनी आध्यात्मिकता को, इस एकात्मता को समझते हुए ही आगे जाना होगा। इसलिए स्वामी विवेकानंद कहते हैं कि हमारी सारी पुरानी व्यवस्थाएँ तोड़-मरोड़ दी गई हैं। Swami Vivekananda explains it and exhorts us to continue the work of our Rishis.Swamiji says,

> "This is my method to show the Hindus that they have to give up nothing, but only to move on in the line laid down by the sages and shake off their inertia, the result of centuries of servitude. Of course, we had to stop advancing during the Mohammedan tyranny, for then it was not a question of progress but of life and death. Now that that pressure has gone, we must move forward, not on the lines of destruction directed by renegades and missionaries, but along our own line, our own road. Everything is hideous because the building is

unfinished. We had to stop building during centuries of oppression. Now finish the building and everything will look beautiful in its own place. This is all my plan. I am thoroughly convinced of this". (*CWSV,* volume III, p. 373).

We also have to use our discretion while rebuilding our systems. Not everything is to be thrown out or is outdated. Swami Vivekananda said, 'The degeneration of India came not because the laws and customs of the ancients were bad, but because they were not allowed to be carried to their legitimate conclusions. ... At their inception, these laws were the embodiment of a gigantic plan, which was to unfold itself slowly through time. The great seers of ancient India saw so far ahead of their time that the world has to wait centuries yet to appreciate their wisdom' (*CWSV,* Vol. IV, pp. 324-25).

फिर से हमारी कुटुम्ब व्यवस्था, ग्राम व्यवस्था, शहरी व्यवस्था – शहर तो उस समय इतने नहीं थे – हमें वो भी देखना होगा। चाहे शिक्षा व्यवस्था हो, सामाजिक व्यवस्था हो; ये सारी व्यवस्थायें एकात्मता पर आधारित कैसे हो सकती हैं, यह हमारी सबसे बड़ी चुनौती है। When we say we have to rebuild the nation, this is what it entails. All these systems are to be based on an Indian ethos, on oneness. अभी तो हम अनुकरण ही कर रहें हैं। लेकिन हमें विश्व का मार्गदर्शन कर सकें, ऐसे कार्य करने हैं।

विश्व के विद्वानों की भी भारत से यह अपेक्षा हैं। Will Durant, the great American historian, said,

> 'It is true that even across the Himalayan barrier India has sent to us such questionable gifts as grammar and logic, philosophy and fables, hypnotism and chess, and above all numerals, and our decimal system. But these are not the essence of her spirit; they are trifles compared to what we may learn from her in the future. Perhaps in return for conquest, arrogance and spoliation, India will teach us tolerance and gentleness of the mature mind, the quiet content of the unacquisitive soul, the calm understanding of the spirit, and a unifying, a pacifying, love for all living things. (*The Case for India*, 1931)

The Methodology for Nation-Building

Swami Vivekananda aroused national consciousness, motivating us to see the commonalities that bind us together inspite of various beautiful diverse identities. Secondly, he gave direction to national regeneration. Third, he gave the methodology to do so. स्वामी जी ने देखा कि ये भारत राष्ट्र एक भयानक मोड़ पर आकर खड़ा है। दो रास्ते हैं उसके सामने और दोनों रास्ते खतरनाक हैं। एक से वह बंध कर रह जाएगा, दूसरे से वह समाप्त हो जाएगा। ये दो रास्ते कौन से थे? एक तो जिस प्रकार से हम ऑर्थोडॉक्सी में, जकड़ गए थे, उसपर स्वामी जी बहुत कड़क प्रहार करते हैं। अस्पृश्यता को लेकर; he said you have reduced everything to a kitchen religion. नहाने के पहले हाथ कितनी बार धोना है और कुल्ला कितनी बार करना है, क्या पागलपन में हम अटक गए हैं? यह सब क्या हो गया है?

ऐसा भी हुआ है कि इतिहास में जब-जब आक्रमण हुए तो उस समय हमें कुछ उपाय–योजना करनी पड़ी। दुर्दैव से उन तात्कालिक उपायों–योजनाओं को ही हम परंपरा समझने लगे। जैसे हमारी महिलाओं की रक्षा के लिए हमने उनको स्कूल भेजना बंद कर दिया क्योंकि वो बाहर जाती थीं तो आक्रांता उन्हें उठाकर लेकर जाते थे। ऐसी स्थिति में वो घर में सीमित हो गई और हम कहने लगे कि यह हमारी परंपरा है कि स्त्री बाहर नहीं जाएगी, पढ़ेगी नहीं। यह एक छोटा सा उदाहरण है। इस विषय में हम काफ़ी बाहर आए हैं और आ रहे हैं। लेकिन ऐसे ऐतिहासिक काल में जो कोई तात्कलिक उपाय स्वीकारे थे, उनको हमने परम्परा बोलना शुरू कर दिया, इनको पकड़ के हम जकड़े हुए बैठे थे। ये एक मार्ग, जिसको हम पकडे हुए रहेंगे तो, बंधकर रह जायेंगे।

दूसरा जो मार्ग भारत के सामने था वह था कि पश्चिम में सब कुछ अच्छा है और उनका अनुकरण करते हुए हम उन्ही की तरह करने लगे। इसमें विज्ञान और तकनीकी की बात नहीं हैं। वह तो सारे ही देशों ने एक दूसरे से सीखनी हैं। ये जीवन मूल्यों की, जीवन पद्धति की बात हैं। हम उनकी जीवन पद्धति अपना रहे हैं, ऐसा सोचकर की वही श्रेष्ठ है। उस जीवन पद्धति से व्यक्तिवाद आ गया, उपभोक्तावाद आ गया या फिर वैचारिक स्तर की सारी विचारधारायें भी आ जाती हैं। स्वामी जी ने उस समय जब बात की तब जितनी भी विचारधाराएँ थीं और उसके बाद भी जो आईं, वो सारी हमें नष्ट करने वाली थीं और हैं। हम फिर भी उनका अनुकरण करेंगे, follow करेंगे और अपने विचारों को भूल जायेंगे तो यह भारत राष्ट्र, भारत नहीं रहेगा। यह भारत अपनी आत्मा, अपनी पहचान खो देगा। ऐसे दो खतरनाक रास्ते पर हम खड़े थे।

हमें तीसरे रास्ते की आवश्यकता थी, जो स्वामी विवेकानंद ने हमें दिखाया। उन्होंने कहा कि हमारी संस्कृति ने, हमारे राष्ट्र ने ऐसी समस्याएं अनेक बार झेली हैं, सिर्फ याद करिये हमारे यहाँ तरीका है श्रुति और स्मृति का। श्रुति जो शाश्वत है उसको पकड़ना है और स्मृति जो है, उन शाश्वत मूल्यों को, बदले हुए काल में फिर से जीवन में लाने के लिए व्यवस्था हैं। अलग-अलग काल की अलग अलग स्मृति है। मै मनुस्मृति की बात नहीं कर रही हूँ। फिर से बताती हूँ, यह व्यवस्थाओं की बात है। हमारे यहाँ अनेक स्मृति हैं, अनेक काल में एक–एक स्मृति हुई है, स्मृति यह बड़ा शब्द हो गया है, जिसका स्वामी जी ने उपयोग किया। परन्तु एक और संदर्भ में वे कहते हैं कि 'as per the need of time, we have to modify or create proper systems, practices which help us in practicing our eternal values'. यदि हम वह नहीं करते हैं तो हम नष्ट हो जाएंगे।

श्री रामकृष्ण परमहंस का दिया हुआ एक उदाहरण है। यह शाश्वत को रखते हुए कालानुसार बदलने वाली व्यवस्था क महत्व को समझने के लिए बहुत अच्छा है। हम सब चावल खाते हैं। अभी हम सब चावल कैसे खाते हैं? धान को कूटकर हम हस्क निकाल देते हैं और बचा हुआ चावल खाते हैं। कोई ऐसा, जिसे डेढ़-सयाना कहते हैं या ज्यादा सोचने वाला कहते हैं, यदि ऐसा सोचता है, कि हम तो चावल खाते हैं फिर धान को क्यों बोना है? फिर धान कूटना पड़ता है, तभी चावल मिलता हैं। इससे अच्छा तो सीधा चावल बो दें, तो चावल मिलेगा। ऐसा सोचते हुए अगर हम चावल बो दें तो चावल नहीं मिलेगा। चावल चाहिए तो धान लगाना ही पड़ेगा। तभी एक फसल से दूसरी फसल में हमें चावल मिल सकता है। Similarly, certain customs, rituals, practices are necessary at the family and societal levels to transmit eternal values from one generation to the next.

लेकिन आज क्या हो गया है कि हम ये सब करने की जरूरत नहीं है, ऐसा समझते हैं। हम कहते हैं ये सारे विधि-विधान की क्या आवश्यकता है। केवल ज्ञान चाहिए और उसके लिए तो

गीता है, उपनिषद है, हम वह पढ़ लेंगे। परन्तु यह इतना आसान नही है। जो मूल्य प्रसारित करना चाहते हैं वे भाषण से नहीं आते या पुस्तक पढ़ने से नहीं आते, अपितु क्रिया–कलापों से; विधि-विधान से; नीति-नियमों का नियमित पालन करने से आते है। मैं आपको छोटा सा उदाहरण बताती हूँ, मैं एक पुस्तक पढ़ रही थी *Battle Between God and Gods.* The book explains how Christianity spread in Rome. During that period, the Romans were all struggling to somehow stop this monotheistic invasion on their polytheistic culture. Christians were claiming that their God is the Supreme Being of the universe and Romans did not have the Supreme Being as they have many Gods. The Romans did not know how to face this challege of Supreme Being. Some emperors tried to declare one of their Gods as the Supreme Being but it did not go well with some others. इन देवों के विविध रूपों से परे जाते हुए एक Supreme Being को पहचानने में वो बस थोडा चुक रहे थे। अंततः वे अपनी संस्कृति नष्ट कर दिए। So, ultimately, they lost their culture. बहुत अच्छी पुस्तक है, पढ़ने लायक है।

भारत में भी अनेक देवी-देवता हैं लेकिन 'एकम सत विप्राः बहुधा वदन्ति', यह तत्व जानने के कारण यहाँ एकेश्वरवादी लोगों के आक्रमणों के बावजूद यह समस्या आयी नहीं। वह पुस्तक पढ़ते समय मेरे ध्यान में आया कि इतने बड़े–बड़े लोग पश्चिम में जो बात समझते नहीं हैं या बहुत प्रयासों से समझते हैं, वह बात हमारे देश का छोटा तीन–चार वर्ष का बच्चा भी समझता है कि भगवान के अनेक रूप और नाम हो सकते हैं परन्तु भगवान एक है। घर में, जैसे हम सबका अनुभव है – बच्चे का जन्मदिन है तो उसे नया कपड़ा पहनाकर कहते हैं कि जाओ भगवान को नमस्कार करके आओ। बहुत सारे घरों में पूजा–घर होता है, जिसमें भगवान के अनेक रुपों के चित्र या मूर्तियाँ होती हैं। बच्चा पूछता नहीं कि किसको नमस्कार करू! बच्चा अंदर जाकर एक नमस्कार करके बाहर आता है।

अर्थात इतने सारे भगवान के नाम और रूप हैं लेकिन भगवान एक है, इतना बड़ा तत्व जो अन्य देशों के बड़े–बड़े विचारकों से भी छूट जाता है, वह हमारे देश के बच्चे कैसे समझते हैं? क्योंकि हमारे घर की जो विधि-रीतियाँ हैं उसे वह समझता है।

Practices in themselves may be meaningless. However, when done with faith, they transmit values. For example, माँ अपने एक वर्ष के बच्चे को कहती है कि चलो भगवान के दर्शन करने जाएंगे। फिर वो निकलती है, जाते समय वो मन्दिर के पास आती है तो पहले दहलीज़ को नमस्कार करती है फिर वो अंदर जाती है, वहाँ पीपल का पेड़ है, उसको नमस्कार करती है, फिर गणेश मंदिर में गणेश जी को प्रणाम करती है, फिर जो भगवान की मुख्य मूर्ति है उसको नमस्कार करती है, प्रदक्षिणा करते समय और जितनी मूर्तियाँ दिखे उनको नमस्कार करती है, और ये छोटा सा बच्चा देख रहा है कि माँ ऐसा कर रही है, तो वो भी वैसा ही करता है। यह सब करके माँ घर में वापस आती है, आते समय कोई गाय दिखती है उसको वह नमस्कार करती है, फिर कोई पहचान के मामा मिलते हैं, उन्हें भी माँ नमस्कार करती है। शुरू में माँ ने बोला क्या था? भगवानों का दर्शन करने जाएंगे नहीं बोला था, भगवान के दर्शन करने जायेंगे, यह बोला था और नमस्कार सबको किया, इससे ये बात सहजता से बच्चे ने सीख ली कि भगवान एक ही है और वह अनेक रूपों में प्रगट होते हैं।

घर में जो पूजाएँ, उत्सव होते हैं, उनमें हम पहले गणपति की पूजा करते हैं, कलश की करते हैं फिर पूजा सामग्री की भीं करते हैं, जब अपने घरों में ऐसी पूजा बच्चे देखते हैं तो इन

सारी छोटी–छोटी चीजों से जीवन दर्शन – ईश्वर सर्वत्र है, जीवन मूल्य – सबके साथ आदर से व्यवहार करना हैं, निसर्ग की रक्षा करनी है इत्यादि आत्मसात होते हैं, संक्रमित होते है। अभी डर यह है कि हम तथाकथित पढ़े-लिखे कहते हैं कि हमें इन सारी चींजों की आवश्यकता नहीं है।

Swami Ji says, "it is perfectly alright if you do not want to follow certain earlier practices; you can leave them. Certain things have truly become outdated and cannot be followed in today's context, then you can leave them. Or as I said before, those practices that were adopted as temporary measures during invasions are not our traditions and therefore should be given up. However, in their place we must have different systems capable of transmitting vision and values of life. You can change or modify the system. You can give up the old and bring in new practices, but practices should be there, certain regulations in life, self-restraint in life which come through family and social practices, customs, traditions etc. should be there. Only then can we transmit the values. If we lose our vision of 'Oneness' and our values, India will not be India".

The vision of 'Oneness' and values can not be transmitted through lectures, books or such means. If that were the case, nothing further remains to be given to the world. Books on our culture and philosophy are available in various media to people in all countries. The therotical knowldege regarding spirituality and Hindu dharma are available to them. However, as the values are abstract, the theoritical knowledge cannot give clear understanding. They are expressed through certain behaviour, practices, and systems. A family lives together, but why do a husband and wife accept each other and live together for 30, 40 or 50 years? Unless children see that, they will not understand what family is. In the West, they say that the probability of divorce increases by 50 percent if the parents are divorced. If the grandparents are also divorced, it goes up to 80 percent because children have no example before them of why a wife or husband should accept the other with all their shortcomings and still live together happily. Thus, the words acceptence, love, surrender etc. can be understood only if these are seen in action, behaviour and practices. It is being and becoming.

The contribution that India has to make to the world is spirituality. But what is spirituality? It is not any religious activitiy but a life lived with Oneness. Swamiji talked about how everything in life becomes spiritual if Vedanta becomes practical, i.e. if we work with the vision of Oneness, 'If the many and the One be indeed the same Reality, then it is not modes of worship alone, but equally all modes of work, all modes of struggle, all modes of creation, which are paths of realisation. No distinction, henceforth, between sacred and secular. To labour is to pray. To conquer is to renounce. Life is itself religion. To have and to hold is as stern a trust as to quit and to avoid'.

This is the realisation which makes Vivekananda the great preacher of Karma, not as divorced from, but as expressing Jnana and Bhakti. To him, the workshop, the study, the farmyard, and the field are as true and fit scenes for the meeting of God with man as the Ashram of the monk or the door of the temple. To him, there is no difference between service of man and worship of God, between manliness and faith, between true righteousness and spirituality. All his words, from one point of view, read as a commentary upon this central conviction. 'Art, science, and religion', he said once, 'are but three different ways of expressing a single truth. But in order to understand this we must have the theory of Advaita' (*CWSV*, Vol I, pp. xiv-xvi).

This Oneness that we are talking about, यह एकात्मता, आत्मीयता हमें हमारे परिवार, समाज और शिक्षा व्यवस्था से प्रकटित करनी होगी। एकात्मता परआधारित और आज के काल के लिए सुसंगत नई व्यवस्थायें हमें खड़ी करनी होगी, ऐसा जब हम करेंगे तब जो हमारें लोगों ने कभी कहा था कि कैसा जीवन जीना है, वह हमारे देश में आकर देखिए, हम फिर से बोल पाएंगे। ऐसी व्यवस्थाओं से ही लोगों को समझा पायेंगे की एकात्मता क्या होती हैं, एकात्मता के ऊपर भाषण सुनकर नहीं। आज यह तीसरा कार्य, तीसरी चुनौती स्वामी विवेकानन्द ने हमें दी है।

There are many others, very relevant directions that Swami Vivekananda has given us for nation-building and also for making the human life purposeful. But for want of time I am not going to touch upon it. But many topics such as women, development of youth, character development, education etc. all are to be understood in the context of these three points.

Last but not the least, स्वामी जी कहते थे कि किसी में भी यदि बदलाव लाना है ...if we want to bring life back to our people, we must love India as she is. उस पर पूरे हृदय से प्रेम करो, स्वामी विवेकानंद स्वयं ऐसे थे। ऐसा प्रेम था उनका, इस देश और देशवासियों के ऊपर जब उनको खाना खाने को मिलेगा कि नहीं, ठंड से बच पाएंगे कि नहीं, शिकागो धर्म परिषद में सहभागी हो सकते या नही ये स्पष्ट नही था, तब भी उनकी चिंता और चिन्तन भारतियों के लिये था। वे अपने पत्र में लिखते हैं, 'I may die of hunger and cold.' But in the same letter he writes, 'Hundred thousand men and women fired with the zeal of holiness, fortified with eternal faith in the Lord and nerved to the lion's courage by their sympathy for the poor, and the fallen and the downtrodden, shall go through the length and breadth of our land preaching the gospel of equality, gospel of social raising up, gospel of help'. यह सपना वे देख रहे थे। वे जीवित रहेंगे या नहीं पता नहीं, लेकिन उनका सपना क्या है? अपने देश के हजारों युवक-युवती इस देश के लिए काम करेंगे, कोने–कोने में जाकर कार्य करेंगे।

वही स्वामी विवेकानंद कीर्ति के शिखर पर पहुंच गये और सब लोग उनसे हस्तांदोलन करने आ रहे, उनके भाषण के बाद बड़े–बड़े पोस्टर शिकागो में लग गए किन्तु स्वामी जी रात भर सो नहीं सके उनके आँखों से आँसू झर रहे हैं, जब उस घर के यजमान अंदर आए और पूछे, 'Swami, what happened?' He said, 'Nothing, I remembered the people of my country'. 'कुछ नहीं मुझे मेरे देश के लोग याद आ गये'। कौन याद आए? छोटे–छोटे बच्चे जिन्हें खाने के

लिए खाना नहीं, गंदा पानी पीकर सो रहे हैं। अपने देश की स्वर्णहृदयी माताएँ, घर में खाने के लिए नहीं है, फिर भी एक संन्यासी आया है, तो खुद भूखे पेट रहते हुए सन्यासी को खाना खिलाने वाली, अपने देश के युवा, उनको याद आए, जिनके आँखों में 'बस मुझे एक सरकारी नौकरी चाहिए' इसके अलावा कोई सपना नहीं। 'कब मेरा देश फिर से इससे ऊपर उठेगा?' यह सोच के स्वामी जी उस दिन सो नहीं पाए।

ऐसे अनेक उदाहरण स्वामी जी के जीवन में हैं। जोसेफिन मैक्लियोड, उनकी एक शिष्या कहती है, जब स्वामी जी 'इंडिया' बोलते थे, वह जिस प्रेम से बोलते थे, हमारे हृदय में भारत के बारे में प्रेम जग जाता था। ऐसा राष्ट्र प्रेम यदि हम कर सकते हैं, तभी हम राष्ट्र के लिए अपना समय और उर्जा का योगदान करने के लिए तैयार होंगें। तभी हम निरपेक्ष भाव से कुछ करने के लिए खड़े होंगे और राष्ट्र की आत्मा को पूरे वैभव से प्रगटित कर पाएंगे। तभी यह राष्ट्र खड़ा हो सकता है। ऐसे स्वामी जी के विचार आज भी अनेकों को प्रेरित करते है। विवेकानंद केंद्र का यह अनुभव है, जब स्वामीजी के विचार युवाओं के पास उनको समझें ऐसी भाषा में लेकर जाते हैं तो युवा उसको प्रतिसाद देते हैं। The youth respond vibrantly to the thoughts of Swami Vivekananda. The natural desire in the heart of the youth to dedicate, to sacrifice is awakened by Swami Vivekananda. The magic in his words continues. People still get motivated by them. Reading Swami Vivekananda is relevant today because he is relevant. Following Swami Vivekananda is relevant today because he motivates and makes our life purposeful and applying his thoughts for nation-building is relevant today because that is what would make India shine again in spiritual glory and bestow peace and benediction on the world.

(This talk was delivered by Ku. Nivedita Bhide at the VIF on October 13, 2018)

*

II. Governance

4

IMPORTANCE OF GOVERNANCE IN INDIA'S FUTURE

Dr Mahesh N. Buch

Distinguished ladies and gentlemen, to be honest I am not too confident talking about governance to an audience which has representatives from all walks of government and academic life. However, I take courage from the fact that at least in one area, I have seniority that probably cannot be matched, and that is in retirement. I voluntarily took retirement 26 years ago, and therefore General Jacob may be ahead of me in this. Otherwise I enjoy great seniority in this matter and I use it most shamelessly. I've never said why I left government. One major reason was that I found I was increasingly marching to my own drumbeats. The value systems and things we were taught when I joined the service had changed completely, so either I could change myself or I could quit. I certainly couldn't expect the world to change its tune and march to mine and changing myself would not allow me to be myself. Therefore, I left service and have had 26 very happy years, and I'd happily repeat them.

What I have been experiencing since then is brought out by an experience I had when I went to the National Academy of Administration some years ago, to address the probationers. One of the probationers got up and said, "Please don't talk to us about ethics. Tell us what we can do in order to win the confidence of Ministers and how to stay put in a good post for a long time". Whatever 'good post' means, I was so furious with that thought that I told them they were all scum and said really harsh words. I came to the conclusion that it's not that people entering the services are not bright. They are in fact brighter than I am and come from better educational backgrounds. Somewhere down the line, however, there was a motivational change.

Unfortunately, I had this experience also in the College of Combat, where something similar happened. Then again at the National Policy Academy, Hyderabad. I went to Hyderabad and was told by the Director that the probationers and directional staff are at war. Being in uniform, they can't do anything else. They'll sit there like wooden people and wouldn't react I walked into this class, wandered around a bit. Then I looked at them and I said, "What a pity! You take a perfectly good batch, a bunch of bright young men and women, put them in khaki and they become bloody zombies!" Immediately one of them stood up and said, "You can't speak to us like that." I said, "That's what I wanted. I wanted a reaction." Then it became very lively. I'm just giving this as an example because I have been observing the change that has started taking place in the services.

To revert to governance per se, I'm going to start with one example of how government functioned once and how it functions today. It's not an apocryphal example. It is from Madhya Pradesh, Central Province (CP) and Berar. It's quite a famous case in the archives of CP and the present Madhya Pradesh (MP). Twynam was the Governor of CP and Berar. The SP of Buldhana was an irascible gentleman of Irish descent. He got annoyed with his bearer and punched him in the stomach. In those days, malaria being rampant, his spleen was enlarged; it burst and he died. He rang up the Thana and told the Thanedar to come along as there had been an incident. His Thanedar came and looked around. The body of the man was lying there, and he promptly sat on the sofa in the drawing room. Here was a desi sub-inspector sitting in front of the SP on his sofa. The SP was furious and told him he couldn't do that. The Thanedar responded by saying he was a station officer of the police, investigating a death under suspicious circumstances. The SP asked if he was suspecting him. The Thanedar responded with a "could be". This man investigated the case, came to the conclusion that it was a rash and negligent act and there was nothing more to it. However, because it was the SP, an IP officer, the matter was reported.

The Governor sent for the SP and handed him his letter of resignation telling him to sign it. Handed him his tickets for the Imperial Mail from Nagpur to Bombay, told him he would be on it that evening, which officers would escort him and the tickets for the P&O Liner for the next day, when he was to leave India. Think of what would happen today. The newspapers would splash this news. There'd be an investigation and a call for CBI investigation. At the end, the case would end like the Superintendent of Police of Pind, who forced the suicide of a woman sub-inspector of the district because he had made a pass at her. That man is today the DIG and has got the Police Medal for Distinguished Service! This is the difference. The British governed; we do not govern. I am not making out a case for the British to come back and rule us again. However, one has to look at the business of governance from this perspective.

Therefore, I start at a macro level. First we examine what are the objectives of government? Why do we have a government? When Margaret Thatcher became Prime Minister of Britain, she had a five-point program. She said that she would dismantle socialism. You may agree or disagree with this or even violently disagree with it. But she stuck to her program. She broke the coal miners' strike that had lasted for 900 days. At one time, the police were used quite brutally there. She changed the paradigm. Even Tony Blair, when he became Prime Minister, had to follow the neo-conservatism of Thatcher. The entire picture changed in Britain from then. Here was a Prime Minister with an agenda, a programme and who stuck to it even at the cost of losing an election, if necessary. Now that is the first objective of governance. Britain is a democracy; I have not given an example from China.

First and foremost, the government has to decide what its programmes are. I am not using the word ideology, because there are no ideology-based political parties in India today. In a democracy, you should have ideology-based parties. We don't have these, even the Communist Party of India (CPM) is not an ideology-based party anymore, nor is the Bharatiya Janta Party (BJP) or the Congress. If you don't have an ideology, at least have a program. What is your programme? Is your programme development? If so, what do you mean by development? Define it. If you define it, that is when you decide what are your priorities. Having decided your priorities, you can then look at your delivery mechanisms. In India, we decide that slogans must replace programmes. Therefore, every manifesto is just a slogan.

I remember when Mr. Uma Shankar Dixit was a very powerful person and I asked him why is it that people always vote for the Congress. He told me that they were a useless group. However, if you looked at the manifesto of any other party, it read exactly like that of the Congress. The BJP has never said that it does not believe in secularism, that they would establish a Hindu state or that they subscribed to the idea of nationalisation. They didn't state that they would give priority to the private sector. The CPM has never said that if they came to power, they would completely dismantle the Indian Constitution. The people of the country therefore say that if all the parties have the same agenda, you can't go wrong with the most tried and tested party of them all. Therefore, we win. In other words, no programme, no ideology, but offering the same as anyone else and since they are already in office, let's go along with them. That is not governance. This leads to some absolutely ludicrous situations.

Take development, for example. The government decides that it is going to build a dam. The Narmada Project is a very good example of how not to build a dam. You decide to build a dam or a series of dams because you think you need water for irrigation and hydel power. That is a decision. Now government should not take this decision in a compartmentalised manner, with the irrigation department and power departments working separately. If government takes a decision like this, it must take into account everything that is involved in the process. This would include the environmental impact, the displacement and rehabilitation of people and so on. Then having taken everything into account, a decision should be made and the dam should be completed within a year.

The Three Gorges Dam is the largest project of its kind in the world. I am given to understand, this is what I read, that the Chinese have displaced 3 million people. There has not been one single protest that has been broadcast. I am told that environmental groups in China had protested, but nothing is known and they have built the dam. Here is a government that took a decision and because of the system, it could take a decision that could ignore 3 million people. We can't do this in India.

Governance obviously cannot follow the Chinese model. It must take into account what Medha Patkar will say. It will have to take into account what will happen to the people displaced by the project. You can't take up a project and go on wasting money on it without getting any results. If government takes everything into account and then takes a decision, then that is governance. I'll give you a very small example of this. My wife has a farm 23 kms from Bhopal, near a Central Reserve Police Force (CRPF) camp. We had gone there once and there was a havildar from the CRPF who asked if we could give him a lift. I said yes and asked him to get in. We got to talking and I asked him where he was from. He said he was from Radhanpur in Sabarkantha district. Radhanpur was a predominantly Muslim princely state from the British Raj. He said his name was Noor Mohammed; I told him that where he comes from is all a desert. He told me that it wasn't. They have water now because Narendra Modi has brought a canal and they manage to grow three crops a year. I was surprised at a Muslim mentioning Narendra Modi's name. He said that because he had brought water to their town, they would vote for him. A person, whose name is an anathema to a lot of people because of the Gujarat Riots, but who at the micro level of a village has the head constables of police appreciating something that has been done, that is what you call governance.

At the present moment, we are in a situation in which we have no governance. Government cites, and this is before Mr. Kapil Sibal came on during Mr. Arjun Singh's time, that they would open a large number of IITs and IIMs. It's a good decision, but all of them are operating on a 50 percent shortage of faculty. In an IIT or an IIM, you cannot employ a person below the rank of Assistant Professor. The person must have a PhD and three years of experience. The number of PhDs in technology that this country needs is 8,000 per year. The number we produce is only 800 a year. Not all of them go into teaching. Here is an example of government taking a decision to set up institutions, without even bothering to find out whether there are going to be enough teachers for them. Mr. Sibal is going through hell trying to find ways of meeting these requirements.

You don't take decisions this way. It reflects lack of governance. I am saying this because in every example you will find that decisions are taken ad hoc. Nobody thinks things through to their conclusion. Due to this, cumulatively, we have come now to a stage where the most easily governable country appears to be ungovernable.

This is probably an apocryphal story that I am going to tell you. When Maharaja Hari Singh was ruling Kashmir, there was a protest that there were no Muslim units in the Kashmir Army and the army consisted exclusively of Dogras. Then it was decided to set up a regiment to recruit Kashmiri Muslims; they were asked to go to Gilgit, but they didn't move. When asked why, they said they needed the police to protect them when moving. You now have a situation in which Kashmir is becoming ungovernable. This is not a talk on Kashmir, so I won't give my views on it here, which are rather extreme. They would certainly not be liked by Prem Shankar Jha. However, the fact remains that it is not that Kashmir has militancy or that it has this demand for Azaadi. The question is that there is no government response, policy or pronouncement as to what we think about Kashmir and what we intend to do about it. Why not at least try and tell the people of Kashmir where they stand vis-à-vis India and the Government of

India? We don't do it. We make inane statements from the Red Fort saying that Kashmir is an integral part of India. Has anyone ever said that Maharashtra is an integral part of India, or Tamil Nadu is an integral part of India? Why do you have to keep saying this about Kashmir? Why don't we lay down the bottom line, whatever it may be? I am no one to determine policy, especially in terms of such highly political questions. However, why doesn't the government lay down the bottom line? We keep saying we will talk. But with whom we will talk and about what?

Let's take this whole business of Naxalism. I had been Director, Tribal Welfare of Madhya Pradesh. My brother had been DC of Bastar and Commissioner of the Division as well. I would say that I can claim to know Bastar and all the sub-districts it is divided into, almost like the back of my hand. I've done plenty of touring there; I've been Forest Secretary of the state as well. In December 1983, Vishwa Ranjan, the present DG of Chhattisgarh was SP of Bastar. Mr. Arjun Singh asked me, and this was shortly before I left the service, to go around Bastar and tell him how we could deal with this incipient Naxalism that was creeping in. I did go around; however, let me take you back a bit. In Bastar specially, as well as other tribal areas, Verrier Elwin has written about the Murias, Gotus and others, and the theory that he touted, which Jawaharlal Nehru accepted, was that the tribal people have to be kept, if not isolated, at least cocooned away from normal society. Therefore, the normal paradigms of development need not apply in these areas.

Abujmarh, which is now a hotbed of Naxalism, was the only Inner Line Area that we had inside the country. You could not enter Abujmarh without the permission of the District Magistrate. Abujmarh had no normal revenue administration, it had no forest administration, land was commonly owned by the tribe and the only government presence there was of the Tribal Welfare Department, through its schools. Due to this, our entire policy towards development in tribal areas became very ambivalent. Do we develop these areas or we don't? Should we put in roads, power and telecommunication, or shouldn't we? The policy towards tribal areas remained in a flux. This happened in the North East as well. Now, fortunately or unfortunately we got the Dandakaranya Project, and a large number of Bengali refugees were settled in Pakhanjore. Forests were felled for them. The local tribals, and the whole of Bastar is part of the Gondi belt with Madia, Muria, Hill Maria, Dand Muria and all the other Gonds; these people found that the forests that they were not allowed to cut were being chopped down for outsiders. They were being displaced for outsiders.

Then came the Bhola-Dila Mining Project. Entire tribal communities were uprooted. The Dankani and Shankani rivers were polluted by the trailings of the mined ore. Bastar went into a state of extreme turmoil at that stage. As Director, Tribal Welfare, I toured extensively. I remember going to Dantewada where all this trouble is taking place. It was then a very peaceful district. I was told by the tribal people that there were 58 minor irrigation dams, as part of minor irrigation projects. I wanted to see them, but the officials couldn't show me even one out of those 58 projects in a span of one week. There was Block headquarters called Kathi Kalyan, where on paper we had a Block Office, a Primary Health Centre, the entire paraphernalia of staff quarters, an ashram, a school and more. I was told we couldn't go there because there was no road, despite the fact that we had a four-wheel drive jeep that can go anywhere. I told them I would walk and I went to Kathi Kalyan. To my horror, I found that the only dwelling in that place were two huts for the local tribals. There was no Primary Health Centre, no Block Office, no staff quarters, no ashram or school; in fact, 100 percent of the funds had been diverted.

It is true that I can't stand Arundhati Roy. However, it is also a fact that the actual delivery of development to tribal areas has been largely on paper or substantially only on paper. In some places, which are more advanced, some work would have taken place.

The second part of this issue is that we have a Planning Commission, an organisation that I think should have been abolished 30 years ago. In fact, it should never have been created. If you were to take up a project of extending electricity in Haryana, Punjab or Western UP, inter-village distance would be about half a kilometre or maybe 1 kilometre. The number of people it would serve would be maybe about a 1000 per kilometre. You go to a district like Bastar, the inter-village distance will be 10 kilometres with three intervening hills and thick jungles. Maybe there are only seven families in a village. The cost per unit of development in districts such as Bastar, Kalahandi or Betul is multiple times that of the cost in a more settled area. Therefore, if one were to do a cost-benefit analysis: that one kilometre of powerline costs so much, divided by the population; in Bastar, this cost would be 30 to 40 times what a normal calculation would be.

Surely governance demands that you take this factor into account and give that powerline, knowing full well that (a) it's going to cost much more, and (b) the returns on it are not going to be much, if any. You take a village like Chunalohma in Betul district. I was DC in Betul for three years. It's got 36 hamlets all in an area about 10 km^2. Maybe one hamlet is within 1 km as the crow flies; however, by the time a child would have climbed two hills and waded through a river, he'd probably have travelled 6 km. How do you extend education in such an area? Do you have 36 primary schools or do you have 1 primary school? Do you go in for the Navodaya Model School where you actually are bringing the child into a hostel environment and providing infrastructure there, so that the child can study? We have not taken any such decisions. We say we've given Chunalohma a primary school. You locate it in one hamlet or in the main village, and the children of 35 hamlets will be left without any education and infrastructure.

My point is if you are going to think in terms of equity in development as a part of your policy, program or ideology, as the Constitution demands you do, then surely you have to take these factors into account and fund them accordingly. We don't do it. Therefore, we ultimately find that the state of Bihar, where the Ganga flows for a distance of 586 kms from East to West, has only three bridges across this length. I do not know how many flyovers there are in Delhi now, because of the Commonwealth Games. Supposing half that money had gone into building more bridges across the Ganga, wouldn't South and North Bihar have been better integrated? If you go to North Bihar, you have these rivers flowing from North to South. It reminds me of a toast rack! If you want to go from Champaran to Katihar, you go from Champaran through Danapur, then Patna and go across Mokamah, take six ferries and then you get to Katihar. Doesn't governance demand that you look at this geographical reality of Bihar? Instead of saying that Bihar is a basket case, do the kind of investment that will bring about equity. That is governance.

My point is that you take any area, there is no clarity of vision for it. I see some very distinguished police officers here; my friend Ved Marwah is also here. I don't claim to be an expert here, but take policing. Prakash Singh has been shouting that we must bring about police reforms. I was a member of the Soli Sorabjee Committee that made certain suggestions in this regard. I don't necessarily agree with everything that was said. But for god's sake, let us decide whose servant the police are, under the 1861 Police Act. Mr. K.F. Rustomji was the IGP of Madhya Pradesh. I was Under Secretary who dealt with police, under a very strong Chief Secretary, Mr. H.S. Cama and R.P. Noronha was the Additional Chief Secretary in charge of Home. This was a very powerful team. In that entire year, there was only one case in which the Home Department differed with the IG of Police. As the Under Secretary, I was told to go and meet the IG. He was kind enough to receive me and I explained the matter to him. He said I was right and he was wrong and that he was withdrawing his proposal. Otherwise, whatever Police HQ said, it mattered. We have not decided how we're going to run the police force. We haven't decided whose servant the policeman is.

It's not merely a question of changing the Police Act. What would we change in it? For example, one of the suggestions we had made was that the DG Police, who is selected from a panel, should be selected by a committee. You know how these are manipulated. I have been on three Committees for the selection of Vice Chancellors. A Vice Chancellor in a State University is selected by a Committee. In this committee, the University Grants Commission (UGC) is represented, the Chancellor is represented and there is one representative of the Executive Council of the University. I'm going to give one very small example, and I'm going to take names. It doesn't matter. This was for the selection of the Vice Chancellor of Bhopal University. The then Chief Minister and Education Minister wanted a particular person to be selected. There was no way in which he could be selected; he didn't qualify. The three members in the Selection Committee were a judge from the High Court, myself and Dr. Moolchand Sharma who is now Vice Chancellor of a Central University and was then the Director of the National Law Institute University, Bhopal. We shortlisted people and the next day was for taking a final view. I opened the newspaper the next morning and saw that Moolchand Sharma had resigned, saying that one of the members had pressurised him. I called him up to confirm whether he'd said this, and he said he'd been misreported. The fact remains that he resigned, and he was the UGC representative. The UGC did not send a replacement for him, so after 2 months, the Committee stood dissolved. Then the Governor was able to put in his own man as Vice Chancellor.

No one can tell me that the selection of a DG from a panel will make any difference. The only thing that will make a difference is when the DG Police of the state gets up and apologises for intervening, but says that it should not be done. There have been cases where this has happened. I'll give you two examples, P.R. Rajagopal was IG Delhi and there was a Punjab National Bank strike going on. Mrs. Gandhi called him. She said she wanted him to arrest some of the ring leaders. He told her that if there is an FIR in the Parliament Street police station, it shall be investigated and if it is found that there's a case, then he would certainly arrest them, to which she replied she wanted them arrested right then. He said he couldn't as they were doing nothing; they weren't obstructing traffic, nor disobeying police orders. They were only sitting quietly and agitating. He was told that he was a very good man, too good for the Delhi Police, and he was transferred. So as you can see, he had the courage to say no. We had P.M. Shukul in MP, a very gentle person who had been promoted from the State Police. When Govind Narain Singh led his revolt against D.P. Mishra, Mishra told Shukul to detain 38 MLAs which he refused. Mishra told him that he thought he was their man, to which Shukul responded saying that just because he was their man, he would not do this. If you want to reform the police, bring in all the legal reforms that you want. But reform the officers that are going to head the police first. This brings me to my next topic.

If government has no agenda or programme, there is one programme they've had that has succeeded beautifully. And that is to subvert the services. In 1967, when this entire 'Aaya Ram, Gaya Ram' started, the Members of Legislature suddenly discovered that they commanded a price. If you want to remain in power, you pay us that price. Now how could you pay that price, unless you subvert the state. You can't subvert the state until you demoralise the services. It is to my eternal shame as an IAS officer that this applies to my service and *mutatis mutandis* to all others. The IAS succumbed not to guns to their heads, but to orders of transfer. I cannot think of anything more pusillanimous than this. You won't get a good posting or you'll be transferred – and the services fell to their knees. This is one programme in which the politicians succeeded very well down to the cutting-edge level of government, and I am talking cutting edge not at the level of DG or Chief Secretary only, but right from the constable to the heads of the civil services.

The services are not carrying out the functions that the Constitution has vested in them. The Indian Constitution is the only one in the world that creates federally controlled services to man all the senior posts, in both the States and the federation. This doesn't happen anywhere else. Besides, there is a guarantee that you can't be thrown out. If you want to be thrown out, there is a due process. Unfortunately, it is very difficult to remove even a corrupt officer. Despite all this and the special position given to them under the Constitution, the civil services don't even have the courage to take a piece of paper and write an advice against something. If they do that, in 8 out of 10 cases, wrong things won't happen; it's very difficult to rule out something on paper. From 1967 onwards, we have had this phenomenon of the politician thinking he can command a price, of the civil servant trying to retain his own position and prosperity, and therefore, not caring about what happens to governance.

In all of this, what happens to the people; who cares for the people? Does anyone care for the people of this country? Where are the kinds of ministers we had in older times? We had a man called Takhatmal Jain, who was a Minister of Madhya Bharat and went on to be Industries Minister of Madhya Pradesh. He sent for his Secretary in the Department of Industries. There was a friend of his whose case was pending with him. Could he examine it? Well, within 15 minutes the gentleman came and examined the case, called it perfect and said they should sanction it. He looked at it and told Mr. Chatterjee that he'd asked for the Secretary to examine this and not his *musahib* or his courtier. He warned him against pleasing him by writing such a note. He ordered him to go back and examine it properly. If the case merited sanction, he had to state the reasons for this and similarly, if it didn't. If he wanted to favour his friend, he would do it, but not at the cost of correctness of procedure. It was the Secretary's job to follow due procedure and provide apt inputs. Where are such Ministers and where are such officers?

Mr. Narayan Murthy said recently that there should be an Indian Management Service. By all means abolish the IAS if that is going to improve this country. However, do you really think this Indian Management Service would be any different than the IAS? It is a very resilient service; we know how to oil our way back. In any case, unless you change the paradigms of government and methods of governance, will abolishing a service achieve what you want to achieve? This is like my saying that the Indian Army is not bashing up the entire Pakistani Army right now, so let's abolish the entire Officers Corps of the Indian Army; we'll have a people's army instead. It's not going to solve the problem. This is something that you have to give very serious thought to, and this is where I will come to that micro level of government, which is now beginning to hurt. You'll be surprised to know that one of the most efficient governments in terms of delivery, and also one of the most corrupt in India is that of Tamil Nadu. You go to Tamil Nadu and visit a District Office; you'll find that it actually functions.

The Tamil Nadu government decides there are going to be mid-day meals and honestly, you'll see that mid-day meals are given to all the children. Their PDS works, though the District Officers are told very categorically that they shall work, and so the delivery systems are still functional. They have not disturbed the relationships between officers, or indeed even their hierarchy. If they want to make money in the state, they tell the politician to go and rack off 20,000 crores from elsewhere. That's how they make the money. Compare this to what Mr. Digvijay Singh did to the government in Madhya Pradesh, especially the police. One fine day he decided that there will be a Zilla Sarkar. He was a great believer and called himself the first Chief Minister to have brought in a Zilla Panchayat. Then he wanted to decentralise government up to the level of the district and he put a Ministry in charge. The reason why he put a Ministry in charge is because the Minister was very unhappy with the Panchayat system, and their powers got reduced.

Therefore, he brought in the Ministry and they collected all the District Secretaries for a meeting, but actually, only one of the powers was being discussed, that is, every transfer in that District would be done by the Zilla Sarkar (that is the Ministry in charge). This included the police. Unfortunately, the then DG, S.C. Tripathi very readily agreed to giving up his powers. He said one SP had made 400 transfers and instead of suspending the SP, he threw the baby out with the bath water. The net result was that the command structure of the police got destroyed just with this single order. Not a single policeman at the subordinate level now thought anything about his SP as he had no power left. I talked to Mr. Digvijay Singh about this and he said that they are all interested only in postings and transfers. They don't take disciplinary action. I said, "if a man can't transfer a head constable or constable, you think the Sub-Inspectors or Inspectors are going to allow him to take disciplinary action." The minute he does, he's got four MLAs in his pocket, and the SP will go. Therefore, I advised against disturbing the hierarchy, unless you want to have a revolution and completely change the entire system of government. A legitimate government can decide that. However, he didn't leave it alone and therefore, the police are in shambles. Prakash Singh can hang himself upside down. What would you be able to do in a situation like this?

I am being anecdotal, I shouldn't be. My wife says I am in my 'anecdotage' now. The fact remains that we want to try and understand what is happening to governance. You take any area, say health. Health doesn't mean power. When you are a doctor, you can't go around arresting people and sending them to jail. You're supposed to treat them. The government has deliberately run health services into the ground. This is an accusation I am making. The district hospitals, community hospitals and block-level hospitals, which were functional in the past, do not function now. Why is this? Ministers want private hospitals to come up. It's alright for a super-speciality hospital like Escorts or Hinduja to come up, but what about primary healthcare? Which country in the world leaves primary healthcare to large, commercially minded, medical institutions? Health is not a priority, so you run the government hospitals into the ground and the average man gets nothing. Then you evolve a system in which you want to make money. Which are the money-making departments?

It's not the police, in case the senior police officers think it's them. They should come down several pegs. Surprisingly, it's the transport department. Here I must again give you an anecdote. We had Mr. B.P. Dubey, who went on to be a very good DG Police of the state. He was Transport Commissioner and was a very stiff-necked man. He was annoyed with the head constable of the Transport Department, called him and banged him in the orderly room. He told him that as a punishment he was posting him to a distant corner of the border. The man gave him a smart salute and the next day a whole crowd of people pushed forward. They all said they were defaulters and wanted to be sent off to these check posts. These check posts are where you make the most money. One party's government in Madhya Pradesh is changing things, and I won't name the party. They decided that the Transport Commissioner must give 9 percent of the revenue for the party to function. Then the next party came in and said that was not enough, and to give 11 percent. These are absolute facts that I am quoting to you. I am ready to face a libel suit, if you like.

Do you expect the Transport Department to function and function honestly under such circumstances? Don't you think that in every case they have to make money? Owing to our lack of governance and reviewing systems of governance, we have now reached a stage where in every walk of life, nothing gets done without paying. I came to know this perception very early, when I was Director, Tribal Welfare in 1968. My Minister sent for me and I went from my office to the Secretariat. He naturally gave me a chair to sit and said that the other gentleman seated there had got a problem and I told him I'd take him to my office and help sort it out. In this man's mind, I was a '*sahab*' because the Minister gave me a chair. However, I was driving the car myself as there was no driver, so I couldn't be the '*badasahab*'. We came to a place where there were some restaurants and eateries. He told me to stop and when I asked why, he said he needed to have some '*chai-nashta*'. I told him we could have the same in my office, but he insisted and I suddenly realized what could be brewing in his mind. He must've thought if he didn't give me '*chai-nashta*', I wouldn't do his work. This is the perception of the common man.

This was in 1968; what do you think has changed today? Since we're talking of governance, I must give this example. The NREGS – the National Rural Employment Guarantee Scheme now called the Mahatma Gandhi National Rural Employment Guarantee Scheme, under an Act of Parliament – states that everyone below the poverty line will get 100 days of employment per year and minimum

INR 100 per day. This scheme is operated through the Panchayats. I wrote to the PM warning against this, for you cannot run a muster-roll–based scheme honestly. This can't even be done in Britain. We could instead go in for a scheme to create village assets. In Madhya Pradesh at least and elsewhere as well, we have run a very successful watershed management program that aims only at this. This has created a lot of assets and we have been able to conserve water in a large number of villages that were chronically drought prone. Given that the beneficiaries are the persons that do the work, the work is honestly done.

But it was decided that there would be a muster-roll–based scheme. It functions like this: The Sarpanch of the village decides he'll take up earth work mainly and he takes up a JCB machine. He doesn't do it manually, which he's supposed to. The cost of the earth work is 30 percent of the total amount sanctioned, which leaves 70 percent of the amount. The INR 70 should go to the villagers. However, they are called and told they will get INR 25-30. The Sarpanch takes INR 25 and the rest goes to the government officials. The proportions can change. The government in its wisdom woke up and said they'd deposit the money directly in the accounts of villagers. That's when the Sarpanches said they wouldn't do the work. If you don't do the work, the money isn't deposited. Then via media was found, where the money would go to the villagers who would keep 25-30 percent and the balance would be given away and the same cycle repeated. This is a story in all the states of the country.

This is otherwise a Scheme which is good; it gives rural employment and I am all for that. Ultimately, money does reach the villagers; it's not as if they remain empty-handed. However, village assets are not created. Instead you get corruption going right down to the lowest functionary. Therefore, the whole system of government honestly performing disappears, which should not be treated as something minor. I am not here to preach ideology or the best forms of government. The only good thing about India is that we have been able to maintain a democracy in which I am able to say these things and not get locked up. That is the positive part of it all. I don't want to live in China; I don't want to displace three million people in one go. I disagree violently with Medha Patkar on a lot of things, but I agree with her on one thing – she has awoken the conscience of this country to the fact that people do get displaced and they have the right to be in the Indian sun as well. Let us sit down very seriously and think, who is interested in the people of India. Who is interested in India? It's certainly not the politician, because the politician of older times was prepared to leave power. The politician of today will sell his grandmother for four annas if that enabled him to retain power.

Power and what you can buy with it is the sole objective of government today. The civil servant is very much a part of this nexus. I am covering the entire gamut of the services: the IPS, IFS, State service and Central services. I am covering everyone when I say the word civil servant. The future cannot be so dark, because things can be done. I will end my talk with one more example. When I became head of the Delhi Development Authority (DDA), I got many complaints regarding Completion Certificates. You can't occupy a building until you've got a Completion Certificate, a sewage connection, telephone and power connection. This is where my planners used to make lots of money. I, therefore, took a decision, where I would accept the Completion Certificate from any Chartered Architect. He had a form with a checklist. I said we'd accept this, and later on if we found that he had given a false certificate, we'd take action against the architect and not the property owner. There was a tremendous hullabaloo. My Lieutenant Governor almost got a fit. I used to keep giving him fits, which was good for his health!

My planners and the Municipal Corporations resisted this and told me that there would be a lot of corruption. I asked them what did they think was happening now? Why would people pay them money? People paid money to get the certificates because there were irregularities. An architect would charge a fee. However, instead of taking 5,000, they'd do it for 1,000; otherwise somebody would go to another architect. Architects went running to the people saying they'd do it for INR 500. There were few architects who gave false certificates. In 19 months, I didn't get a single complaint on the issue of completion certificates. When I left, the first thing they did was reverse my decision. I am giving you this example because it is about time that we all get together and start thinking, what are the areas of interface between the government and the people? Can we reduce this interface? Can we make a lot of things automatic? If I have any dealings with government, can I just go to the government and get it done? I shouldn't have to pay anyone.

Even in decision-making, there are norms laid down. If I am working by the norms, I can get it; if I am not working as per the norms, there is no way in which I can get it. Can we not do this? If we start doing this, and start looking at rules and regulations and make a small beginning from there, you'll find a lot of things we can do. What we do not need, however, is the present amendment that the Prime Minister and the Law Minister are bringing to Code of Civil Procedure. I really wish police officers read the Code of Civil Procedure. The powers given are not by the Police Act. The Police Act only gives the organisational structure to the police. The Code of Civil Procedure, Chapter 14 and Section 154 onwards, is what gives police the powers they can exercise. Under Section 154, I cannot give the exact wording as I do not have it, if information of a cognisable offence is given in writing or verbally to the officer in charge of a police station, he shall take this in writing and enter it in a book that shall be prescribed as per the FIR Code. A copy of the FIR shall be given to the person who gives the information, as well as to the Magistrate. There is no discretion with the Station Officer in recording the FIR. He has to take it down, and this is the law.

If he says no, he must investigate to check if there is prima facie case, and only then will he file an FIR. He is bound by the law to file the FIR. He can under Section 155 of the Code say that he will not investigate the offence and can provide the reasons for this. However, if he chooses not to investigate, then under Section 156, he is bound to investigate it as the FIR opens the investigation. I violently disagree with the CBI that they will hold a Preliminary Enquiry before registering the FIR; that is not legally permissible. My point regarding the present amendment being brought is that if the station officer does not register the FIR, then he has to give reasons. This means you are diluting the Code. They claim they are strengthening it, by protecting people from the arbitrariness of the police. This is handing arbitrariness to the police. I don't think we need this.

We need governance that is rational, logical, based on programmes and ideology of the party in power. Having said that much, still has civil services and police which act impartially? The decision to do something or not do something about a policy is a political decision, and one needs to respect that. However, once you take that decision, for example, with the Urban Ceiling Act, then it is with the Revenue Officer to apply it or not. This leads me to my final story. Amongst other things, the Revenue Department was in my charge. Arjun Singh was Chief Minister. I was summoned to the Cabinet and was asked if I had sent some Inspectors to Bilaspur, under the Bonded Labour Abolition Act. The Bonded Labour Abolition Act is the best piece of legislation after Macaulay made the Indian Evidence Act, which cannot really be amended. It is extremely well thought out and tells you how to identify bonded labour, defines it, lays out who will adjudicate it and gives exclusive magistrates the power to summarily try cases and give up to three years of rigorous imprisonment.

I said I had sent 5 and I was told they were harassing cultivators. The Minister asked me to tell them to ignore that. I told him I couldn't do that, since both him and I had sworn an oath to uphold the laws of the land. In any case, if I told them to ignore it, they would do so once. In other cases, they wouldn't. In many cases, they would take money; how would I distinguish between them? I told them if I did this, all agricultural activities would come to a halt. I asked them to give me 15 minutes to draft a letter to the PM, suggesting why this Act is not in favour of cultivation and it should be repealed. They immediately told me not to do that. It is a fine piece of social legislation they said at which point, I lost my temper. I said the law has been violated and the man who keeps Bonded Labour after this clear-cut Act can even ask a person to send his wife over to see him. Even she is murdered; there is nothing the victim can do, and now the culprit knows nothing will happen to him.

If you know a law is not going to work, then don't put it in the statute book. However, if it is put in, then don't give anyone the discretion. The law must be enforced. Period. Police officer in charge of the police station has to enforce the law; he cannot refuse it. A tehsildar has to enforce the law; he doesn't have discretion. We need to go back to that kind of governance. For that, we need interlocking accountability. It shouldn't matter if a Thanedar, SP, or anyone else doesn't follow the law. If they don't, they should suffer for it. The SP, ASP and DCP should suffer for it. Build this into every department. If an Assistant Engineer doesn't do his duty and a building collapses, then his superior must also be suspended. Put in interlocking accountability and you will have much better supervision, and we will start moving towards improved governance.

Thank you.

(This talk delivered by Dr Buch at the VIF on March 30, 2010)

*

5

VISION INDIA 2025: NEED FOR LEGAL, JUDICIAL AND CONSTITUTIONAL REFORMS

Shri Soli J Sorabjee

Ladies and Gentlemen,

May I thank the Vivekananda International Foundation for doing me the honour of addressing you on the topic of 'Vision 2025'. Now even if I become a super yogi and take various Ayurvedic medicines and tablets, I don't think I will be on this planet in 2025. But there's one advantage; I won't be criticised in 2025! But 2025 is still a rather large order.

Well, before attempting to discuss 'Vision India 2025', let us first consider what was the vision of our Founding Fathers. Well after a long night of waiting, a night full of faithful portents and silent prayers, we completed the challenging task of framing a Constitution for the people of independent India. Our Founding Fathers had a grand vision of India, where poverty, hunger, disease, exploitation would be eliminated. This vision is beautifully encapsulated in the Preamble to our Constitution and I think it is among the finest pieces; apart from the legal language, it is really literally an expression of that vision, and let me read what does the Preamble proclaim: *"Justice, social, economic and political, Liberty of thought, expression, belief, place and worship, Equality of status and of opportunity, and Fraternity assuring the dignity of the individual."*

You can see, each of these concepts is pregnant with meaning. Our Constitution comprises 395 articles and along with the schedules appended, it is one of the largest Constitutions in the world. But the quintessence of our

Constitution lies in Part 3 that guarantees certain basic human rights or fundamental rights. And Part 4, which sets out Directive Principles of State Policy, embodies the goals and ideas for making our country a better state in the right sense. In fact, Directive Principles incorporate socio-economic rights. But, under the Constitution itself, Directive Principles are not enforceable by courts, but the Constitution says they are nevertheless fundamental to the governance of the country.

Now friends, it is important to be aware of the distinction between governance and government. The distinction was recognised in a statement made way back in the year 1701, and I quote, it said, *"Wise princes ought not to be admired for their government but governance."* You see governance is a qualitative expression and a normative concept. It is different from government. Good governance means achieving goals and delivering results while working with established rules and parameters. To my mind, there can be no good governance if the state instrumentalities persistently fail to protect the fundamental rights of the people and also default in implementing the Directive Principles.

The state as you all know has three wings – a Parliament, the Executive and the Judiciary. Let me start with Parliament.

The essential function of any parliament is legislative business. Our parliament devotes little time, I am afraid, to legislative activities, and when it does, it rushes through Bills without adequate debate and without mature consideration. The only time when there is unanimity is when there is a Bill to increase the emoluments of the Members of Parliament (MPs)! Those are passed with alacrity and, with good humour and bonhomie. No problem with that. But then comes a problem.

One of the things that is really distressing is that some important Bills remain pending in the parliament for years; some of those are essential for good governance. The parliament seems to be in no hurry to pass these Bills.

Take the example of the Lok Pal Bill; it's been there for years, debated for decades. The Bill, when finally enacted into law, will go a long way to combat corruption that has really spread like cancer in our body politic.

Another instance is the Judicial Standards and Accountability Bill whose passage is imperative for enforcing accountability in the judiciary. Legislation in respect of appointment of judges in the higher judiciary is also necessary because many of the ills that prick the judiciary result from the appointment of judges who lack competence, character and integrity. The subject has been discussed, debated; many proposals have been put out. The National Commission to review the working of the Constitution, of which I was a member and which was headed by former Chief Justice Shri Venkatachaliah, made a proposal and you see what happened. I must tell you one thing – if the power of appointing judges was totally in the hands of the executive, then it would have been a bad experience as had happened during Mrs. Gandhi's regime. Then the Supreme Court gave a judgment in what is called the "Judges Case", and it turned a full circle in that the power of appointing judges must rest solely in the hands of the Supreme Court.

The Collegium system that we all supported, quite frankly, happened as a reaction to what had happened during Mrs. Gandhi's regime. But experience shows that the Collegium system has not worked satisfactorily. So a suggestion was made that let a National Judicial Commission be appointed, consisting of five persons. This was made by the Venkatachaliah Commission. It was to have as members the Chief Justice, two more judges of the Supreme Court in order of seniority, Union Minister for Law because the government must have a word, a say in the matter, and an eminent jurist to be appointed after discussion between the President and the Chief Justice of India (CJI). So there were to be five members; but some people said there should be seven, by including an academic, and there should be someone else. Now, we are all agreed in principle; there may be some difference of opinion, there may be five, seven, but please tell me, what are you going to do with this? I know complaints are coming every day about appointment of judges. I am sorry to say this, but these shock me sometimes. Why? Because we require a lady. Yes, sure appoint a lady because she comes there on merit, not on other considerations such as state of origin etc.

What are these considerations? If you are talking about the Supreme Court, you require people of high integrity, experience and caliber. If necessary, have three people from Punjab, have three ladies, but not on considerations other than merit. Unfortunately, that does not happen many a times. So, we said, let there be a National Judicial Commission of good composition where one can expect that these factors, which have vitiated the appointment processes as a result of the Collegium system, will disappear. Nothing has happened; we are still waiting for the Bill.

Let me give you another example. The Judicial Standards and Accountability Bill – what happens today? When I started practice, at that time if anyone had said that this judge is dishonest, '*isne paisa liya*' etc., we would really say that this man is a disgruntled litigant or '*zyada piya hai*'. It was unthinkable those days. I'm sorry to say and I say with anguish that today when we hear such reports and such stories, we can't dismiss them as we then used to. These are not the outpourings of a lunatic or a disgruntled litigant. In some cases, there is substance in such allegations.

Now what happens today under the Constitution? If you want to remove a judge for misbehavior, there is a process known as impeachment, a long process – the Judges Inquiry Bill (Act), *report karo*, this and that. The procedure is cumbersome and time consuming, and it gets politicised. It happened in the case of Justice V. Ramaswami. Under the Judges Inquiry Act, three judges reported about him, recommending impeachment. The Congress party abstained and the process fell through.

We don't want such things to happen. That's why I must say to the credit of the government that it introduced the Judicial Standards and Accountability Bill. It requires a lot of changes, requires a lot of things, because we must be very careful that while trying to enforce accountability, the judicial independence must not be compromised.

So, again the composition of the body of the houses of parliament is extremely important and to my mind, this should be a semi-judicial institution. In this, we don't want any spokesperson of a political party, no leader of the opposition, no academic, no member of the bar council, because removal of judges is a very serious matter. It must be entrusted to people of high caliber, high integrity. But the question is whether this is being done? That's what I have been trying to emphasise.

Let me give you another instance of the lethargy of the parliament. You know, there was this pervasive phenomenon of sexual harassment at the workplace. The Supreme Court, CJI J S Verma, in what is known as the Vishakha's Case, a very celebrated case, delivered a very good judgement laying down certain guidelines. It was actually a bit of judicial legislation. It stated what constitutes sexual harassment: who can complain, what should be the penalties. And Justice Verma made it very clear that these guidelines or these directions will hold the field till the Parliament enacted the requisite legislation. The court felt some need in the time being, to fill the gap.

Harassment of women in the workplace is perniciousness, pervasive. Very well. When was the judgement delivered? On 13th of August 1997. When was the Bill introduced? Last year in 2010, after 13 years. Of course, now that it has been introduced, it will go to a committee, or whatever it is, which it should. But the fact remains that the law is not yet enacted even after 13 years. So, what I am trying to highlight is this sort of lethargy of parliament, lack of activity, especially in matters of Bills, which are really of importance to the country. We need early enactment in such cases.

Now let me come to another problem that we are all familiar with. Parliament has been stalled on numerous occasions. In the past, parliament was stalled for 45 days in 1987 on account of the Bofors Scandal. In 2001, the Tehelka Scam led to the stalling of parliament for 17 days. Of course, both the parties do it; in Tehelka Scam, the Congress did it, the latest regrettable instance being the stalling of parliament by noisy, rowdy behavior that practically wiped out the entire winter session. Chairman of Rajya Sabha Hamid Ansari's statement that "Peace prevailed only when obituaries were read", I think, is a sorry reflection on the behavior of MPs. Lok Sabha Speaker Meira Kumar who is a fine person, was very anguished. But we are all anguished. The point is, "*Raasta Nikalo Na*". That's the whole point. If this does not take place again, what will happen? I don't know, but the session is in the offing; it's on the anvil.

The question is how do we prevent repetition of this regrettable phenomenon? One suggestion was that MPs should not receive emoluments for the period the parliament is stalled, but that would lead to unsavoury consequences like deciding on who was responsible for the stalling of parliament, which seems a little unworkable. The reason for parliament's non-functioning in the last instance was the opposition's persistent demand for a Joint Parliamentary Committee (JPC) to look into 2G Spectrum scam and the government's obstinate refusal to concede to the demand. Whatever be the merit or otherwise of the demand for a JPC, preventing parliament from undertaking legislative activity for practically the entire winter session, I think, was unjustifiable. This is one of the few matters where I disagree with my good friend Arun Jaitley. After all, parliament is the place to work; it's our institution. I can understand for one or two days you mark your protest, but not for the entire session. Now let us hope that reason and a sense of proportion will prevail and we do not have a repetition of the same phenomenon this time.

Now that I have talked of parliament, let me tell you another thing. You know, in our Constitution, there is no provision for educational qualifications for our MPs. I wanted to consider the credentials and attributes of the representatives of the people. It was discussed in the Constituent Assembly and was rejected and I suppose rightly so because in India, to insist on educational qualifications would result in the exclusion of a large segment of the people. May be there is something in it. But I ask myself a question – should there not be a minimum literacy qualification? If a member cannot read or write, how will he or she take any meaningful part in the debate and discussions that precede the enactment of laws? Not necessarily BA, it need not be this, need not be matriculate, but at least he or she must know how to read and write. Otherwise, the person can't read the Bill and simply goes to sleep. Not being able to write, he won't really exert himself. If someone tells him, "*Haath Upar Karo*", he just does that; he does what he is told to do. I mean it is a serious business in parliament. So this is one area in which I really think some reform should be made. I really don't see how can there be any meaningful participation by a Member who is ill equipped, when it comes to reading and writing. Possibly there are very few like that. But we must address this issue of educational qualification.

Now I want to refer to the present electoral system. The majority of those elected gain entry into the legislatures with minority of votes cast. The other issue is of a number of persons with criminal antecedents entering the legislatures, including the Lok Sabha, through use of money and muscle power. These trends show an alarming increase. You see the records. There are some history sheeters, some of them with very colourful background. Why don't we suggest to the Election Commission, or even in the National Review Commission, that if a person against whom charges have been framed by a court of law in respect of an offence of moral turpitude and an offence for which the sentence could be five years or more, mind it not an FIR because FIRs could even be bogus, nor even the case having been merely chargesheeted, such a person should not be eligible to contest an election – to stand for election. Overspeeding, or such others should of course be excluded. Mind you, Supreme Court has held that standing for elections is not a fundamental right. The person should get himself cleared of the charge. In this law, we must insist that charges must be framed by a court of law, to make him ineligible.

I want to make it very clear. I'm not saying against whom an FIR has been lodged. What I am saying is that when a court of law has applied its mind and framed charges for a serious offence, a person should not be eligible to contest elections. That's all! What fundamental right is affected here? Unless one says politics is his fundamental right like carrying on trade and business, but then I think he will not seriously take that. This is one thing that is very important.

Another issue relates to defection. Defection is the worst form of political immorality. It amounts to a betrayal of the trust placed in him by the electorate. He gets elected on the ticket of a certain party and thereafter, he defects. Of course, the Constitution makes certain exceptions like a merger of parties. But defection is both the cause and effect of corruption. We amended the Constitution to deal with this menace of defection. Actually, in one parliamentary committee, there is a report that a person changed sides three times in three days – crossed the floor in three days – *Dal-Badal or Aaya Ram-Gaya Ram.* So the Parliament thought we should do something about it and they didn't make an ordinary law.

The constitution was amended with a good majority. Everyone agreed with this, and we got the Tenth Schedule. In short, the Tenth Schedule says that a person can be disqualified if he has voluntarily given up the membership of the party which he is from. What is giving up voluntarily? That's the key question. Did he disobey the orders of a whip? Now, what I am trying to say is that the power of disqualification under the Tenth Schedule is given to the Speaker. Let me tell you Ladies and Gentlemen, it is my experience that the Speakers, especially of some states, have not shown the requisite degree of impartiality when it comes to matters of discussing/determining disqualification.

I have appeared in a number of cases arising out of disqualification. Unfortunately, most Speakers think that they have been appointed by a certain party and therefore, they owe their loyalty to that party. In England there's a convention – once you are appointed Speaker, you have to sever all political ties with the party. That we have not done here. No convention has come up. And let me give you a very amusing example – there was one matter in which I was briefed. So I came to the meeting and enquired about the presence of one gentleman there. He told me that he was the Speaker of the House. I persisted, asking him, "Mr. Speaker why are you in this conference? You should not be here." He promptly said, "No sir, I am on your side, I am on the chief minister's side." I told the advocate who was instructing me in the case to advise the Speaker to leave the place. That was done tactfully. They got him out of chambers though he was furious and complained to the chief minister, "Sorabjee insulted me, I was there to help you, I was on your side." But when he said I am on your side, I said, "Mr. Speaker you are not supposed to be on anyone's side."

Then, what is the way out? I made a suggestion to give this power of disqualification to the Election Commission. It is a very important power to disqualify any member and also has serious consequences. If that is not feasible for some reason, please entrust it to an independent body – a three-member independent body. When certain members of government were in opposition, they readily agreed. When they got into government, they changed their stand. They are still thinking about changes. But the fact is that this provision is very important and it is very necessary to reform it. Defection really cuts, really hits at democracy. It's really, as I said, the worst instance of political immorality. But this is what happens. It is not a very difficult issue to resolve. You can vest this power in another body. We suggested the Election Commission because it is an independent body. And a three-people committee – that's another thing that hasn't happened.

I have talked enough about parliament, the legislative wing of governance. Let me now turn to the judicial wing. Herein, I think, the most obvious malfunctioning is manifested in the horrendous backlog of cases. There is no question about it. Access of seeking affordable justice is a basic human right, but it is unavailable to a large majority of people of India, especially the needy and the indigent. There has been some improvement at the level of the Supreme Court but Hamlet's lament of laws delays, haunts us in the high courts, and is a terrifying spectacle in the subordinate courts.

This phenomenon is certainly not indicative of good governance because delays in securing justice have compelled people to take recourse to extra-legal measures and employ services of the mafia. I give you a case in which I was involved: Mr. A secured an assignment to a foreign university for a year or so and he sent for Mr. B, and said, "okay you can stay in our premises, I'm not going to charge you anything, you just pay the outgoings." So, it was a gratuitous license. After Mr. A came back from America where he had gone for his assignment, he told B, "I have come back now, I'd like to have my premises back." Mr. B says, "Yes, yes, I'll do it, I'll do it". Mr. A had to live with his relatives. Then he had to move to the Parsi Dharamshala. When he asked Mr. B, "What are you doing, when are you going to give me back my premises?" What was his reply – "Why are you getting so impatient, don't you know how difficult it is to get premises?"

Then Mr. A came to me. I saw the papers and assured him that he had a clear case. Mr. B had no defense. He asked, "Soli, how long will it take?" I said, "If your lawyer doesn't take adjournments in other courts, it should be over in five, at the most six years, five to seven years, it may take 15 years." I told him a little white lie. He thanked me but never came back. Then one day I saw him at some wedding function and asked, "Hey, what happened to your case, did you file it?" He hesitated but when I pressed, he said, "You will get angry with me." I said, "No, no tell me what happened?" He said, "Bhai, I got fed up, I couldn't encroach on the hospitality of my friends and relatives, and so one day that fellow – Mr. B – while he was away at work, I took some people, threw out his belongings, furniture, everything and told him you go to court and take ten years." So this is what happens in real life.

Whenever I relate this incident, there's an applause; there is acceptance, and that's the tragic part. This incident shows the complete, abject failure of the rule of law. It's a mafia system. I know these people call the person, the tenant and say, "*Kabhi khali karega, kitna mahina chahiye, seedhe baat karo, teen mahina, chhe mahina,*" – then of course they may negotiate and get the job done.

People say, you must follow the rule of law, but this way, we get instant justice. That's the problem. These sort of mafia, we call them mafia, obtaining mafia justice, dispensation of mafia justice meet the approval of the general people, apart from the man who has the benefit of getting back his premises.

May I give you another instance? Look at the way the system works. A person is given Rs. 10 lakhs. There is no dispute, the man has, more or less, admitted. Then the matter reaches the court after 10 years and he submits his plea of admission. He gets time for payment in installments. People say this is too much. They go up to the lawyer. They say, "*Usne 10 lakh liya hai, nahin deta*". Lawyer says, "*Naam kya hai, kahan reheta hai, achcha, bulao usko*". The lawyer asks the person, "*Kabhi paise deta*", the person says, "*Nahin nahin nahin de sakta*". Lawyer says, "*Dena padega, baki hum log kya kaam karte hai, aise toh hamara chhuti ho jaegi.*" Browbeating, and everything, the fellow agrees to pay something or the other. The man gives the money; he's very happy. But, it's really affecting the roots of our system because people get to believe that you can get quick justice this way.

This is something that needs to be taken up on priority. We require a crusade, there must be a crusade, not merely speaking at seminars and lectures, and passing resolutions, but a crusade to wipe out the arrears and backlogs to ensure that people get quick redress and do not have to take recourse to the Mafia route. In this crusade, there are three peers. First is the government that must ensure that there are no unfilled judicial vacancies. Second are competent and able judges. What happens today is that a matter, which should normally not take more than two hours, goes on for two days, three days and even beyond, due to inexperienced/incompetent judges. In the third, I refer to the subordinate courts that need to be provided with the necessary judiciary-related infrastructure. You will be surprised to hear that the poor judges of the lower courts have to take down notes in their own hands since they have no proper stenographer, and no or ill-equipped library with old racks. Even work premises are not decent enough as a result of which the judges are too hard-pressed to give a judgment and yet they give it. So this is where the government can make a difference – in improving infrastructure, appointment of proper judges and providing other facilities.

The second player also includes the judges who sometimes haven't developed the right work ethic and are very easy in granting adjournments, especially to keep lawyers in good humour, keep them happy. It's a terrible thing if a judge is sick and doesn't give adjournment; the lawyers threaten to go on strike. It's a bad syndrome, but that's the way it has been with my community, the legal fraternity.

The legal fraternity is the third player and is also to blame because once a stay order has been obtained, every trick in the book is used by them to seek continuation of the stay order and here lies the real disease for arrears of cases.

There has to be a three-prong attack by the three players. I don't know whether it will ever happen; it should happen, otherwise the mafia will increase and *laws bhi khatam ho jaeyega.*

Now, let me tell you the encouraging part. The Supreme Court is not that bad; arrears have come down; government has made some changes like legislative changes to set up fast track courts for delivery of justice. But, as I said, this is not enough. Much more needs to be done. Its success will depend greatly on the attitude and response of the government, the bar and the bench.

I have covered parliament, I have covered the judiciary. Now let me come to the executive wing. I think the absence of good governance is most evident in the working of the executive wing. There is miserable non-implementation of laws made by the parliament, especially of beneficial legislation for the protection of children, legislation to protect the environment, and legislation aimed at improving the health and wellbeing of our people. The failure of the executive branch is vividly brought home to us when we witness the filth and garbage in our cities, absence of sanitation, the miserable state of health service and the horrifying spectacle of starvation deaths, despite surplus food stocks that are rotting in the warehouses.

These are functions of the executive. What happens because of non-implementation of such legislations, willy-nilly, the matter comes up before the judiciary in the form of Public Interest Litigation (PIL), because the laws are not implemented and the court's role is misunderstood. The court and the PIL in such cases do not make laws; it doesn't run the government. All it says is that you made the laws, so implement them. Non-implementation of laws for protecting the children working in hazardous occupations and various other things provide a glaring example of bad governance and abject failure to enforce law and order. There is total non-governance when no action is taken against a bunch of intolerant vandals, who, acting as the moral police, ransack offices and theatres of people who display objects, or screen movies that appear objectionable to these vandals. Inaction to take prompt and stringent action against these law breakers is a classic example of failure of governance. These offences should be made non-bailable. And these things keep happening. In Maharashtra and in other states also, political leaders and their workers go to the offices of news channels, destroy properties, manhandle the people. Why doesn't the government take action? That's a failure. If you don't act against the law breakers, how do you maintain the majesty of the law otherwise? Frankly, if you ask me Mr. Sahay, ladies and gentlemen, respect and observance of the rule of law, to my mind, is the foremost requirement and essential ingredient of good governance.

The essence of rule of law is that every person, a private humble individual or a mighty minister or influential bureaucrat should all be subjected to the equal discipline of the law. The basic tenet of the rule of law is that howsoever high you may be, the law is above you. But then there is absence of rule of law if a political leader can stop a train to allow his ticketless supporters to board it. There is subversion of the rule of law if highly placed influential persons preach and promote communal hatred and disharmony with impunity. There is a mockery of the rule of law if persons expressly guilty of red-handed corruption can prolong their charge inordinately and roam at large in luxury. For example, in a recent instance, if a building or a structure is illegal, if there is an encroachment which is harming the public and if a court orders it should be removed, it should be removed. That's the rule of law and that's the court decree. But you know what happens in reality: agitations, this-that and the other to show the power. I am taking a hypothetical case in which it has been established that the structure was unauthorised and was an encroachment. Then it has to be removed, no matter what it was and which community it belonged to. It may be a mosque, a church or a temple. The rule of law makes no distinction unless you say it is not me who's done it, it's another man. If you do not do this, you don't have respect for the rule of law.

Let me give you an example. I was in Oxford. At that time, I had problems with my feet, so couldn't go around and walk much. A taxi chap asked, "*Kahan saheb kahan jaega*"? I asked, "What's your name?" He said, "Jahangir Khan." Because Jahangir is my son's name, we became friendly. The Pakistanis are very warm-hearted that way. So he told everybody, "*Soli saheb ko paise charge nahin karo*". Then you know what he told me? "*Saheb Ek cheez hai, idhar Duke ka ladka bhi hoga, aur traffic signal torah, issko pakad liya, chhodega nahin*". So that's what impressed him. That's what impresses me too. Even if it is a Duke's son, if he breaks the law, he will be booked. *Apna desh mein nahin hota, hota toh hamara desh bhi improve ho jaata.* This is what I mean by observance of the rule of law. This is what really gives credibility. You can't break the rule of law.

Now there is another thing that I had referred to earlier. One of the directives of the Directive Principles is to minimize inequalities in incomes and wealth and to ensure that the country's wealth and resources are not concentrated in the hands of a few. Now friends, there can be no good governance when there are vast inequalities of wealth and income. Social justice is the signature tune of our Constitution. It still eludes us after 60 years. On the other hand, we witness the spectacle of obscene and lavish display of wealth by industrial houses and bureaucrats, when crores are spent on a wedding reception and when the media reports it, they gain an admiration. Why can't there be an expense tax on such events? If you can spend a crore on a wedding or some social function, shouldn't there be a rate of tax of 5 percent – a tax which can be earmarked for some social project? Continued absence of social justice leads to alienation, frustration, anger in the people and then anger is directed against the system, which leads to extremism, of which Naxalism is a proof. No one approves their methods but please remember they see we can feed our children, but we can't make provision for their children's education and health; this vulgar, ostentatious display of wealth by this expenditure – this is one thing where we can pass a law on expenditure tax. Why don't we do it?

I am sorry to say the one person who did was Gadkari. Some 5000 people came in airplanes – what is all this? Actually, I had refused to go to the parties; it's no use going there having good food and wine and coming out and presiding – boycott these functions. Whatever we may say, Mr. Doval, this is an important element in ethical norms and their observance is most needed in administration to ensure good governance and impart it with ethical dimension.

There was a very important report in England. I am referring to it because our Supreme Court has also referred to it. Lord Nolan's report on Standards in Public Life is very instructive. It mentions seven principles of public life – Selflessness, Integrity, Objectivity, Accountability, Openness, Honesty and Leadership. When I think of these, the ones that I find most essential are Integrity, Accountability and Leadership.

The real problem is about devising the appropriate mechanism for enforcing these principles. Needless to say, the efficacy of any mechanism to achieve ethical norms will be the inner driving force of any individual rather than the external sanctions of any disciplinary authority. You see democracy, unfortunately, is regarded as a periodic, ritualistic exercise of casting the vote. But remember, there cannot be a genuine democracy and good governance without an ethical content and dimension. And who said this? Justice Louis van Duys of America – he was a great American judge – and let me quote his words, "Democracy in any sphere is a serious undertaking. It substitutes self-restraint for external restraint. It is more difficult to maintain than to achieve. It demands continuous sacrifice for the individual and greater obedience to the moral law than any other form of government. Success in any democratic undertaking must proceed from the individual. It is possible only when the process of perfecting the individual is pursued."

Now, I have said all this ethical law being grandiose, but it is impossible to speak about ethical norms without mentioning corruption – a subject that we have discussed, debated and spoken about *ad nauseum*. Ethical norms and values cannot meaningfully exist in a society affected by corruption, and corruption is associated with every walk of life. One thing which can be said in favour of corruption is its universality and observance of principle of equality! It doesn't discriminate on the ground of sex, colour, age, community, ethnic origin, affects all, males, females, religion, any caste, anything and in a way, jokes apart, you see it is not generally realised and this is what I want to talk about. Consequence of corruption is not of the bank balance of the person concerned, or the corrupt official, or that the beneficiaries of corruption have gone up. No. The effect of corruption is really the denial of the socio-economic rights of the people. Funds that are supposed to build bridges, schools, hospitals, various other things, for the betterment of the people, have been siphoned away. So really, a person who after a fair trial has been found to be corrupt, I think, should be regarded as a human rights violator. He violates the human rights of the people. He should be treated that way, regarded that way. Don't call those people to inaugurations. Such people, even if they are not convicted, but who have very wholesome, well-deserved reputation of corruption, don't call them to inaugurate schools, colleges and hospitals. It's sickening.

Social ostracism will work well. Treat them like rats. They have plundered our people; they have plundered the country. One necessary provision is we must make sure that the person doesn't reap the fruits of his misdeeds. Sending him to jail, the corrupt official, or corrupt beneficiaries, won't meet much – *ye to jailor ko bribe kar dega, ghar se biryani aaeyga, and TV set bhi lag jaega.* His wife, sister, daughter, will be shopping in London, New York, Paris. Make it impossible for him to reap the fruits of his misdeeds. How do you do it – confiscate it, confiscate his property. That has been tried in Australia; the Law Commission has recommended it; that will make some difference, otherwise it will just go on and go on as it has.

The other thing I want to say, and I have already said that, is regarding crisis in governance. I would like you to read from the report of Mahboob Haq Human Development Centre – Crisis of Governance – since we are talking of governance. Just let me read from there, "It is a cruel injustice when the economy is continually raped by corrupt officials and politicians, by drug mafias, by loan defaulters, by those who appropriate state patronage, and they are creating new unethical norms which destroy the very fabric of a society."

We have seen how corruption has spread in many places, and is not necessarily restricted to the state. It happens in corporations giving dealerships; this is the case in banks – whether to give a loan, not to give a loan, whether to recall a loan – in school admissions. So, I think, the corruption laws should extend to other sectors, not merely confined to the state, and include anyone who by power abuse makes a public deal and deprives the people of their just entitlements.

Now having said all this, the question is how shall we do these? Frankly ladies and gentlemen, I feel that the root cause of the absence of good governance is that we are facing an acute crisis of moral leadership. We search in vain for a person who embodies certain ethical values and who can provide inspiration to the people. The prime need in the new millennium is for men and women who will relentlessly struggle against the onslaught of materialism and corruption, personalities who are sound enough and profound enough to generate ethical ideas that radiate from them as a force and thereby impart a fresh intellectual, spiritual and ethical dimension to democracy.

Unfortunately, in the present times, there are no men and women to match our Himalayan peaks. Our political system has more crooks, criminals and hypocrites per capita, than at any time in our history. Mere growth is no good when the moral universe is shrinking. Please remember that in the history you read, as so many of you are in retirement, if you go through Gibbons, the Roman Empire, you will see how the fabric was corroded by these factors.

As I conclude, I am reminded of the concluding remarks of Dr. Rajendra

Prasad in the Constituent Assembly. He said and I quote, "India needs nothing more than a set of honest men who will have the interests of the country before them. If the people who are elected are capable and men of character and integrity, they will be able to make the best of even a defective constitution. If they are lacking in these, the constitution cannot help the country." I think this was said in 1949; there is resonance in the ring even now in 2011.

I think our endeavour should be to allow re-entry in our public life of the ideas of fruit, goodness and beauty. It seems we have banished them and we regard them as silly slogans of impractical people. But then we are paying a heavy price for their banishment. So today, let us resolve in all seriousness and sincerity to restore our sense of values and see their implementation in all walks of life. Otherwise, it will be a case of just words, words of fury, signifying nothing. But let it not be that way. I know it's very depressing, it's very disappointing, and people have sometimes given up *ki nahin, kuch hoga nahin*. Don't do that. We must try, we must strive to see that the Constitution that our founding fathers gave with a beautiful preamble is still living and vibrant and realise the pledges made to the people of India in the constitution.

(This lecture was delivered by Shri Sorabjee at the VIF on January 11, 2011)

*

6

INDIA: SLOWING DOWN AN UNDER-HEATED ECONOMY

Dr Bibek Debroy

Thank you Mr. Doval for that very kind introduction. Ladies and gentlemen, thanks to you also. Initially when Mr. Doval invited me, I tried to duck, well not exactly try to duck, I tried to postpone it because I thought for God's sake, it's 30th of December; who is going to be interested in such a boring subject like the Indian economy, and I was expecting not more than ten people. So I am very pleasantly surprised. The weather outside is pretty dismal, foggy, bleak, a winter of discontent and no immediate sun, so to speak, to offer a silver lining in the clouds. The reason I am mentioning that is it is exactly reminiscent of what is happening in the Indian economy today.

There will be absolutely nothing new in what I will tell you; you know all of it, except that I will mention certain points to you, flag them for your attention, and perhaps I will articulate the issues somewhat differently. The first point to note, and having mentioned it, I will promptly forget about it, is what is happening in India today has got very limited relevance with what is happening in the United States; with what is happening in Europe, of course there is some relevance, but it has got limited relevance. Certainly one is talking about real growth in the Indian economy and one is not talking of volatility in exchange rates; one is not talking of volatility in capital markets. What's happening globally is largely irrelevant. It is a very convenient Red Herring. It is a very convenient scapegoat, because the problems that are plaguing us have less to do with what is happening globally and much more to do with what is not happening domestically. So the next time you see, or hear, or read that the Finance Minister, the Prime Minister, or the Deputy Chairman of the Planning Commission, or the Chief Economic Adviser has blamed it on the external world, please treat it with a healthy degree of skepticism.

You might have noticed a few days ago that there was a report in the Indian newspapers about a research institute overseas that has just carried out a study according to which in the year 2020, India will be the fifth largest economy in the world. Wonderful news! It was reported about four days ago, but if you step back let us say two years ago, you will find that there were a plethora of reports talking about the bullish prospects that the Indian economy has had; all of those bullish reports that used to float around a couple of years ago have generally tended to disappear.

This particular report or study that I mentioned was a bit of an outlier. Most reports about India now are somewhat skeptical. Indeed, Fareed Zakaria wrote a piece which is much more symptomatic of what is the take on the Indian economy today. Several years ago, Goldman Sachs coined the term 'BRIC' – Brazil, Russia, India, China – and everyone talked about the explosion of income growth, explosion and consumption growth that would happen in the BRIC countries. This particular piece said that out of the four, the BRIC country that was likely to miss the BRIC bus, so to speak, was going to be India. And this negative piece by Fareed Zakaria is much more symptomatic, is much more representative, of the external world's take on India. Also, this particular piece was written in the aftermath of the fiasco and then deliberately using the word fiasco, over opening up of Foreign Direct Investment (FDI) in retail. Again as I will argue later on, the issue is not FDI in retail, as there are other issues that are much more important. However, the basic point that I had made about the external world being much more skeptical about India remains valid.

The situation is pretty bad. How bad is it? Data in India invariably come out with a time lag. The last data on GDP growth that we have are still for Quarter 2, which is the second quarter of this particular financial year and what does that figure tell us? That figure tells us that in the second quarter of this financial year, growth was 6.9 percent. Of course, the normal tendency is, 'Hey look at all the happening across the world', look at the dismal state of most of the economies of the world are in, and that 6.9 percent is not that bad. May be yes, may be no. When the budget was framed at the beginning of this financial year, we already knew that the world economy was in a bit of mess. So, when the budget was framed, we expected a rate of growth of about 9 percent. Compared to that 9 percent, we are down to 6.9 percent. People within the government are still talking about the rates of growth this year of 7.5 percent, recovering to 8 percent or more next year.

Economists are bad at making predictions; they are far better at predicting the past. Having said that, let me assure you that there is absolutely no way that we are going to get that 7.5 or 8 percent growth rate. Let me assure you that we are now settling down for at least the next couple of years on a rate of growth of around 6.5 percent. That's the baseline now, and remember, of course, that not very long ago, over a sustained period, a relatively sustained period of 4 years, we used to do 9 percent. Those were days when we talked about double-digit growth. And mind you, these are not just numbers, because if you grow at 10 percent, you create about 15 million new jobs a year. If you grow at about 6.5 percent, you create about 10 million jobs a year. So, there's a difference of 5 million jobs that aren't going to be created. So, it's not just numbers.

Mr. Doval mentioned that in the year 1991, we were insulated somewhat from the global economy. Since 1991, we have become much more open. There are much more of exports and imports happening. Today, net exports, which is exports minus imports, adds to 2-3 percentage points to GDP growth. These are the Reserve Bank of India's (RBI) figures. Let me repeat that; net exports today accounts for 2-3 percent GDP growth. And what did I say a little while ago? I said we are settling down on a growth trajectory of 6.5 percent, and remember Q2; I said these are CSO figures of 6.9 percent. If you take away that 3 percent from 6.5 percent, what are you left with? You are left with 3.5 percent. What is the point I'm making? If you remember before the reforms, we use to talk about the so-called Hindu rate of growth of 3.5 percent and the point I am making before you now is the somewhat startling revelation, so to speak, that we are back to that Hindu rate of growth and the reason we don't notice it is that today the Indian economy is much more exposed to the global economy. If in 1991 and before 1991, our export-import GDP ratios had been of the levels that they are today, we would have then also grown at about 6.5 percent. So don't get misled by the 6.5 percent; if you take away the external factor, we are going at 3.5-4 percent. That is how bad it is.

And remember in 1990-91, when we went into that crisis, the growth rate was 5 percent. When we got into that crisis of 1990-91, I will get back to this point later on, there was at least one decade of fiscal profligacy that had triggered that crisis. The fiscal profligacy and I said I will come back to this later; the fiscal profligacy of today is very reminiscent of the fiscal profligacy in the first half of the 1980s. The fiscal deficit numbers are not as bad yet as in 1990-91, but they are getting pretty close to being as bad as in the early 1980s.

Let's step back a bit and ask why did we grow so fast between 2003 and 2007? What were the reasons? Between 2003 and 2007, we attained an average rate of growth that was 9 percent. So why did we grow by 9 percent between 2003 and 2007? There are different ways of looking at the problem, but one reason was that investment rates went up sharply to about 38 percent of the GDP. Those investment numbers are down by about 3 percent of GDP today. The investment rates went up because the savings rate went down. Savings have three components – there is the household savings part of it; there is the public savings part of it and there is the private corporate savings part of it. One of the reasons behind the growth of 2003 and 2007 was the increase in public savings and one of things that have happened recently is that the public savings have dramatically dropped. Quite often it is argued, particularly by people within the government, that the crisis, the global financial crisis hit us in 2008, and therefore in an attempt to neutralise the shock of that external crisis, we needed to step up public expenditure. That's absolute rubbish. Because if you look at what had happened, if you look at the timeline, you find that the increase in public expenditure had actually predated that crisis in October 2008. That increase in public expenditure had begun to happen ever since the United Progressive Alliance (UPA) government came into power in 2004. And I am using 2004 because in several respects, UPA-2 is only a continuation of UPA-1. If the growth is to be sustained, if the growth is to continue at 9 percent levels, we need a switch away from public expenditure that is fundamentally consumption expenditure because it does not lead to creation of any productive assets towards consumption, private consumption, and towards investment. Unfortunately because of the increase in public expenditure, neither private consumption expenditure nor private investment expenditure has been happening.

Earlier, whenever I used the term PPP, people who knew I was an economist, thought I meant 'purchase power parity', which is a favourite expression of economists. These days, whenever I use the term PPP, people think it means 'permanent policy paralysis', which is an expression that has been applied to the present government. So let's try and figure out what is this policy paralysis about. At one level, the policy paralysis seems to be about silly attempts to control inflation.

Why am I saying silly attempts to control inflation? Because if you look at the components of inflation, these are of three different types: one is the manufacturing type, other is the food type and then there is the imported kind of stuff associated with increases in global prices of various commodities. None of these is readily amenable to monetary policy measures. Monetary policy is singularly ineffective to address these kinds of inflation.

Today, and you might say what is this guy talking about, I read in the newspapers that food price inflation has come down. Of course it has but this has got nothing to do with what the RBI has done. It is purely a statistical fact, because when you look at these inflation numbers, they are expressed on a base of what the index was exactly one year ago. If one year ago the inflation levels were high, if the price levels were high one year ago, it is an almost statistical inevitability that the inflation numbers will come down. It has absolutely nothing to do with the RBI tightening the monetary policy. And indeed in those terms, you will see inflation come down further from the next month onwards.

But if you look at investments, has that really been affected by interest rate hikes? Interest rates generally do not affect private corporate investments that much. So it is fine to say that monetary policy is singularly ineffective to address inflation. It is also fine to say that hikes in interest rates discourage private consumption expenditure such as in consumer durables or housing – that's fine. But so far as interest rates adversely affect private sector investment decisions, there are huge question marks. There must be something else that is happening in the nature of the policy paralysis because the private corporate sector is sitting on large quantities of cash. If you ask the banks, they say that there are no demands for credit. In this context, let me give you a startling number: do you know how much the Indian corporate sector invested abroad in 2010-11 – outward investments from India – 44 billion US dollars. How much was it one year ago – 18 billion US dollars. These are RBI figures. So compared to one year ago, from 18 billion US dollars, it has shot up to 44 US billion dollars. The simple diagnosis today is that people are not investing in India; people are investing abroad. And the question to ask is why? Why are people investing abroad? Why aren't they investing in India? Of course there are things like the world's banks doing business indicators that document all kinds of problems that we have with investing domestically. But those have been constant over a period of time. What on earth has happened in the last couple of years so that no one is willing to invest in India?

There is an organisation called PRS Legislative Research. PRS does a lot of work on legislative activity and has this long list of legislation that has not happened. Bills have been withdrawn, Bills have lapsed, Bills have not been placed in parliament; there are 117 of them. It is very tempting to jump to the conclusion that we have got a funny kind of coalition government going on and hence the legislation is not happening; is it really the lack of legislative activity that is behind this policy paralysis? But then this kind of absence of legislative activity is also not that new either; so that's not a very convincing explanation either.

So we have disposed of the interest rates, we have disposed of coalition and legislation. Then what are we left with? Almost everything that I am going to mention now is in the nature of executive decisions. They are not legislative for the most part. The first one I'm going to mention is environmental and forest clearance. Coal India Limited (CIL) says that there are 168 projects that are awaiting clearances on either forest grounds or environmental grounds. If legitimate environmental clearances, legitimate forest clearances are perfectly legitimate, there shouldn't be any question marks. But if you talk to industry off the record, they will all tell you that the forest clearances, the environmental clearances have just become an avenue for rent seeking and bribery.

Related to this is what I will call sanctity of contract. What I mean by that expression – sanctity of contract – in this particular context means that if a project has been cleared, there should be a finality about it and it stands cleared. I cannot choose to examine it de novo and change the policy and apply that to a particular project with retrospective effect. On both forest clearances and environmental clearances, this is exactly what has been happening.

The second item that I will mention is the complete killing of land markets. Land markets are being completely killed, once the Land Acquisition Bill that has been proposed comes into play. And splice that with what is being done on the mining side. So at the top of my list of that paralysis agenda, I will have forest clearances, I will have environmental clearances, the killing of land markets and the killing of mining sector. To these, I will add one more that is in the nature of the Mahatma Gandhi National Rural Employment Guarantee Act/Scheme (MGNREGA). Let's not debate this as this is not the right forum to debate the efficacy or otherwise of MGNREGA. Let's leave that debate aside. Apart from food inflation, one of the things that the MGNREGA has done is that it has led to an increase in wages. Again let's not debate whether that is desirable or undesirable, but then what that has led to is an acute shortage of labour in several sectors. However, in passing let me mention that the structure of MGNREGA is such that it does not allow for the creation of any productive assets.

Going back to the fiscal side, we have this sword of the Food Security Bill dangling before our eyes and what worries me about this is not much the fiscal costs; it probably will go up to Rs. 100,000 crores. That is important, but what's even more important to me is that we have decided to push this bill through because we want to do it before the Uttar Pradesh (UP) state assembly elections without having even figured out who are the poor! There is a social economic census that is supposed to be happening. So why could we not have waited for that social economic census to evolve? Why could we not have figured out for a delivery mechanism independent of the Public Distribution System (PDS), which we know does not work, before trying to ram this decision through?

We can all have our views on the UID (Unique Identification). It has utility; but was there any need for this fiasco between Nandan Nilekani on the one side and Ministry of Home Affairs on the other? Would this have happened had we had the legislation in place first before trying to push through the UID?

Let me also mention the corruption part of it; I'm not getting into Lokpal issues, but there is evidence, significant evidence to show that corruption has been increasing. Corruption at the lower end of the scale has been coming down, particularly in the delivery of public goods and services, but higher up the ladder, the corruption has been going up. If I'm going to give an example of that, corruption has been sort of kicked up. If I'm going to give an example of that, let me put it to you in very simple terms: I no longer have to bribe to get a telephone because that shortage has gone, that monopoly doesn't exist; the bribery associated with the telephone has gone. So the bribery has been kicked up because now the bribery has moved to selling of the telecom licenses. Let me also mention the Right to Information (RTI) Act. And I'm mentioning the RTI because it is undoubtedly a fact that the RTI has led to a situation where the bureaucracy is extremely, extremely reluctant to take decisions.

I want to make two or three more additional points and then I will stop. This government is supposed to have a great deal of economic expertise. With all of this economic expertise, could I have not anticipated or should I have not anticipated the food price inflation that would result from something like the MGNREGA? Should I have not been able to be a bit more convincing about what is happening on inflation? I could have had a PowerPoint presentation here with all kinds of announcements about inflation being made by all kinds of people

– Prime Minister, Finance Minister, Chief Economic Advisor and Deputy Chairman of the Planning Commission – all of which have been proved to be wrong. So the signal that is being conveyed is that despite all this economic expertise, this government simply does not know what is making the Indian economy grow and what should be done to control inflation. It does not even seem to be able to make up its mind about what the 12th Plan document should contain. As a result, the 12th Plan document has been pushed back because it is being revised. With this particular government, I never expected the opening up of FDI in retail. I never expected the labour market reforms interpreted as Chapter 5B of the Industrial Disputes Act; I never expected the opening up of pensions and insurance. What I did expect, and there is no conflict with what this government wants, is improving the efficiency of delivery mechanisms, targeting the subsidies better, reforming the civil service, weeding out unproductive schemes. All of these have been documented in a large number of reports brought out by the Second Administrative Reforms Commission. Have those recommendations been implemented? The answer is no. Why have they not been implemented, because it seems to me that several decisions, and I can name at least six, are being driven completely with the UP elections in mind.

UP may be important; there may be several people here from UP, but India's economic future should not become contingent on what the electoral outcome is in UP. What worries is something else. What worries me is that in terms of government intervention in the Indian economy, not the fiscal part, in terms of government intervention in the economy, you're back to the late 60s and early 70s. One can document this. That doesn't worry me. What worries me is that exactly like the 1960s and the 1970s, no one is contesting or very few people are contesting the government policies. I don't mean just ordinary people, citizens like you; I also mean the economics fraternity. Just as in the late 60s and early 70s, the economic fraternity went along with those policies, supported those policies; that is exactly what seems to be happening now. More than anything else, what worries me is why India is slowing down despite it being under-heated in the sense that 9 percent is not what India should be aspiring to. India should be aspiring to something like 12 percent. In that sense, the economy was under-heated at 9 percent and is now slowing down to as I said 6.5 percent.

Finally, as in the invocation at the beginning, '*Nimittani ca Pashyami Viparitani Keshava*'. That is what works for me.

Clarifications: Q&A Session

Replying to a question on RTI having resulted in reluctance in taking decisions, Dr. Debroy said that the view was held not only by the then Prime Minister but also two of his cabinet colleagues. They should have thought of it in 2005, instead of suddenly discovering in 2011 that it was causing a problem. His own personal take was that if there was transparency in decision making, there should be no problem with the RTI.

On the question of the Rupee going down, leading to lower capital inflow, it was clarified that the exchange rate was not market determined. It was heavily subjected to intervention by the Reserve Bank. And yes, there are various things that could have been done to broaden the market, to develop the Forex market and make it less susceptible to RBI intervention. Capital inflow was typically not a function only of the exchange rate but several other factors also. It is true that if the Rupee depreciates, inflation to the extent that the Rupee costs of imported items go up but simultaneously, it also makes exports more price competitive. So there is always a trade-off. In the present instance, the problem has been that the RBI has done what one would call "One-way Intervention" in a sense before this recent episode. So they prevented the Rupee from appreciating because exports would have suffered. The trouble with doing something like that is it creates perverse incentives, because people do not take forward cover. If 'RBI had not intervened to prevent the sharp depreciation', it would have been only a short-term solution. In the long term, the exchange rate will be what it will be and any intervention is not without its costs. Whether we intervene to prevent the appreciation-depreciation, there will always be costs in one form or another. Higher liquidity in the system is one example of that. In the present case, I do think, after all those qualifying remarks, we had enough foreign exchange reserves for the RBI to intervene and cushion the sharp depreciation, not prevent it completely.

Replying to another question on the role of judiciary in the context of land acquisition and environmental issues etc., Dr. Debroy said that whenever there is ambiguity in the legislation, the judiciary tends to step in. The clearer the legislation, the lesser the scope for the judiciary to step in. Even in the cases relating to environmental issues, if there was ambiguity in the legislation, the judiciary steps in. In several cases, the judiciary has stepped in where either the executive or the legislature has not delivered. But the follow-up to your question is, whether the present Land Acquisition Bill will solve the problem. He doesn't think it will; it will make it worse. He gave one instance of that – What is urban and what is rural? How does one know what is urban and what is rural? Census has a definition of what is urban and what is rural, but that's for census purposes. Right now about 7 percent of Delhi is "rural". Does it make sense to artificially segment rural from urban? And that is just one example of that and related to that there are various other clauses in the Bill. So he didn't think this Bill will limit the intervention of the judiciary.

On the questions of whether India is an under-heated economy; Indian investment abroad has increased manifold compared to domestic investment, and whether this could be viewed as a positive development or otherwise, the speaker clarified that the latter can be regarded as a positive development. After all, capital is mobile; it should go to the best location possible, so why not? The trouble of course is that is not what is happening, because if in one year we have FDI of 18 billion going out of India and next year it shoots up to more than 40 billion, then this not a trend. This suggests that there is something internally wrong which is why the capital is exiting. In other words, it is not being driven by a pull factor; it is being driven out by a push factor. Therefore, he interprets it as a negative. And on the first part of the question, typically an overheated economy is an expression that economists use for an economy that is growing too fast. What it means is that the demand for goods and services is going faster than the supply. In macro terms, the result will be inflation. So one needs to cool it down by controlling the growth so that the demand keeps up with the rate at which supply is growing. That's the classic notion in which he uses these expressions. India was growing at 9 percent; there was enough slack in the system to suggest that 9 percent was not India's capacity – India was capable of growing faster and he gave a figure of 12 percent. In that sense, India was under-heated. And inflation was certainly not due to, in the macro sense, demand being unable to keep up with market supply. So there was no reason for the monetary tightening policy in that macro sense to cool down the economy.

(This talk wad delivered by Dr Debroy at the VIF on December 30, 2011)

*

7

India's Biggest Challenge: Water Management

Shri Suresh Prabhu

Director Dovalji and distinguished friends, I am really overawed by the fact that as I look around, I see so many faces who are qualified to speak and offer advice on these issues more than I can. I really feel that it is innovation that is currently required in managing water problems. The innovation being suggested is that the person who needs the least, knows the most, and he should speak and others should listen. That is probably what Shri Dovalji thought and hence invited me to speak today. He has also called such a distinguished audience to be present here. I thank you very much for giving me this opportunity. I consider this as something that we all have to think on together.

Water is a very big challenge in India. In fact, if you tell somebody in India that we have this problem, nobody gets affected. This is because there are so many problems plaguing us that probably now there is an immunity to understanding and getting disturbed by a problem. For a long time now, we have worked in a system where we have been told not to get troubled, until trouble troubles you. However, now there are so many things troubling us that we have decided to forget about trouble. Therefore, we let things just happen and cease to worry about them. In fact, now the rupee has fallen almost by one-third and our Prime Minister has not even made a statement. When inflation is constantly going up, the so-called great economists of India have been predicting that it is going to fall after 17 days. Thus far, we have been thinking that such predictions are normally made by astrologers. Economists would largely decry astrologers by saying that they go by theories and they have science. Astrology is fake and they don't believe in that. For now, astrologers can take up the economists' jobs for they can probably better predict what the Rupee's future is going to be! Meanwhile, all these economists have become like astrologers and they would do their jobs better.

In this context, even where you have so many problems, if there is an additional problem and if it is going to affect you, you're going to talk about it. So, if I had to talk about a single problem that cuts across all other problems we face, it would be the water problem. I hope I will be able to convince you of this by the time I finish my speech.

As the Minister of Power of India, the biggest challenge is power. Obviously, I had to say that because I understood it, and I have been the minister responsible for it. Those were not the days, when Vajpayee ji was the Prime Minister, when we spoke about other's ministries. The concerned minister used to normally speak about his or her own responsibilities. Nowadays, we are seeing that ministers are making promises they are not concerned with. Some minister would ask why we are not trying to open up the administrative prices on petroleum products that are high, even though we have a Petroleum Minister to look into that, and all this while the Petroleum Minister says the opposite. Those were the days when we would confine ourselves to our own responsibilities.

In those days, I used to think that Power was the biggest problem. This was because 44 percent of India was not connected by electricity, with 44 percent households without electricity, and that situation continues even today. When I say 44 percent, sometimes statistics defy on-ground reality. So with 44 percent at a time when the population was less, one can only imagine what the situation today is. Those who do have power, they may only have connections and no electricity. If you add the numbers up, we have a serious situation. Hardly any other country in the world faces difficulty based on population size. Therefore, it was always a matter of concern for me.

Subsequently, I got into the water issues and I realised there is no other issue more pressing than water. Imagine, even power generation cannot be done without water. Almost two-thirds of the power generated in India is through thermal sources, mainly coal, some gas and also some nuclear. However, even in the case of thermal power, for cooling purposes you need water. We have almost 23,000-24,000 MW of electricity generated in India that uses water, so without water one cannot have hydroelectricity. However, when we use water for hydroelectricity, it is for non-consumptive use. The same water can be used for agriculture and drinking purposes once the electricity is generated. Power generation is, therefore, more or less dependent on water, unless you are using solar power, which doesn't need water.

However, even thermal or concentrated solar power will require water. Without water, generation of electricity is not possible. Of course, this doesn't mean that we have to just rely on this situation. We have to think about new technologies. Secondly, none of us can survive without food. In fact, more than 82-83 percent of water in India is used for agriculture. This means if we do not have water, we cannot have agriculture. We keep talking about Israel and there is a lot we need to learn from them. They use less water to generate more food. Even Israel has not mastered any technology where food can be grown without water. No agricultural activity in the world can be carried out without water. Therefore, even food needs water. Of course, without drinking water, none of us can survive, so primary consumption of water is needed for us. The ecosystem needs water and if the ecosystem doesn't exist, water itself will not be available. The only way that we can actually get water is by making sure that ecosystem is alive.

Water is one of those rare, precious commodities that we cannot manufacture and cannot import, like we do with oil. There is no technology in the world that can manufacture water. You can recycle it, desalinate it, use it in its many forms, but cannot manufacture water. You could technically manufacture it in the laboratory, but definitely not in the volumes that it is required. What other problem then can be more serious than this? My friend Dr. Anubha will tell you that there are a few countries in the world that actually import water; for example, Singapore imports water from Malaysia. Now of course, they have realised the folly in this. Singapore used to import the water, process it and again give it back to Malaysia. Singapore has now decided to be self-reliant in terms of water. They are only a small city-state, but even they are now virtually self-reliant in terms of their water needs. The point I am making is that all these things, like agriculture, all economic activity, bulk of manufacturing, our social life and even our cultural life, are dependent on water. In India, if you take culture away from humanity, what will the humans living here be like?

This leaves us with having to manage with what we have. That is our biggest challenge right now. How do you manage water, required for so many critical activities? I have been to almost 80 percent of the districts, if not more, over a period of time, and out of interest and used to find out what were the big challenges in each district. I have not yet come across a single district where people say that water is not a problem for them. Some districts in Assam may have a different kind of water problem. During the monsoons in the months of August and September, there is so much flooding that it causes a water problem. None of the districts that I have visited can be said to be free of water problems. This is a serious challenge all over the country. Yesterday, I was in Dehradun. It was a very interesting meeting regarding the forest-dwellers. People from almost 25 states, a few from other countries and other participants had come. The forest-dwellers were saying that they have only three problems – '*jal, zameen aur jangal*' (water, land and forest). I will come to this later how this is going to snowball into an international problem very soon.

These three problems are agitating them so much that they are willing to go to any extent, even challenge the authority of the state itself, just imagine, because of these three fundamental things. Of course forests are not threatened all over, because there are no forests all over – there was a time when India had almost 80 percent forest cover, but that was several centuries ago. Today, forest cover has gone down so much that one cannot say that forests are causing any kind of problem. However, land and water remain problems everywhere. In fact, the relationship between water and land is very critical. Where do we get water from? Almost 85 percent of the precipitation in India is rainfall, while most of the remaining 15 percent is in the form of snow or snowmelt. However, in order to receive precipitation, we need land. Where else can we store water? Even underground water settles in when there is land. For water to be properly harvested, we need several types of rainwater-harvesting solutions. The relationship between land and water is inseparable, and that is what is causing problems all over.

In fact, water is now becoming a major social and political issue – an issue that is probably threatening the authority of the state itself. Water problems are therefore the biggest challenge we face today. I think the situation is only going to get worse and not the least because of human issues. Humans are responsible for a bulk of the problems, but the divine hand is also going to cause a serious problem when it comes to water. Climate change, which has become a reality, also contributes to the water problem in a way that is not felt in any other walk of life. Almost 40 percent of weather patterns are changing. Approximately 40 percent of the population of the world, either on this or that side of the Himalayas is getting water from this water tower of the world. The Himalayas themselves have become vulnerable as a result of climate change. Water is now not available as it used to be; it is either scarce or is received in torrents at a particular time. Too much of it at a time or prolonged periods of scarcity are going to become a norm.

What are the effects of climate change? Climate change is largely manifested in the rising temperatures across the world. Rising temperatures mean all crops need more water and water availability is therefore going to be a problem as all water resources will be under stress. Moreover, rise in sea levels poses the danger of salination of coastal areas and other water bodies. Some of our freshwater resources, which are already scarce, can no longer be used for agriculture or in fact not even be potable. Climate change therefore increases the stress on already scares resources, especially water. In the next few years, water is going to be our greatest priority. As you correctly said, we have only about 2 percent of land and 4 percent of water, but 17 percent of the global population. Population is rising and is projected to reach 1.6-1.8 billion by 2050. Purely because of this rise in numbers, our per capita water availability will go down by 50 percent. If we add another 600 million people in the course of the next 40 years, presuming that availability of water remains intact, then this would be the scenario.

However, more population also means that more land will be required for habitation and agriculture, and this will be at the expense of water bodies. This is already happening. Most of our real water bodies have gone away mostly due to overpopulation where people have reclaimed land. Bangalore used to be a city of lakes once upon a time. Earlier when we asked which place in the country gets the highest rainfall, the answer used to be Cherrapunji, but not anymore. Water bodies are no longer available; therefore, population increase is going to add to our already serious water issues. In the next few years, our biggest challenge is going to be to alleviate water issues. The other very important issue, which has already happened because of industrialisation, is pollution. Industry perhaps does not use as much water as we have been given to believe. Agriculture takes the bulk of it; power generation comes second in terms of water use and then comes industry.

While industry may not be the largest consumer of water, the negative influence of industrial activity is very profound. The types of effluents and emissions they release in water have, despite not reducing the quantity of water, made less of it available for use. This is again not a localised issue. Effects of pollution are felt in a certain place, though the source is elsewhere. Recently, Hong Kong citizens discovered that fresh water on their island was getting contaminated. The cause of this was not Hong Kong itself, but mainland China. Some of the effluents that were being released into the waterways flowing into Hong Kong were causing this problem. While we may not notice, there are local populations who suddenly realise that their water is no longer potable. The cause may not be industries nearby either; it could be something else entirely. If at all industry is set up and there is an economic benefit that is accruing from it to that locality, even that benefit is not enough to face the consequences of pollution.

I must add one thing here. We recognise our rivers from the fact that they are flowing. Perhaps in the future, once the monsoon gets over, we will have to put up a signboard saying there is a river here, because there would no longer be water flowing in the rivers after the monsoons. When the rivers are not flowing, most of the water bodies are taken over by encroachment. How then do we get the water we need? The water we regularly use is groundwater. This is also why for the longest time we didn't realise that we are facing such a serious problem. Surface water has already disappeared, but ground water, which is not visible, is still quenching our thirst. However, now as NASA has pointed out, most of our groundwater is no longer available. In some places, groundwater has been exploited beyond the level of replenishment. We are truly facing a challenge in terms of desertification. In fact, Punjab, which is considered the granary of India today and produces the bulk of our food grains, will probably not be able to, because the water needed for these food crops may not be available. This is the state of India, the second largest irrigated country in the world.

Currently in Punjab, almost 80-85 percent of arable area is irrigated. This is where we are using groundwater for irrigation. One very interesting estimate was done by economists on how much groundwater is used normally in India. It turned out to be two and a half times the annual flow of the Yangtze River, one of the mightiest rivers in the world. Two and a half times of that is our groundwater usage! When we keep drawing it without realising that it is not going to be replenished, what do we think will happen? Suppose you keep going to the bank and drawing money; because the manager is your good friend, he allows you to keep doing so, and probably extend facilities to you for a while. But after a while, he will allow you only to draw the equivalent of a month's income that you can first put in to the bank. However, if you keep drawing 2-6 months' worth each month, then after two years either the bank manager will be sacked or the bank will be closed. This is the kind of situation that has arisen in India. We are drawing unsustainable amounts of water.

When we are drawing groundwater from a plot of land and we think that this is our land, and therefore we have the right to draw the water, we don't realise that the aquifer from which we are drawing probably has its source elsewhere. It may not even be originating in Chanakyapuri. Maybe the source could be Faridabad or Gurgaon. I am drawing water here and benefiting from it at the expense of all those who are entitled to it. Our use may be depriving so many other legitimate users of water of their share.

There are several other issues related to water, including gender disparity and others. With the knowing audience that sits before me, I will share a few of these issues so that these can be discussed. I remember when I was looking at the interlinking of rivers, the Tamil Nadu Chief Minister told me that they felt I should do justice to them. They have been agitating for so many things, but on this count, they expected justice from the national government. Tamil Nadu is a part of India and among its most important states. None of the major rivers of the country originate in Tamil Nadu. The state, after a few years, is not going to get enough water. They are obviously going to question that as a part of India, why are they not being treated fairly.

If India is one nation where a state like Assam is suffering from excess of water and a state like Tamil Nadu is suffering from a lack of it, are we not going to find solutions within the sovereign land of India for such problems? These issues will keep cropping up over a period of time. Water issues can threaten the edifice of the setup of our institutions and systems. This is going to be among the major political issues of India. You must already know that whenever the monsoons fail, Tamil Nadu and Karnataka begin fighting over water. They keep quiet until the monsoon fails and then they get into action. Then both Chief Ministers have to be brought together for talks, and hopefully by the time this is arranged, monsoon arrives and the need for the talks abates. I don't even want to suggest this, since I am talking in front of an internal security think tank. However, I want to provide a glimpse of how serious this could become. There was also a fight of a different kind about 3-4 years ago.

Imagine if there is a situation where neither state has water! It could even be that a state chooses to mobilise its police force because it needs to get its water. That would be a disaster. This is something inconceivable. Therefore, if water issues are not addressed, sooner rather than later, our internal civil situation will be exacerbated. This is because people cannot survive without water. Tamil Nadu does not have any oil, and they import oil from other states. While there has always been chaos, they could still survive. Imagine a similar situation in the state where for 8 days, no water is available. I am not saying this is possible, or trying to oversimplify the situation. What I am trying to put across is that we really need to understand the ramifications of these problems and how these could snowball. Secondly, we need to consider the international dimensions of water issues. All the major rivers of India originate in China, actually not even really in China, but in Tibet – which is why we must say China. We ourselves offered that great concession to China by saying Tibet is their territory.

We are therefore downstream from China. I remember, a major source of conflict between India and Bangladesh is water. When I was looking at the interlinking of rivers, I used to speak with the Ministers in Bangladesh. They used to be so angry with India, and their newspapers would call me, when they hadn't even seen me, a rightist, RSS man. I have never belonged to the RSS, so I do not know where this came from. Their perception was that India sought to finish off Bangladesh through this scheme. Then I started explaining a few facts to them. I reminded them that we are all worried by the annual floods, but if the water overflow is reduced through diversion or linking, then there won't be flooding and everyone benefits. If China diverts rivers, then water will not flow and therefore there may be no floods. That would make China a better friend than India, as they divert water but whatever water comes to you, comes through India. India will also not get water, as they are not doing any of this for India. They have never looked at India as a friend. They are probably doing so for Bangladesh as they have just formed a new friendship with them. But their solution is worse than the problem.

Water problems are already creating serious conflicts with our neighbours. Bangladesh is just one of them. Yesterday I met a delegation from Pakistan of about 11 people. They are the ones who are always promoting good relations with India. They belong to the Labour party and are traders. They were telling me that we must now try to do something about water, because now the fundamentalists in Pakistan are using water as a device to create anti-India sentiment all over Pakistan. They said that if this continues, then after a while the effect will be irreversible. Water issues not only have internal security implications but also international security effects. The other important issues that water scarcity gives rise to are food and soil security. In Punjab, due to the greater use of water for irrigation, there has been an increase in the salinity of the soil. This makes the soil lose its fertility. What makes land fertile is not the land itself; if that was the case, then even the desert should be fertile! It is the top soil that makes land fertile, and top soil is a result of the accumulation of millions of years of ecosystem activity.

Therefore, soil security must also be a major consideration. Another issue is cropping patterns across India. This is the time when we must review India's various cropping and irrigation patterns. Use of groundwater for irrigation, as is the norm in Punjab, requires electricity as the water needs to be pumped up to ground level – first consuming electricity to pump water out and then using that water to raise a crop like rice that is a water-guzzling crop. It is not necessary for it to be grown in Punjab. Therefore, we need to come up with cropping patterns for India based on a proper understanding of soil composition, water levels and resources. Water management can then be done with the perspective of cropping patterns. If we are unable to understand agriculture and water use linkages, we will not be able to moderate consumption.

Next is food security that is also related to water issues. There are certain controversial issues when it comes to water management. One of these is pricing. If water is a common wealth, then it should be available for free. Is it, however, true that everyone gets water free? In urban areas, people who are most poor and live in slums (and Vijay ji has been Lieutenant Governor of Delhi, so he will tell you), even they have to pay for water. People like us are lucky enough to be living in government houses, where we get water free. The government is, of course, paying for it. Compared to us, those who get piped water supply, for them pricing is an issue of importance and it remains a topic of discussion. There are, however, those who do not have piped water, but must still pay so much to gain access to it. Pricing can therefore be used as a tool for water management, through management of demand. The other issue is the rural-urban divide in terms of water consumption. Most of the water that we get in urban areas comes from rural areas. Even for Delhi, now we are thinking of bringing water from Tehri. In Mumbai, much of the water comes from Nashik, which is about 250-300 km away. It is almost as if we are presuming that there is no water scarcity in Nashik.

There is definitely no such situation in which Nashik has a surplus of water that it would want to give it away. Soon there will come a time when farmers in Nashik will protest against water being sent to Mumbai, because they are going thirsty. Why would they want their water supply to be shared? If they physically stop the transport of water, even through pipelines, imagine how bad that situation can get. We have to figure out a system where the conflict between urban and rural areas can be avoided through proper water management. For this, we need to think differently, and I am only making one suggestion. I have already shared this with several people but it hasn't been worked upon yet. When we get water from rural areas to urban areas, we use a bulk of it for drinking and sanitation.

Water that has been used for sanitation should be sent back to the rural areas, where it could perhaps be used for irrigation, if not for potable uses. If not the same volume, at least 80 percent of the volume can be returned. This way only the capital cost of transport will be incurred. Incurring this cost is better than having social conflict develop between urban and rural centres.

Now, there can even be a situation where farmers from Punjab say that they do not want to farm rice anymore. It is time, therefore, that we think about subsidies for non-farming in certain areas where it might be disastrous for the land, water and overall ecology. Giving subsidies for desisting from agriculture in such areas will be much better for the country as a whole. If such a system can be developed, we must consider implementing it.

Water rights is another issue. One of the last points I am going to touch upon is a controversial one. The honourable Supreme Court recently gave a judgement regarding interlinking of rivers. If you recall, the then Prime Minister Mr. Vajpayee had initiated the idea about a decade ago during one of the worst droughts the nation saw. It was also during that period that the Supreme Court had directed the government to look into the matter. This is the context in which we must look at this issue. Today we are generating power from hydroelectricity. Our potential is 150,000 MW. Thus far, we have only tapped into 23,000-24,000 MW. I understand that it is not possible to tap into the entire 150,000 MW potential because there are several environmental and social issues involved.

Despite this, we are already implementing several new projects. We need to irrigate at least an additional 25 million hectares of land in order to meet our agricultural needs. The Power Ministry is looking at hydroelectricity. Ministry of Renewable Energy looks after projects of less than 50 MW because they are supposed to be micro projects on renewable energy. We are already thinking about our shipping. The Shipping Ministry is looking at developing waterways for India. This is only to remind you, in 1857, during our First War of Independence, the British Government was not officially here. At that point, it was only the East India Company. The war started in Kanpur, while the East India Company was in Kolkata. How did they move their soldiers? They were moved from one location to the other via waterways. They went via the Ganges from Kolkata to Kanpur. Waterways are desirable, for when we move our traffic away from our roads, it will help reduce pollution and make us energy efficient. Similarly, the Agriculture and Water Ministries are working together to try to make production of crops efficient via better managed irrigation.

All these activities are happening independently at several Ministries, but only at the Central Government level. Each state has at least a few departments that look at similar issues and activities. If we can combine the efforts of all such departments to do a multi-purpose project, it will definitely help. Each state has its own rights over water, as most of our rivers are inter-state rivers. The Tribunal gives awards, based on which any state gets the rights to use of water from a particular river. The award is also made based on the caveat that if a state fails to use its water rights, in the next round of awards those rights can be handed over to another state. Therefore, states want to assert their water rights. In my state, I am now trying to put in greater sugarcane production so that its water rights are maintained. However, it is hardly a good idea to put sugarcane production in a state or location where it is not desirable.

If you look at all these issues together and think about them, interlinking of rivers is already being implemented. Therefore, doing it together will make the process more efficient and thus make sense. One of the issues that will be raised when interlinking of rivers is underway is the displacement of people. Our record of rehabilitation of people is awful. When I was the Power Minister, I had seen this for myself in Tehri, where we had done a very bad job. We were willing to give two contractors up to four times the cost of original quote in the name of cost escalation. However, we are not willing to give 5-10 percent of the total cost of the project in order to rehabilitate people displaced by it. There is a solution to this that I had given to Chairman of the Taskforce of the Supreme Court. There are three reasons why rehabilitation is not implemented properly. First, there is not enough money. Before the project begins, you appoint a judicial committee to evaluate what the rehabilitation package should be. This package is to be worked out in a way that the people who are going to be displaced will be able to build a better life.

I must tell you this from the Chinese experience. We think that in China, because it is not a democracy, they just lift people and throw them anywhere. This is not true. In the Three Gorges Dam project from which they are generating 18,600 MW – the biggest hydro project in the world – the rehabilitation programme carried out by the Chinese government has actually made the lives of the people displaced by the project much better than they were before. In our case, the judicial commission will first evaluate the cost of rehabilitation, and then the project implementing agency will have to pay the entire amount of this money upfront. Once the project has started, they will start an organisation to disburse this. A special purpose vehicle (SPV) will be created only to handle rehabilitation. This is because normally the project implementing agency has no interest in pursuing rehabilitation. For them, this is a distraction from the main project that they need to complete. In this way, enough money is made available, first through legal process of quantification, and those who are displaced receive the money they have been promised. Since the SPV has been created, no money will be diverted and will remain with this organisation until the project and rehabilitation are completed.

We now come to how to ensure that the SPV does the job it has been created for. The people that run the SPV should be elected by those that will be affected by the project. Elect from among those who constantly agitate or are active members of the civil society, and let 50 percent of the Board of Directors of the SPV be constituted from these elected persons. For any rehabilitation work, this can be the new model.

While these issues are controversial, if you put your mind to it, you can come up with solutions for them. I am, however, concerned by the fact that water does not seem to be recognised as a priority area. By not doing this, we are relegating it to the back burner, as an issue to be dealt with over a period of time. I think we are sitting on a ticking time bomb, which may explode in a manner we can never foresee. The only way we can deal with water issues is through judicious management.

There are a lot of misconceptions regarding the interlinking of rivers. I have conducted 5,000 meetings across the country. There are 2,000 points we have identified for environmental impact assessment. The Indian Institute of Management (IIM) was asked to look at how the organisation for handling rehabilitation should be structured. We asked several experts on transparency on how to ensure high-level corruption does not take place. We have tried to cover ground on legal issues and how to tackle them and looked at several aspects and facets of water issues in the process.

The first problem is the name given to this concept. It should not be referred to as interlinking of rivers, but inter-basin water transfer. Normally, water flows into a basin. If you are making use of the water in the basin, that is the optimum and right way to do it. After you use the water in the basin, there is a possibility that water from other basins can be transferred in and used to the mutual benefit of both basins. Which are the basins that have surplus water? This is a natural question that is asked. In the North East, post-monsoons when there are floods, if even a part of the flood water can be transferred to other basins, it will help take care of the excess in that area and addresses the shortages in other areas. Floods have been a mainstay of certain basins. Since 1947, there hasn't been a single budget that has not had an allocation for Flood Relief. Similarly, there hasn't been a single budget that has not provided for Drought Relief. Thousands of crores are spent by the States and Central Governments on droughts and floods annually.

I do not deny the fact that whenever you attempt to play with nature, there are hazards involved and we must be extremely careful. On this count, we had ordered a comprehensive study of various aspects, but this was unfortunately not completed. The Supreme Court, when they passed the judgement, was looking at all these reports that we had filed with them. I personally feel that we must look at several options to help solve India's persistent water problems. There cannot be a singular solution, so we need to look at situations village-by-village by village mapping, remote sensing, GIS and satellite imagery and try to find out the water catchment and watershed areas of various clusters of villages. Incidentally, if you invite me some other day, I can give you a presentation of six districts of India where we are trying to work on soil, water and land holistically. We are looking at cropping patterns, credit, training and even at those farmers who do not want to continue farming and giving them alternate employment. We are trying this in six districts currently. If any of these models works, this will be another solution to our water problems.

I am not saying that interlinking of rivers is the only solution. This is a misconception. At the same time, looking at some of the major challenges that we face, it is imperative that we keep all our options ready. We should refrain from ruling out any options. We must look at water management as a comprehensive solution and manage the issues that come our way. I hope we all will succeed in shaping a policy that will be able to address the water problems we face today.

Thank you very much.

(This talk was delivered by Shri Prabhu at the VIF on May 29, 2012)

*

8

MAKING HEALTHCARE AFFORDABLE

Dr Devi Prasad Shetty

I am extremely grateful for the opportunity to speak before you all. I don't wish to talk about affordable healthcare alone; affordable healthcare will become a by-product if our policies are revolving around creating employment opportunity for millions of boys and girls from here to work outside India and bring in 100 billion dollars every year. We can become the first country in the world to dissociate healthcare from affluence just by policy changes. All this country needs are policy changes.

If healthcare emerges as India's largest employer, the by-product will be healthcare for everyone. I'll just give you an idea how this can be achieved. Just for your information, this is where we are today. In the World Health Organisation (WHO) ranking of health systems of countries, we are at 112, well below Venezuela, Iran and Iraq. We can never become a superpower with this kind of a healthcare indicator of the nation.

I have had the privilege of interacting with some of the knowledgeable people. Which is the largest industry in the world? Is it the IT industry or the automobile industry or the oil and natural gas industry? Just guess which is the largest industry in the world? Any guesses? Yes, the global healthcare and wellness industry is an 8 trillion-dollar industry; it is the largest industry in the world and IT is only 3.4 trillion dollars. Oil and natural gas, which everyone thinks is a big industry, is 2 trillion dollars. People think automobile is big, but it is also a 2 trillion-dollar industry.

The economy of the 21st century will be driven by the health sector, but there is a problem. The problem is that this industry, after spending 8 trillion dollars, serves the needs of only 20 percent of the world's population. If all the governments get together and decide that almost 50 percent of the world's population should have access to decent healthcare, we need 14 trillion dollars, which doesn't exist.

Therefore, something dramatic has to be done to reduce the cost, make it affordable and accessible and that will only happen by using technology. Now, there is an impending crisis that is going to happen in the next 10 to 12 years. The World Bank predicts that in about 13 years, there is going to be a shortage of 80.2 million healthcare workers. For a country like India, which produces 26 million babies a year, this is a great opportunity. We should not look at it as a threat, but if you want to get into it, you have to start acting now because the demand comes after 13 years.

For your information, we run a licensed industry. In this industry, to train a hand surgeon, it takes 14 years. So if we start training people now, we have a phenomenal opportunity. Irrespective of how much we do in this country, irrespective of how much money we produce, or spend on manufacturing and other things, believe me, we simply cannot give meaningful jobs to 300-400 million young people in this country. And the greatest threat for this country is going to be unemployed youth. Unless we can look at industries that can create millions and millions of jobs for extremely skilled and unskilled people, we will have a serious problem in this country, so here we have that opportunity to train 80 million workforce. PricewaterhouseCoopers studied the issue and, in their opinion, we need 2 million doctors and 6 million nurses today. Our own country is facing a shortage. The healthcare mess that we have in our country today is only because we don't have that many specialists. Boston Consultancy in association with the CII did a study and found that Indian healthcare will generate 40 million new jobs by 2020. That's just 2 years away. That is the requirement.

I am fascinated with this industry! Cuba trains six times more doctors than what is required for their country and 45,000 doctors and nurses from Cuba, working in Central America, have been remitting 8-9 billion dollars of foreign currency back to Cuba, that is approximately 30 percent of their foreign currency earning comes from doctors and nurses.

Now, say world is the market; they need people because Indian doctors have already created the brand all over the world. A recent study by the Harvard Business School shows that Americans treated by overseas doctors, that is Indian doctors, live longer than the ones treated by their own doctors. So we are recognised as healers in Europe, in the US. We have created the brand, so we just have to produce doctors. Essentially, if we make a strategy today that we just have to train five million doctors and nurses in this country, we can earn 100 billion dollars of foreign currency a year within the next 7-8 years. Currently we earn only 250-300 billion dollars of foreign currency. Healthcare can be one of the largest revenue generators.

Now, there are many industries that earn foreign currency but these are all listed companies, oil companies, software companies. When they earn 10 billion, or 20 billion dollars, that money goes to the shareholders who already have enough money to spend. But if 100 billion dollars comes to India through the doctors and nurses, it will go directly to five million households, where each and every penny will be utilized for the right reasons.

When I look at our government's strategy to create millions of jobs, even by mistake, they do not mention about healthcare as an industry, or a sector, for which we need to make the right policies. Please note that this is the job profile in the US; I am talking about the US here because if you want to get accurate data, you have to go to the US or Europe. We don't have accurate data. In the US, the largest employment generator today is the healthcare industry. That is right on the top and Manufacturing in the US shows negative growth, as Manufacturing cannot create that many jobs. If we have to create millions of jobs, we have to have the right policies to reform medical, nursing, paramedical education. That's all what we need, and everything else comes in as a by-product.

The shameful thing is that if you look at the US Bureau of Labour statistics, out of the 15 fastest growing occupations in the US, nine are in healthcare and none of those training programmes exist in our country. On one end, we are saying we need to create jobs for millions of people, and on the other, our universities and the education system do not allow structured training programmes and license to these people. Because if you do not have the license, you cannot touch the human body, and we do not provide it because institutions called universities, which are giving the current degrees, are controlled by institutions offering training programmes for a fee. So they would like to control and restrict the numbers. Government as the custodian of healthcare has to take charge.

The next question is what the hope is; is there an alternative model? There are hundreds of models available. Why do we have a shortage of doctors? We have a shortage of doctors because it costs 400 crore rupees to start a medical college. When you spend 400 crore rupees for a medical college, how can children from poor families ever hope to become doctors? Why children from poor families should become doctors? Because, outstanding doctors across the world with magic in their fingers generally come from deprived backgrounds; because these kids have the fire in their belly to work 24 hours and change the rules of the game. But those children of today have stopped dreaming about how to become doctors because medical education has become an elitist affair.

In the process, we will all grow old, older and weaker; we will have third-class doctors treating us. This is the reality. Is it that expensive to build medical colleges? No. In the Caribbean region close to the US, there are 35 medical colleges training doctors for the US. Some of these medical colleges are built and are running in only a 40,000 square foot rented space in a shopping mall. And these medical colleges train doctors for the US, and interestingly, most of the doctors are from India. All we have to do is to try to convert our 600 district hospitals into parallel medical education institutes to train doctors, nurses and technicians. Convert all of our 600 district hospitals into medical schools. These schools should have very rigid entrance criteria because, as a doctor I am telling you, 80 percent of the graduating doctors from Indian medical colleges will not be able to pass tests like USMLE or the PLATH or any other entrance exam – 80 percent.

So we need to have a different kind of a system, identifying children from poor families, from the rural part of the country, and the brightest ones should get into those medical and nursing schools with the idea that when they finish their education, they will be straightaway appearing for USMLE and PLATH exams and all the rest of these, and they will work outside India.

Now as a pilot project, we should identify 150 district hospitals that are located in areas infested with Naxalites. Naxalism is not a law and order problem. It is largely an economic problem. Irrespective of what incentives government gives, no industrialist will ever set up an industry there. But if you convert the district hospital of that region, 150 districts, into medical schools, in 2-3 years' time, there will be 2000-3000 children doing the MBBS, pharmacy and nursing courses, and the entire economy of that region will change. The value of land will increase; people will get jobs – accommodating people, the taxi drivers, movie theatres, everything. Children bring the greatest excitement. Just keep 10-20 percent of seats for kids only from that region; that's all, and this can transform the society. And how much is that going to cost? It'll cost nothing compared to what we are currently spending in dealing with insurgency.

So we already have a model and we just have to copy and paste; we don't need to invent something new. People cannot ask question whether this is the way to run medical colleges. This is the way medical colleges are running in developed parts of the world. Around 10 years ago, we wanted 2000 children from villages of West Bengal to join medical colleges every year. What we did was got these kids commit to us that they would become doctors. When they went into 8th and 9th standard, we gave them a stipend of 500 rupees each and we mentored them. We have kids who were selling trinkets in trains, now working as doctors.

Essentially, I am not against reservation, but going to rural schools and identifying kids who are bright, who have the passion, and encouraging them to work hard can have a long-lasting impact.

As an organisation, we started around 17 years ago. We started the hospital; my family put forth the condition that all the jobs should be given to women. At one point of time, 90 percent of our employees were women. So why give the job to women? Suppose for the floor-cleaning job, you give a man Rs. 10,000 as monthly salary; he would spend Rs. 5,000 on himself and the balance of Rs. 5,000 will go to the family. However, if you give the job to his wife, she would spend the entire earning of Rs. 10,000 on the family's welfare. And more than the money, a woman who is employed, becomes an empowered woman. She ceases to be a doormat. And an empowered woman will teach the children the art of making choices. She becomes a disciplinarian; she will teach the children to differentiate between what is right and wrong.

If you look at children from knowledgeable, wealthy families, they make right decisions and prosper while children from poor families always make wrong choices. Then you wonder why? So many of them may be working for you, and you have got great plans for them; all of a sudden, they quit the job, and you don't understand why; it's because they haven't learnt the art of making choices. Why some people become successful and why some people fail is all about the art of learning and making right choices, and kids learn that from the mother.

So if we want to build a great nation, we have to invest in creating jobs, predominantly for women from rural background, from poor families. And healthcare is the ideal industry to make it happen. As a kid, all my holidays were spent in villages as all my relatives were living in villages. It's very interesting. Today in the newspaper when you read about farm loan waiver and all the support for the farmers, that doesn't make much difference. It is a very pathetic situation for them, for the farmers. I have been observing them. It's very interesting that if you look at a typical farmer, his only worry is about the rain because we don't have that much of irrigation projects in the country. It's an interesting industry, wherein, if there is no rain, there is no crop, there is no money. If there is too much of rain, again there is no crop, no money. If there is adequate rain, there is bumper crop and whatever he has grown has no value. So whichever way you look at it, it is a matter of time before he goes bankrupt. And interestingly, of our GDP, only 17 percent comes from agriculture, but 57 percent of the country's population depends on that. So if we really want to do good for them, we have to help them to look at alternative ways of earning money because today 57 percent of the population depends on agriculture.

That was the case in the US also, years ago. Today only 2 percent of the people in the US depend upon agriculture. That will happen here with automation/mechanisation and all the rest of it. We do not need that many people in the villages.

Now what can we do? There are many things that we can do to help these farmers. I want to give an example of how a simple intervention in skill building can make a difference. In Mangalore, there are lots of agencies that supply '40-Day Ladies'. Who are these 40-Day Ladies? These ladies have only one qualification of having had a child and therefore knowing how to take care of the newborn baby. In Bangalore, there are a large number of young couples working for software companies. They are pregnant, and are going to have babies soon. In the good old days, their mothers, mothers-in-law or somebody from the family would come to look after them. Today, there is nobody to do that. So these agencies bring those ladies to Bangalore, and they spend 40 days educating the mother in taking care of their babies, essentially teaching them the art of taking care of the baby. They also provide companionship to the new mothers who feel lonely because their husbands go for work. And you know after childbirth, women can get very depressed and here she gets company.

So, they spend 40 days. Guess how much they earn for 40 days? They earn 40,000 rupees; that's 1,000 rupees per day. That's the money they earn with no other qualification. So if our Skill Development Council, if our government, can train them for just for 2 months about how to take care of the hygiene, importance of washing hands, importance of feeding the baby on time, along with some other simple things, certify them, and create a website saying that these are the people who are trained, and then introduce them to these millions of young people who want them, we can create jobs. The impact in terms of numbers can be huge since 26 million babies are produced in the country every year. These are essentially very simple ways of creating jobs, provided we develop our education system that takes care of the country's needs and builds a nation.

Nursing profession is on the verge of extinction. Nursing colleges down south, nearly half of them, are on the verge of closure. And those that are running are doing so with great difficulty. Why has the nursing profession become less attractive for the young people? It is because there is no career progression. If we do not provide a young person with job that has career progression, it ceases to be interesting and attractive. In the US, today 67 percent of the anesthetic procedures are being done by nurse anesthetists. In India, a nurse who has worked in ICU for 20 years is legally not allowed to prescribe even a painkiller tablet. We have been fighting with our policymakers for the last 10 years to allow them career progression. If they want to become nurse anesthetists, give them a choice, a path to career progression. But doctors like us do not want anyone else to touch the patient.

We are a very interesting country. If you look at the Drug and Cosmetic Act of India, according to that, only an MBBS doctor can prescribe medicine. You look at the Drug and Cosmetic Act of any other country, and you will find there are about 25 different professionals who can prescribe allopathic drugs. Britain is a very conservative society. Yet, a girl there who has undergone 6 months of British training programme can inject Botox. In India, you need a dermatologist.

So essentially what we have done is that we have allowed professionals called doctors to hijack the entire system and the country suffers, and no one cares. The other problems in policies are predominantly around the priorities of the government. We have looked at healthcare policies of India, all the developing countries. Interestingly, every government is obsessed with malaria, TB and HIV. No government document in any part of the world talks about surgery as an important public healthcare need.

Malaria, TB and HIV every year kill 3.8 million people, but the lack of access to safe surgery kills 17 million people. If due priority was accorded to surgery, we could have extended this vital healthcare to the needy through the existing network of 5,500 community health centers. By the way, I'm not talking about heart operation and brain operation. I am talking about Bellwether procedure to be made available at the community health centers. What is Bellwether procedure? It includes three procedures: emergency severance section, laparotomy for burst appendix and surgery for compound fractures. If we can make these procedures available in 5,500 community health centers, 90 percent of the country's healthcare problems would be solved. Besides, those hospitals can also easily look after malaria, TB and HIV without any problem because they have the infrastructure. But if the thrust is only on malaria, TB and HIV without surgery, they can't make the difference.

The sad thing is we are not alone. Across the world, 313 million surgeries are done. Out of that only 6 percent are done in poorer parts of the world where 37 percent of the world lives. India requires 65 million surgeries a year. All the hospitals put together perform 26 million surgeries. Is it because we don't have the hospitals? No, we have the hospitals, but to do the operations, we need a surgeon, we need an anesthetist and we need a radiologist.

I will give the data as to why this problem exists. If you look at the top 10 causes of death in India, none of those causes of death can be treated legally by a doctor without a post-graduate (PG) qualification. You need to have doctors with PG qualification and we don't produce them.

Let us take the issue of maternal mortality and infant mortality. Every time there's a discussion, we find that our maternal mortality and infant mortality record is worse than even sub-Saharan African countries. Every 12 minutes a pregnant lady dies somewhere in India during child birth. Three lakh children die the day they are born; 1.2 million children die before they celebrate their first birthday. Why does this happen? The moment there is a discussion happening in our parliament, or local state government assembly, it is all about how little our government spends (1 percent of the GDP) on healthcare and that is the reason why we have a very high rate of maternal mortality.

Theoretically speaking, if we were to increase the budget allocation on healthcare to 20 percent of the GDP, do you think maternal mortality will come down in this country? It can never come down because of simple statistics: 26 million babies are produced; if they had a good antenatal checkup, 14-15 percent would need caesarean section; half of the pregnant ladies would not have seen a gynecologist during their pregnancy and half of them don't even know what their blood grouping is. So let's assume that 20 percent of them need caesarean section; that would mean we have to do 5.2 million caesarean sections per year. To do that, we need 2 lakh gynecologists. Currently, we have less than 50,000 gynecologists; half of them don't practice obstetrics and all of them live in cities, while 60 percent of kids are born in rural India. We need 2 lakh anesthetists while we have less than 50,000. We need 2 lakh pediatricians while we have less than 50,000 pediatricians; we need at least 1.5 lakh radiologists and we have only 10,500. And then we expect our maternal mortality rate to come down.

Every year there is a debate. I was part of a Commission set up to look into these issues. We were distributing thousands of crores to the state governments to reduce maternal mortality. They come up with all kinds of figures. You cannot reduce maternal mortality; let's be very realistic.

What is the reason? The reason is vacancy of medical specialists in government hospital which is 80.5 percent. If there is a surgeon, there is no anesthetist; if surgeon and anesthetist are there, there is no radiologist. So essentially the problem of healthcare today is government hospitals are not taking care of the people who can't afford the healthcare. When I was a kid, I went to a government hospital to get my tonsillectomy done. Today no one goes to a government hospital for this because there are no doctors there.

When we look at healthcare, we have to look at availability of doctors. There are two types of doctors – one is an MBBS doctor; the other is a specialist doctor. Government hospitals alone have 65,900 MBBS doctors across the country. These doctors legally cannot give anesthesia, they cannot do a caesarean section. An MBBS doctor without a PG qualification cannot do an ultrasound; he or she can't even interpret a chest x-ray legally. Essentially, an MBBS doctor today legally cannot do more than what a housewife can do. But there are more than 2 lakhs of them and we don't give them an opportunity to become a specialist.

The US has 21,000 under-graduation seats across the country and they have 40,000 PG seats to convert them into specialists. Not only all doctors can become specialists, even doctors from India and other parts of the world can go to the US and become specialists. We have 65,845 under-graduation seats across the country and only 14,500 PG seats. So at any given time, we have more than 2 lakh MBBS doctors spending 2-5 years mugging the multiple-choice questions in Kerala or Kota to get one of those elusive PG seats, which they will never get. So if you go to any private hospital, any government hospital, doctors who are doing the on-call duty at night, are not MBBS doctors, they are Ayurvedic doctors because MBBS doctors are busy mugging their multiple choice questions. Everything is known. People ask me, "Have you spoken to people and are they aware"? I have a very simple answer: "It is very difficult to wake up people who are not sleeping".

But is it all so bad? No. We have fantastic answers; in fact, we have phenomenal answers. I'll just give you one story: I call it the "Maharashtra Miracle". Maharashtra and Karnataka – we are all in southern India. We are supposed to be prosperous states. And maternal mortality in Karnataka and Maharashtra was the same. It was very bad 10-15 years ago. Today, Maharashtra's maternal mortality record is one of the best, coming very close to Kerala, which has the least maternal mortality. How did Maharashtra's maternal mortality come down to 68 compared to Karnataka which is equally prosperous but at 133? These are two states with equal prosperity but look at the odds against Maharashtra. Maharashtra is twice the size of Karnataka; Maharashtra has four times more tribal population than Karnataka. How did they reduce the maternal mortality rate to 68? All they did was to recognise the PG degree from an organisation called College of Physicians and Surgeons (CPS) and convert over 900 to a 1000 MBBS doctors as intermediate specialists. So they have enough gynecologists, anaestheologists and pediatricians across government hospitals as well as outside in private hospitals and they reduce the maternal mortality to this level. We are fortunate that Girish, who is the president of CPS, is here today. Essentially, this could have been done by every state, but nobody did it. This is the beauty of policy for saving millions of lives without money. This country doesn't require any money from Foreign Direct Investment (FDI) or any of those. We just need the right policies.

We have, like all the other countries in the world, a system in which credentialing is important. A nurse who is handing over a surgical instrument during a hernia operation, or appendicectomy, or any of those, needs to be B.Sc. in Nursing. Is it really required? Seeing the credentialing for every aspect of services; making it mandatory? I feel it is the greatest insult to human imagination. I will give an example. There is a beautiful painting in my office. When people come to my office, they look at the painting, and they ask me, "Who is painter"? I ask them, "Who do you think the painter is"? This beautiful painting is done by a trained elephant in Thailand. If we can train elephants to do this beautiful painting, can't we get the girls from villages, who couldn't get into a nursing college, and train them how to hand over a surgical instrument? It is possible. This is exactly what we did.

We had a joint commission accredited hospital. Our nurses work in the operation theatres for exactly one-and-a-half years and they get higher salaries than us and go to the Middle East. My colleague surgeons said this can't go on; we need continuity. So we identified girls from villages who couldn't get into nursing colleges not because they didn't have the merit, but because they didn't have the money. And we trained them for three years to hand over surgical instruments and help us. Today, when I do a major heart operation and ask for a 6-0 Prolene, i.e. a suture for stitching the heart, she knows the steps of the operation I am in. It doesn't need 6-0 Prolene, but requires 7-0 Prolene, and so she hands me over 7-0 but doesn't say anything. She knows what I need rather than what I ask for. And that is what is required. And this is what these girls do. Every day 27 to 35 heart surgeries are done in one building. Twelve percent of the heart surgeries done in India are done by us.

So essentially, if people can assist in heart operation, they can assist in anything. All it requires is passion. We are blessed in producing 26 million babies with the greatest passion. We just have to use them. They are not a liability; they are our asset.

We are obsessed with price control. You are always aware; you read in the newspaper, we have to control the price. Healthcare should be affordable. But looking at the final product is not the answer. You have to look at why something is very expensive. I'll give an example. India produces medicines that are the cheapest in the world. In India, a banana costs 4 rupees, an egg costs 7 rupees, and a cyprofloxacin tablet, which cures infection, costs 3.5 rupees. Now I can tell you that no company on the planet can make cyprofloxacin with the quality it requires at 3.5 rupees. It is not possible. They are subsidising this by making money in other aspects. Because government has pushed them, today none of the companies in India are making API, i.e. Active Pharmaceutical Ingredient. We are the capital of the world to make API. If China wants to hurt India, they don't need to invade us; they have to just stop supplying us API. Our pharmaceutical industry, which has stopped manufacturing a significant number of tablets, medicines that are lifesaving because it is not viable, would collapse. So essentially when we drive down the price of healthcare, we should address what is the input cost? Then we should, instead of looking at the artificial figure to make these tablets available at 3.5 or 4 rupees, find out how to make the tablet in a quality background, how much is it going to cost. To reduce the cost, economy of scale is very important.

Our target is to build one health city complex with 5000 beds and to have 10,000 outpatients per day. We are not anywhere there; we have four hospitals now. The idea is to have large-scale operations to reduce the costs, but we have 100 towns in India with a population of half-a-million to one million where there is no specialty hospital. They can't afford a hospital of the type I have built in Bangalore. They can't afford it. So we worked with L&T. Our target was to build a hospital with 200 to 300 beds and we wanted to build and equip the hospital for $6 million. That's about 45 crore rupees. And traditionally, it takes 2-3 years to build those hospitals. We wanted L&T to build it in 6 months. We built this hospital in a place called Mysore. But we couldn't build it in 6 months; we took 9 months.

So you can build a super-specialty hospital for 45-50 crore rupees and equip it. Now this building is not centrally air conditioned. My house is not centrally air conditioned. Why should a hospital be centrally air conditioned? Central air conditioning doesn't prevent infection in a hospital. In fact, it is the commonest source of infection in a hospital. Fresh air and sunlight are the best sanitisers for a hospital, not central air conditioning. This building, a pre-fabricated building, has only ground floor, so we could build it very fast. There is no additional cost for fire preventions, because if there is a fire, you just open the doors. Essentially, we developed and built this model. Now when I look at government's obsession to build AIIMS-like institutions, in Delhi, I feel all you need is to build a super-specialty hospital like this in every district headquarters. Ninety percent of the patients who are getting treated in Delhi don't belong to Delhi; they all come from all the neighbouring states. Why should they come here when you can easily build hospitals in places they come from? And how much is it going to cost – Rs. 50 crore; make it 100 crore rupees. It is nothing compared to the trouble these people go through. There's a model available.

Now a word about health insurance scheme we launched 14 years ago with a Rs. 5 per month premium. We have 1.5 million farmers paying 5 rupees; we network with 400 hospitals. Essentially, we have proven that in 10 years, 1.2 million patients had varieties of surgery; 1.31 lakh farmers had heart operations. We are requesting the government to launch a health insurance scheme. We have 950 million mobile phone subscribers who spend Rs 150-200 per month just to speak on mobile phones. If we can collect Rs. 30 from each mobile phone subscriber every month, we can pay for the surgical care of 900 million people. Poor people in isolation are very weak, but together they are very strong. Just want to give you a glimpse of how cost goes down. Ninety-nine percent of hospitals in India still use linen drapes and gowns – perceived to be cheaper. So we got hold of some young local entrepreneurs. We taught them how to make those gowns and drapes. They started a company called Amaryllis. We were spending 2500 rupees for linen gowns and drapes. Now we are buying disposables from them for 900 rupees!

So the important thing for all the hospitals, including the government hospitals, is to know how much it costs. Everyone is talking of reducing the costs, but no one knows how much it costs. Before we listed our company in the stock market, we had a policy that every senior doctor, every administrator got an SMS on his mobile phone with previous day's revenue, expenses and the margin. For us, looking at the profit and loss account at the end of the month is like reading a postmortem report. Looking at the profit and loss account on a daily basis is a diagnostic tool. I just want to bring the attention of you all to one thing here – you all look at a hospital as a charity. Charity is never scalable. Good business principles are scalable. Money is like oxygen. Without oxygen, we cannot live for three minutes, but purpose of life is not oxygen. It is very important whether it is a government hospital or a private hospital; we should know how much it costs. For that, we need data. We believe in God, but for everything else we need data.

Coming back again to the policies, we need to create the right policies for digital health because online healthcare will dramatically change everything that we do. All the busy consultation rooms of doctors in the next 10 years are going to disappear. A patient will see a doctor online on his mobile phone and the doctor will see the patient online from his home or the house or the holiday resort. Will this be the reality? We firmly believe that within the next 5 years, smart software will make smarter diagnosis than doctors, and within 10 years, it will be legally mandatory for us to get a second opinion from the software before starting the treatment. It is going to happen. I put this timeframe of 5 years and 10 years mainly because I don't want my colleagues to shoot me down. It's going to happen much earlier than that.

How can software make the diagnosis? In any sphere of life, if the composition of decision making is finite, software will beat us. If it is infinite, you need wisdom. Then human beings will win because they have wisdom. But in a limited number, software can do the calculation very fast. Now is it that complicated to make a diagnosis? If you look at the ICD-9 core (International Classification of Diseases), there are only 6000 diseases you can suffer from. None of you can suffer from anything more than 6000 diseases. We make a diagnosis on the basis of a symptom that you complain about. There are less than 25,000 things that you can complain to us. You can't complain to us on things more than 25,000. Again, that is finite. And then we can make the diagnosis based on the symptoms, that is, when we examine you to look at the tenderness, we look at jaundice, we look at anemia; there are only 25,000 things we can elicit and there are only 1 lakh lab report images. You just have to tally that and come up with the diagnosis. Software in a mobile phone can do it.

So this is going to be the new reality. But for all this to happen, we need the right framework. Every government of the country is talking about telemedicine. We have treated 53,000 patients, but you don't know that it is illegal. You call a doctor and say you have headache and have this problem; the doctor will tell you to take some tablet. Do you know it is illegal? We haven't created the legal framework for the massive transformation in healthcare; we are using online means. So these regulations are very important. We believe that within the next 5-6 years' time, this will be the reality. I just want to explain how the healthcare will move. Uber – most of you use the car service – has no cars. Swiss Book has the largest content but doesn't create content. Ali Baba, the world's largest retailer, has no inventory. Air BNB, which is the largest provider of hotel rooms, has no hotel rooms. And the world's largest healthcare provider will have no beds. It will be a software.

The question is where this will be developed? This will be developed in India or in China. It won't be developed in the US. In the US, they don't allow legally mobile platform to be involved in healthcare delivery because of security or whatever reasons. It is mainly the vested interest. In any case, the US is far, far behind us in developing these technologies. You will be surprised that most hospitals in the US still use pagers. In India, if you want to see a pager you have to go to a museum. But they know how to innovate. So what have they done? They put the EMR (Electronic Medical Record) on a desktop with wheels and they call it as a COW (Computer on a Wheel). That is the latest innovation they have done. In the US, the innovations in technology can only happen if the software engineers can spend lot of time playing with the patient data and looking at the doctors as to how they treat the patients. That is not possible in the US because if you lose the patient data on a mobile platform, the minimum settlement cost will be a few million dollars. So in a country where patient data is more sacred than sacred life, no innovation can happen. So here we have a phenomenal opportunity to make it happen, but then for that to happen, we need the legal framework.

So, in the end, I just want to tell the Indian healthcare providers that we need to train manpower and supply the cheap manpower for the world. We shouldn't do what software companies have done. Indian hospitals, Indian entrepreneurs should take our hospitals to the developed parts of the world and manage them by having our own doctors, nurses and medical technicians. This is what we did in Cayman Islands. Five years ago, the Government of Cayman Islands, the Prime Minister, the Health Minister, all of them, came to our hospital and requested us to build a hospital in Cayman Islands. I went there, made a presentation to the cabinet and said that I would be very happy to build a hospital but we have only one condition. They asked me what my condition was. I said, just one condition, "You have to recognise my Indian medical degree". Most of you may not know that Indian medical degrees are not recognised in any country other than India. Our degrees are not even recognised in Bangladesh and Pakistan. So I told them they have to recognize it. Then the premier said, "Look we are a British protectorate; we follow British rules, so you have to appear for an entrance exam". I politely explained to them, "I didn't come to you, you came to me, and if you want us to build the hospital, this is my minimum requirement. I don't want my senior doctors to be humiliated by asking them to appear at an entrance exam at that stage of their life". Within six weeks, they changed the law and today the Cayman Islands is the second place in the world that recognises Indian medical degrees. This is what will happen all over the world because every part of the world requires doctors, nurses and medical technicians from India. Just want to show you, what is the impact. What is so big about building a hospital in the Cayman Islands? That is a lesson we all have to learn.

A nurse worked with us for 2 years in Bangalore; when the hospital started, we asked her to go to Cayman Islands and work in our hospital. Obviously, they are paid extremely well. Last year, just after working there for 2 years, she took her parents on a holiday to the Niagara and Disneyland. Tell me which girl from a poor family in Kerala, at the age of 24 or 25, can afford to take her parents on a holiday to Niagara and Disneyland? No other profession will allow that to happen. It is only the medical profession that pays the professionals disproportionally high in all these countries. And we have a great opportunity. We have lost out on the First Industrial Revolution; we lost out on the Second Industrial Revolution. This is one window of opportunity for us, so let's not lose it again.

Thank you very much.

(This lecture was delivered by Dr Shetty at the VIF on December 19, 2017)

*

III. NATIONAL SECURITY

9

Strategic and Tactical Responses to Left-Wing Extremism (LWE)

Shri Vishwaranjan

Mr. Doval, General Jacob, Shri Khandelwal, Ladies and Gentlemen. I see many of my 'gurus' in the audience. Mr. Doval has been my mentor in more ways than one when I did a three-year stint in the Intelligence Bureau. I am greatly honoured to be here sharing my views with all of you.

Left-Wing Extremism (LWE) is a simple problem if we look at it from one point of view and a very complex problem if we intend to make it complex. I intend to initially state that there is a great deal of confusion about the problem itself; about its causes, which have led to this kind of violent problem we are facing today. This confusion emanates from certain perceptions.

One of the very common perceptions, according to me, is that this problem is a socio-economic problem. There is also a perception that Maoists are misled; they have gone far away from their original ideology, or have misinterpreted the ideology, hence the necessity of a dialogue. Yet another perception is that the Naxals and the Maoists of the 1960s and early 1970s understood the Maoist ideology. The present bunch of Maoists are extortionists and hoodlums. And there is also a perception that is very commonly aired that because the society, and every institution of the society has become thoroughly corrupt, the Maoists are doing a good thing, that they are doing a good job and that the killing of the innocent by the Maoists may be bad, but killing a policeman or a police informer is okay.

I feel that if there is so much of confusion about how Maoism has come to this state, then our prescriptions would also be faulty. Even among security experts, I find a fair degree of divergence on how to deal with this situation. We can talk of these perceptions and prove or point out their inadequacy or incorrectness. When it is generally believed that ideology is a good thing, and since the Maoists are doing so much of mindless killing, they have deviated from the purest form of ideology, we fail to appreciate that ideologists can be evil and violent per say.

Maoism is an ideology that sanctions violence. History of Maoism in China is replete with examples of chilling and gruesome violence that was perpetrated on those who differed from them. There is a perception that the Maoists have become bad because they have become extortionists and hoodlums. This again emanates from our incomplete knowledge of what Mao did and said. There is a great deal of archival material coming from China as well as from Russia, which clearly indicate the psyche of Mao. In the early days of the Chinese Revolution, Mao called his supporters the "Red Bandits" and allowed looting, extortion and killing of people who were opposed to him. He believed in chilling violence that sent a message that if anyone tried to oppose him or his party, he would be dealt with very severely.

Further, the perception that we must negotiate with these misled people emanates from yet another of our beliefs that the present-day Maoists are deviating from their ideology. As I just pointed out, they are not deviating; in fact, they are keeping quite close to the central theme of the Maoist ideology. And if you read Mao, most of his 33 volumes and the archival materials, which are now coming out, it is very clear that Mao believed in negotiations with "the enemy" only when the revolutionary forces were in disarray and it needed time to consolidate itself. So, if we are aware of this, then we will be very wary of negotiating with the Maoists.

I will later deal with the socio-economic causes of Maoism. At this point, I want to show you what the present-day Maoists have done to Bastar.

These are gory pictures; you will not like to see these. In fact, I have collected over 200 screening hours of such photographs of killings that the Maoists did ever since they took control of most parts of Bastar. This is a scene after a Jan Adalat authorizing brutal killing of a person by the 'Kangaroo Court'.

Many people think that the recent attack on a civilian bus was the first of its kind. The fact, however, is that the Maoists have always been doing that in Bastar. In 2006, a truck was blown off.

And this is the kind of destruction that they have achieved in the last 10 years. They have been continuously subjecting Bastar to this kind of violence. The condition of the state highways, which pass through Naxal dominated areas, is miserable. They have destroyed schools, ashram, and tribal hostels. This is what they have done to rails that carry iron ore.

We must understand that if we allow the Maoists to consolidate in other areas, they can very well do to other states what they have done to Bastar.

We keep debating as to why the police were not able to detect mines and defuse them in time? Well, our boys are trying to do that, but it is not an easy task. These mines are buried seven to eight feet below the surface. That makes it so very difficult to detect. We do not have any equipment that can alert us, although recently an Israeli company has claimed that they can detect mines down to three meters and a trial is going to take place. They are coming to Raipur on the 9th to demonstrate this. If it is so, then we'll have a couple of them, although it is very expensive – each equipment costing Rs. 25 crore.

From the Tables below, you can see the number of blasts that have been carried out. It does show a downward trend as we have been doing a lot of de-mining.

Blast (from 2005 to April 2010)

Year	*No. of Blast*	*No. of killed security men*	*No. of killed civilian*	*No. of injured security men*	*No. of injured civilian*
2005	55	37	04	45	04
2006	122	36	81	108	91
2007	107	85	13	104	27
2008	74	37	02	89	10
2009	56	48	17	71	10
2010 (till 24th May)	22	23	19	16	24

Recovered Explosives from Naxalites

Year	*Landmines*	*IEDs*	*Claymore mines*	*Gelatin*	*Detonator*
2005	112	00	00	00	82
2006	256	03	01	00	388
2007	175	31	07	49	208
2008	119	08	02	04	323
2009	103	03	10	00	263
2010 (till April)	20	03	02	04	69

The land mines recovered show that these are the normal landmines, which include pressure mines and mines of less than 50 kg. And the next column shows the mines recovered that were 50 to 150 kg. Although we have also recovered one mine which was 500 kg, but we have not recovered another of that type.

What kind of damages these mines can cause are shown below. I have only included the big explosions caused by mines that were between 30 kg and 150 kg. The bigger ones are all 100 kg and above mines.

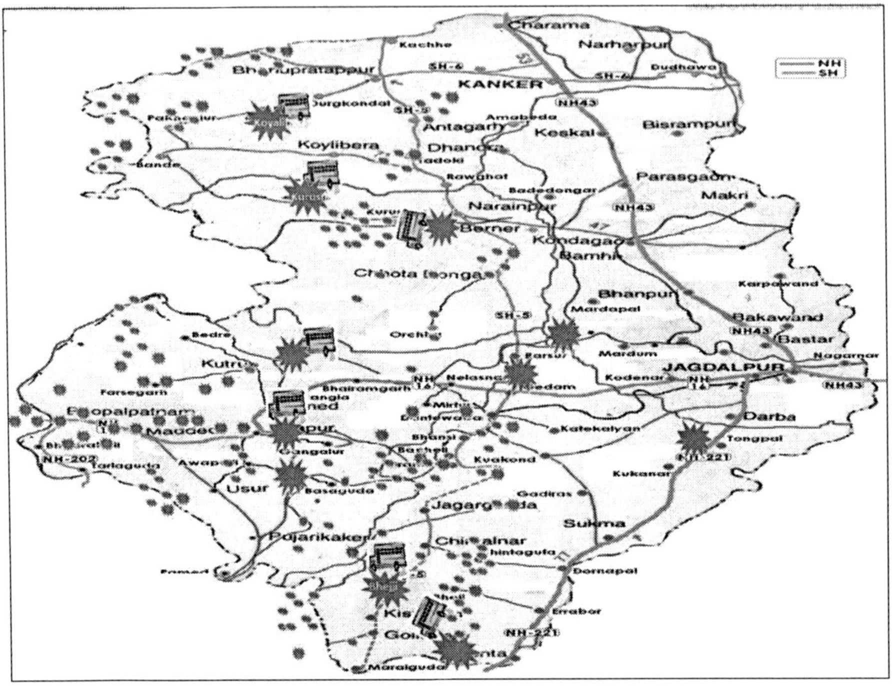

As I said earlier, this may soon become the scene in other Maoist-dominated areas if we do not adequately respond to the problem. What I want to stress is that we cannot solve a problem if we have wrong or inadequate understanding of the problem. Similarly, we cannot solve a problem if our response is inadequate. Do we need to correctly understand the problem and assess if our responses are adequate?

And what are the problems of inadequate understanding? First, as I said, there is a general confusion about the causes. It is generally believed in India that the causes for the growth of Maoism, Naxalism are lack of development in an area or other socio-economic contradictions that exist there. The fact is that the socio-economic contradictions only offer the fertile soil where such movements strike deep roots. That must not be confused with the real causes. A fertile soil is not the cause of a dream – because the logic lies in the seed. The fact also is that in a developing country, we cannot find an area where no socio-economic contradictions exist. The real cause of rise of Maoism lies in its sinister ideology that aims at replacing democratic polity with the Maoist totalitarian system.

This is very clear from what their documents say. These documents normally are not ever quoted by their friends. Many of them belong to the civil society, although I have a suspicion that most of them are aware of the existence of those documents. These define the central task of the revolution as seizure of political power through protracted people's war, the seizure of power by the use of armed force and the final settlement of which should be by war. This is the central task and the highest form of revolution. This is virtually a quote from Mao; some words are changed but virtually a quote from Mao, which you find in his Red Book as well as in his detailed writings. To accomplish this central task, the Indian people will have to be organised into a people's army to wipe out the armed forces of the counter-revolutionary state through war, and to establish in its place, their own state.

Let me clarify that I have quoted these from one of the chapters. The full chapter carries detailed discussion on who are the part-time members and only when the professional revolutionaries and the part-time members are strong, will the party really be strengthened. The professional revolutionaries form the core of the party while the part timers constitute the base. When you read the whole chapter, you will realise that the part-time revolutionaries are those underground cadres who are penetrated into the civil society. In fact, they say, we must only penetrate such people who have not been exposed to the enemy, the state. So, it is quite difficult for a common man to even know if a person, who is part of some organisation or is living in different places or working somewhere, is actually a Maoist cadre doing a part-time job in the civil society networking. The chapter details how he should function etc., and how he should acquire social status in the area where he is living. So, the only way you can detect such a mole is from the activities he is doing – it's like a black hole. You don't see a black hole, but only the activities that go around the black hole.

The book further says – it's a long chapter – that as lakhs of enemies, i.e. state's armed troops have been deployed since long in Kashmir and the Northeast, and as more and more sub-nationalities come into armed confrontation with the reactionary Indian state which is keeping them in a state of subjugation and denying the right of self-determination, it will be difficult for the Indian ruling classes to mobilize all their armed forces against the Maoist forces.

In this context, the book also talks of winning over and supporting these sub-national movements so as to create a powerful united front against the Indian state. So, it needs to be understood that the book hardly talks about poverty, although it talks about exploitation by the ruling class, how to create a united front etc. It does not talk only about getting the help of poor peasants but also of the middle-level businessmen etc. and even anti-social elements.

One of the reasons why we had this confusion is also because of the very well calibrated psy-war unleashed by the Maoists. I will give you one example of this: the much commented upon Salwa Judum that was started in 2005. The Politburo of the party said that this was an anti-people's movement and they will crush it, physically exterminate this movement. Then, in January 2006, the Central Committee meeting decided to initiate a dialogue. Four months later, in April 2006, the Central Committee realised that the movement was still going strong. The Politburo met and decreed that they must isolate and crush Salwa Judum at all India level including in Chhattisgarh. They decided to create a sub-committee to contact Indian and international study teams through their over-ground 'friends' and friendly NGOs after getting them vetted by the sub-committee and the international coordination committee of the party. So, only those selected study teams were provided access in the interiors of Bastar.

The first study team entered Bastar to study Salwa Judum after this resolution. To step up propaganda against Salwa Judum, it was decided to activate friendly NGOs, create a sub-committee, set up web sites and produce propaganda material against the Salwa Judum movement. The interesting part is that most of the attacks on the Salwa Judum started after this decision. Gradually, the Maoists succeeded in changing the perception about Salwa Judum from a tribal movement against the Maoists to a vigilante violent movement. We will have to appreciate that they did it with a lot of finesse, and unfortunately, there was no psy-war riposte from the side of the government or institutions which were trying to support the initiative.

Now we'll come to the inadequacy of strategy among security experts. The basic problem was that the Maoists were still being seen as guerrillas whereas they had already entered the Mobile Warfare stage since 2004. In fact, they started entering this stage in 2000 itself, but by 2004, in most parts of Bastar, they had started subjecting the Bastar area to Mobile Warfare strategy. It was no more a guerrilla kind of thing.

The second problem was that the situation was being seen in the light of the Andhra experience as the ideal strategy to tackle the Maoist menace. The Andhra Pradesh police had tackled the problem when the Maoist movement was still in the early stages of Guerrilla Warfare, when their operating groups consisted of 15-20 members of a guerrilla gang. Today, the Maoists are moving in military companies, sometimes one to three formation supported by 200-300 members of their militia. A Maoist military company today has a minimum of three LMGs, 15-20 automatic rifles, an assortment of SLRS, 315 rifles, 303 rifles, in addition to mortars, crudely fabricated rockets and grenades.

The difference is that up to 2003 in Bastar, as in most parts of India, they had one company each. In most parts of India, they had no military company. Today, Bastar has eight military companies. The total number of military companies that they have formed may be 13-15. But in Bastar, eight military companies are active; 24 military platoons are active. They are trying to create a battalion, but because of some leadership problem, they have so far not been successful in creating that. The North Telangana State Zonal Committee cadres have moved into Bastar. The Andhra-Orissa border cadres also play active part in raids. Interestingly, a lot of linked Naxal military move in from Orissa and Maharashtra whenever they have to do an operation. In one of such operations, we lost our Superintendent of Police and nearly lost our IG also in an ambush that was multi-layered on both sides, extending over 2.5 km. It was a three-layered ambush. The policemen virtually exhausted all their ammunitions before reinforcements could reach. The SP and the IG had only half a magazine left. Had the reinforcements been delayed, I don't think they would have survived the onslaught.

Earlier, raids used to be conducted in extreme cases by less than 50-60 Naxalites. Some raids today are conducted by more than 500 Naxalites. Even landmine blasts that used to be 10-15 per year have increased in Bastar to more than 100. As against low-pressure mines used earlier, today large numbers of pressure mines, anti-personal mines are being used. Multiple blasts too were rare, but today multiple blasts have become common features and are carried out in quick succession. Sometimes the blasts take place on both sides of the road in a zig-zag formation. Their plan is simple. They want to carry out protracted raids in the state. It is protracted people's war, and the form of war depends on stages where they are going. An effective stage is the initial stage when they are creating cells and all that.

Compared to the Guerrilla stage, the New Democratic Republic, as they call their Mobile War, is meant to lead to Liberated Stages. This will be followed by Positional War in which they will confront the 'enemy' to retain areas and advance onto new areas. So, this is their estimated design – moving from Guerrilla to Mobile to Positional warfare. There is no defined timeframe demarcating the three-war stages. This has not been specified in their documents. In the preliminary phase of Mobile War, guerrilla tactics will be more pronounced accompanied by some characteristic of Positional warfare in a quiet manner. This is again from their documents. The aim of the Mobile warfare is not to retain or capture territories. Instead its aim is to wipe out the enemy troops. Fluid battle fronts and deployment are emphasized upon: mobility of attacking the enemy at relatively vulnerable spots, withdrawing quickly, fighting when you can, moving away when you can't, flexibility of tactics with changing conditions, with troops to concentrate in large number to encircle the enemy and melt into guerrilla groups during withdrawal. The emphasis is on higher degree of political consciousness and greater discipline and military training.

It must be understood that in such a situation, unidimensional response cannot work. We have to calibrate it during different stages of Maoist movement. In the preparatory stage of Maoist movement, we can focus on removing the socio-economic contradictions, land reforms etc., though which are only temporary solutions as land holdings take two to three generations to reduce. So, we will have to find alternative means of employment. Various other valid developmental interventions must be taken. During the course of guerrilla to mobile to positional warfare stages, the response has to be security centric, followed by developmental intervention. We must introduce proper developmental initiatives in the peripheral regions to act as a bulwark against Maoist expansion into newer areas.

For effective security response-passive development, the force levels have to be adequately increased along with capability development. Training of forces in counter-terrorism and jungle warfare is essential. You cannot use a normal policeman to fight at this stage, especially from the mobile stage onwards of Maoist warfare.

Enhancing Motivational Level of Police Forces

One of the major problems being faced by the police in Bastar is the extremely inadequate force levels. Let me give you a comparison and Gen. Jacob will well appreciate how inadequate our force levels are. In Bastar, one battalion (1000 or so men) has to operate over a 3000 sq km area. That works out to one company (100 plus) to operate in an area of 500 sq km. As I shift from police-civil ratio to public-police per sq km ratio in the jungle area, it is one policeman for every 4 sq km.

Ratio of Police Force in Bastar Area

Each Bn has to Operate in an Area	3,000 sq km
Each Coy has to Operate in an Area	500 sq km
Police: sq km Ratio Comes	1:4

Some Police Stations in extremely affected Naxal areas Bijapur & Dantewada have to look after about 700 sq km.

Force Area Ratio in Bastar

Area of Responsibility & Operations per Bn	2600 sq km
Area of Operations per Coy	430 sq km

Note: In some areas even more than 2000 sq km segments no force exists.

In the affected areas in Bastar, we have deployed our battalions that have to still operate over 2600 sq km – the area responsibility of a battalion that works out to 430 sq km per company. In some areas of more than 2000 sq km segments, virtually no forces exist. This leads to the first Naxal ratio comparison: one policeman to four force ratios in Manipur, J&K and Punjab, and approximately 12 policemen to one insurgent today. The force ratio as per international standards in Greece, Malaysia and the Philippines was 15:1; this I have got from some books, so I cannot vouch for its authenticity. Manipur and Nagaland combined are smaller than two districts of Dantewada and Bijapur, which have most torturous terrain and one of best tropical forests, or very dense tropical forests. We had asked a retired Inspector General of Police to carry out a study on how much force was needed. He had come to the figure of 70 battalions to tackle the Maoist insurgency in Bastar. In reality, we have just about 30-32 battalions, which includes the Central Armed Police Forces, the state armed forces and civil police. It can go up by another 2000-3000 men if we add the Special Police Officers (SPO), but not all the SPOs are in the class of fighting force. Many SPOs are deployed in defensive postures like protecting the relief camps.

Sinha Committee's Calculation about Requirement of Manpower for Chhattisgarh

Unit of force, which can dominate a particular area	*Total affected area to be dominated*	*Force Requirement*
One BN-600 sq km (Extremely)	30,000 sq km	50 BNs
One BN-2000 sq km (Highly)	17,000 sq km	08 BNs
One BN-4000 sq km (Mildly)	28,000 sq km	07 BNs
L/O & other Security Task	...	05 BNs
Total requirement	70 BNs	...

And now we come to the most talked about incident that took place at Chintalnar, Dantewada on April 06, 2010. I have my own perceptions of this. We have the benefit of having in the audience Mr. Rammohan. I would not talk of what went wrong; I would examine it more from a military point of view.

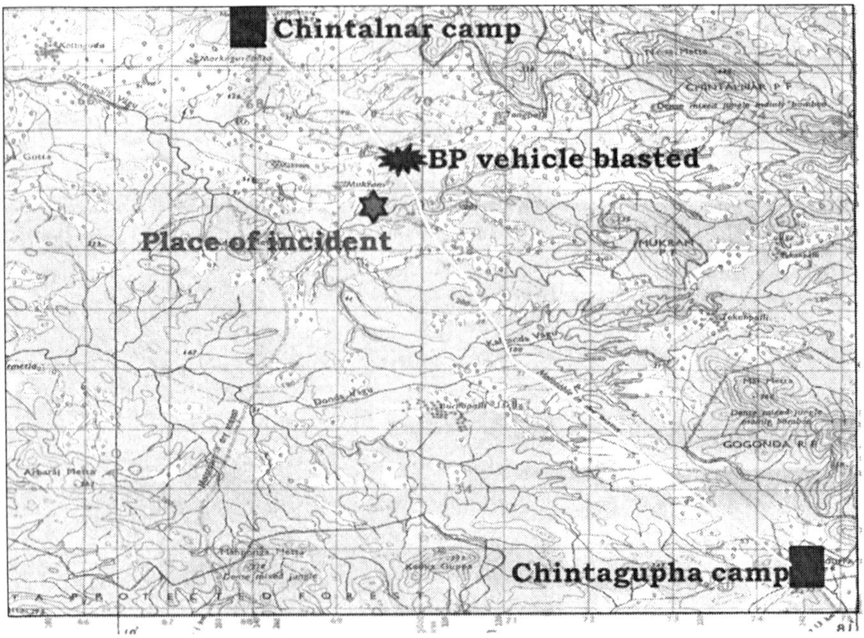

62nd Bn CRPF and Naxal Encounter dated 06-04-2010
Incident Place
Out Post Chintalnar Area Tadmetla Forest, Distt. Dantewada (C.G.)

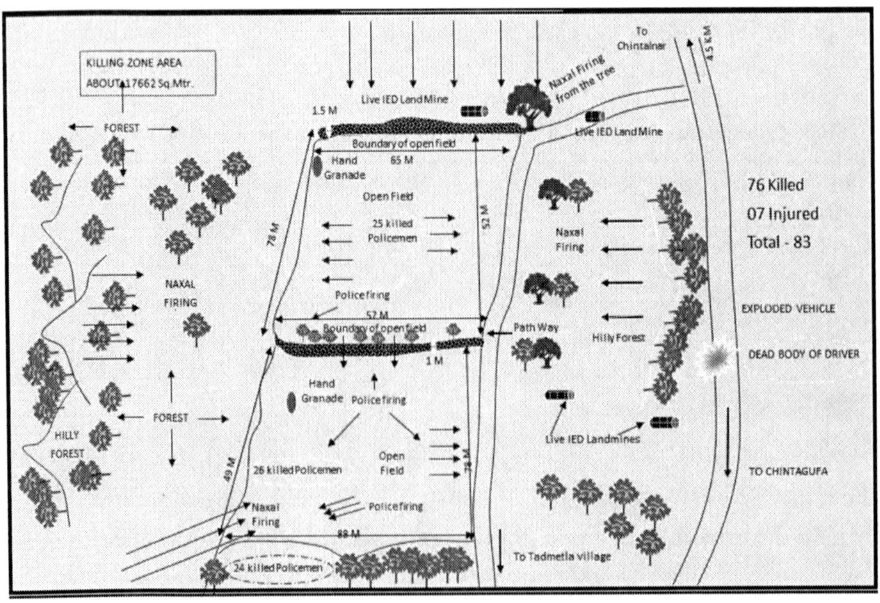

This is the place where it happened. This is a plain area, a kind of a killing zone. We know that Maoists have been laying U-shaped ambush, multiple ambush, so if you enter an area where you don't get any protection, and if by chance an ambush has been laid, then you cannot fight back that ambush. The victims would not have even got time to react properly. They must have obviously fought back because as firing starts from all sides, you will definitely fight back. But there was hardly any place, natural trees, rocks, anything, trenches, from where you can take position and fire back. So, they must have resorted to random fire to save themselves. Nine Naxalites were killed. That we came to know from their spokesperson saying that they lost nine people.

I think even with all the things that happened or what did not happen – omissions and commissions – things went wrong and what is worse, it can go wrong again and again. If your formation in the jungle is dictated by the terrain of the jungle, you keep on changing your formation on the terrain to get the minimum hit if attacked. Your movement should be so flexible that if you identify the enemy, you must be able to encircle them. This needs training in jungle warfare. If the force is not trained adequately, you will make this mistake if you move in a cluster. And if you have entered a cluster with no formation, if you have not been able to identify, it can be a killer zone. Not all killer zones are killing zones. It becomes a killing zone if there's an encirclement by the enemy and you enter the area without due precaution – then you are inviting a mayhem on you. And what I'm trying to say is that even if whatever is being said that they did this and that, even if we set aside all those things, I think, most of our forces, police forces, are not trained for this kind of response. They must be trained.

That is what we did by setting up our own training institution. That is why, for the last 3 years, policemen trained in Jungle Warfare College in Kanker have only had 16 losses, and actually in combat operations, only 4 losses. Most of the losses occurred in mine blasts and all that.

I personally feel that it is the responsibility of each and every police camp to first sanitise the area around. The protection to the camp; should not end at the perimeter of the camp, it should extend slightly into the terrain ahead. You have to secure an area of 5-6 km radius. That way you send the message that if the enemy enters this area, he will be hit very hard. It is the responsibility of the force that is staying there to move around in that area and sanitise it on a continuing basis. This can involve many things – it can involve visiting villages, winning over villagers; it can involve creating sources; it can involve cordon and search operations in many villages; it can involve ambushes being laid at strategic points. You cannot sit in your camp and think that the perimeter of the camp will protect you, but you need to protect the general area around the camp to keep it under your control.

Now we have been doing all that in our stand-alone camps. All this is included in their handbook; in this they have shown how they will maneuver if their headquarters are attacked. They have been trained in what maneuvers to do in L-shaped ambush, how they retreat if they are attacked, or when the first platoon of their ambush is attacked, what movement they have to do, and force maneuvers during attack by Naxal platoon from the flanks. To combat the Maoists in the stage of mobile warfare, police need to be trained in jungle warfare. Unless we do that, we will not be able to adequately respond to the challenge.

And now let me tell you how a trained force can respond. I am giving this example because this is the first group that was trained in Kanker and they were sent there. It was a platoon strength force, and it was able to withstand a very major Naxal attack. We have got from their document containing their analysis of why they failed in an operation carried out by 150 People's Liberation Guerilla Army (PLGA) members comprising one to two local squads, 40 militia men, assault group, four sentry capturing group, three groups for capturing camp, two for capturing kitchen store, one artillery team, two demolition teams, two relay teams, two diversion teams that attacked at two other places, two groups for dummy raids on nearby police stations, four ambush parties to block reinforcement, reserve group, one reserve team with doctor. They had conducted reconnaissance of the post. On the date of the attack, they checked for any last-minute changes. They blocked the road at 72 places; they blasted and fired anti-landmine vehicles at the back-up reinforcement with SP Narainpur.

In their analysis, it was mentioned that they had used 122 automatic and semi-automatic weapons, four Light Machine Guns (LMGs) and a dozen rocket launchers. Their volume of fire was 846 rounds, 12 rocket launches, 20 grenades, two landmine with a rate of fire per minute of four rounds. However, our men didn't lose their cool; the platoon commander was alert. He protected the camp and allowed the Naxals to come into the killing zone and then he attacked. There was also a great deal of fire control on his part. And our forces hit their leader and once their leader was hit, they ran away.

So, if you are fighting a battle, you have to have the courage to enter the combat zones. In this case, the school was completely destroyed by the Naxals. It became our police camp for one year. From here we started building the security around, without concertina wire and with only sand bags and other kinds of trenches, we strengthened our positions. We are still doing it, and now we have everything there anyway. That is how we have to go; we can't say that you give us the facilities and then only we'll move. When you are in that kind of a situation, you are going to fight, so you must have the courage to enter any territory and have the confidence that you will out-maneuver the enemy.

Thank you.

(This talk by Shri Vishwaranjan was delivered at the VIF on May 29, 2010)

*

10

Indigenising Technology and Production in Defence: India's Survival Need

Dr Vijay Kumar Saraswat

A very good evening distinguished audience. I see here some great personalities who have been at the helm of affairs in Government of India, in industry, academia, and administration. I think the whole view of the Indian scenario is present here to listen to the requirement of Indigenisation for defense technology. Actually, we thought of combining both technologies for war and for peace issues, but I think the focus would be more on the Indigenisation of the defense technologies. Ultimately, that is what is going to bring self-reliance as required by all of us.

Basically, I don't intend to discuss why and where the real situation is in respect of the defense technology requirements of the user, in the overall context of the emerging threat scenario. And to solve the problem, what kind of measures we need to take?

It has been years and years since we have been at it. Had we made the right decisions in the past, or did those decisions really result in actual growth? These can be discussed ad nauseam, but the ultimate result is that we are still at only about 30-70 or 40-60 percent. There are different perceptions of different people on this.

Science and Defence Technology

The fact is that we have been late starters as far as technology development for defence is concerned. Why defence alone, everywhere we have been late starters.

It is only post-independence that we started looking at it, and thanks to Jawaharlal Nehru's vision, we found that science and technology was the only way by which we could really make our country strong and self-reliant. The Nehruvian model of development definitely provided direction to making our country modern in all walks. Have we succeeded? To some extent yes; we have pillars of technology centers, whether it is energy, whether it is research and development (R&D), defence, pharmaceuticals or anything else. But whether we, in the last 66 or 70 years, have reached the required level, is debatable. The vision was very clear that it should be a planned growth through science and technology.

So we are looking at science and technology–driven planned growth to achieve the objective of a good life, better living standards, self-reliance, regional development and security through science and technology. Pt. Nehru was of the view that we should have good education, should have coherence in R&D and we should have collaboration. We have good collaboration in many places, but whether the collaboration was really good enough for the technology growth is questionable; whether the coherence in R&D was existing, carries the largest question mark. Standard of education, to a large extent, we can say, was good. But it has been deteriorating over the years.

So these are some of the factors that will actually give us answers to why we have not performed well despite this kind of a vision. The great advantage we had was that people with excellence were identified: Dr. Homi Bhabha for nuclear; Kurien, everyone knows, for the White Revolution; M S Swaminathan for Agriculture, who gave us the Green Revolution and solved the food problem of the country. And in the field of science and technology, for defence we had Dr Kothari, who set up the Defence Laboratories over the years for doing the research and development. That's what we have today as Defence R&D Organisation (DRDO), which came up sometime in 1958-59. For space research, which was an offshoot of atomic energy spearheaded by Dr. Vikram Sarabhai. What we see today as the advancement in the field in terms of *Chandrayaan, Mangalyaan* and so on including our capability in Satellite Launch Vehicles, all that is part of this vision and the mission that was set up by Dr Vikram Sarabhai. In the area of general technologies for civilian and other uses, it was the vision of Dr. Bhatnagar and later Nayudamma, which gave birth to Council of Scientific and Industrial Research (CSIR) in its present form. "Science for common man" was the basic slogan at that time and complimentary in international science and technology cooperation and collaboration ventures.

So these are some of the great people who did great work. After doing so much work between 1958-59 and 1995, Dr APJ Kalam who took up the Integrated Guided Missile Development Programme (IGNDP) migrated to DRDO. He gave a vision for 2020 in which his main mantra was freedom from all technological constraints. Development was the main mantra and that India must stand up to the world; it should not get cowed down in negotiations with respect to whatever is needed for the benefit of the country. These are some of the visionaries who have done wonderful work and what you see as today's science and technology and what you see as India's defence capability technology are due to the collective efforts of these great people who also created institutions that are today churning out technologies in different disciplines.

Now I come to the impact of technology. This lecture was actually prepared for giving you an idea of the impact of technology both on human aspects and in the field of defence. If you look at the technology that has changed our way of life right from 10,000 years down, making use of the gear for hunting, making use of the weapons about 4000 years back and also boats and sailboats, each aspect of the human life has been affected by the technology growth that has taken place for centuries, including the aircraft industry that is for 100 years plus, the automobiles, the roads and mass production of chemical that are today available, nuclear weapons that are there for about 55 years and so forth. These figures I am giving you are from 1998. Extensive use of fertilizers for agriculture, health, and of course landing on the Moon and now the Mars missions, genetically engineered plants and Internet are today's realties, which have affected life in different forms.

All these technological linkages are essential both for achieving the various missions and for setting up the required infrastructure. These linkages as propounded by the visionaries and followed by our country through mission mode programmes have resulted in the growth story that you see in space as a developed system, right from Satellite Launch Vehicle (SLV3) to Polar SLV (PSLV) to Geosynchronous SLV (GSLV) and Indian Remote Sensing (IRS) and communication satellite. Each one has been done in mission mode from the concept note to getting the technology. The missile programme of the country has been a similar story.

And so, even today, what we need to do is to move from traditional infrastructure in power, transport and ports to modern infrastructures. What we are talking about is modern hi-tech materials, electronics, advanced manufacturing methods and info-tech software, sensors, cyber security – all of these need to be taken care of. We need to improve the engineering industry. In fact, we have a real crisis today because our engineering industry still lives in the technological domain of the 1970s and 1980s, whereas the manufacturing methods over the years have progressed so much that if you had to do today's product, you have to first upgrade our engineering industry.

Clean energy is another requirement of today and so are the emerging life sciences because the future lies in the convergence of nano, bio and Information Technology. We need to have complete convergence. Only then will we be able to achieve national security, energy security, space security, economic security, economic growth, and of course agriculture, food for all and finally the desired level of prosperity. That is how the linkages of these various programmes to the final mission of getting prosperity can be done.

Let us now discuss national security as the major issue. In national security, we see how the concepts of modern warfare have changed. Warfare has not been static; it has been sometimes driven by the technology, or sometimes the technology has been developed to meet the warfare requirements. The scenario today is changing rapidly. In the past, it was the warfare priorities that demanded development of new technologies. But today, it is technology that is driving the warfare doctrines. Network-centric warfare is an offshoot of what is happening in Information and Communication Technology (ICT).

Human warfare was there, weapon warfare was there, economic warfare was there, and today, we are talking about cyber warfare. The tools were different; the dominating nations were different. Sometimes it was religion, sometimes it was demographic requirement, and sometimes it was high technology that was the driving tool. Today, what we see is that technology is either controlling the economy, or it is bringing the information ascendancy. So cyber warfare is getting more and more critical. Now nations, depending upon the level of technologies, are having supremacy. Today, for example, in the field of cyber warfare, it is USA, France, Japan, China, Russia and many other European countries, which are dominating. The modern threat profile from weapons of mass destruction are constituted by missiles of different kinds, metal-filled drugs and then electronic warfare, cyber warfare, information warfare, space control and security.

As far as our country is concerned, we have a huge, long border on both sides and we are under attack from two adversaries – from the North as well as from West. The attacks could be by missiles or other weapons of mass destruction. In this scenario, we have our own nuclear doctrine that is of 'no first use' and no use against non-nuclear countries. India needs to defend against these kinds of threats.

When you have multiple threats, you have to determine whether the environment is conducive for self-reliance or not. Our levels of self-reliance are getting strengthened; we have our own control of defence technologies that have been there from 1989 onwards. People say that it is being released to some extent, but my perception is that it is only a different name. We have our neighbours being fed with nuclear and missile technology systems. We have dumping of low technology. To strengthen our country, we have our own constraints – industrial growth, national priorities, technology growth and resource constraints in terms of funding for various programs and projects. A number of countries are acquiring missiles, and nuclear powers are continuously on the rise. Piling up of destructive arms continues inspite of arms reduction treaties. In such a scenario, self-reliance through Indigenisation becomes important.

DRDO was one of the major agencies identified for doing this. Over the years, 52 laboratories were set up. The growth has been from inspection agency to scientific research, to reverse engineering and technology generation. Programmes started in the 1980s now design with concurrent development, leading to production of prototypes, system analysis, new system development, production and delivery. That is the kind of journey that has taken place. Today, the DRDO is expected not only to develop new technologies but also to deliver to the armed forces. If a new system is developed and not delivered, it does not make any sense. So a continuum from development to production, and actually giving the user the final support, is essential.

Through the years, the various products that have been developed and delivered include the LCA combat aircraft, the Unmanned Aerial Vehicle (UAV) Nishant and the complete missile spectrum produced by the DRDO. These have resulted in the development of different kinds of missiles – starting from surface-to-surface missiles to today's AGNI-1 to AGNI-5 and ballistic missiles in defence systems. You have technical missiles like *Akash*, which is under production, *Brahmos*, which is a cruise missile under joint venture, and air-to air missile, which is under development. Two other projects, for long-range Surface-to-Air missile (SAM) and medium-range SAM, are being developed for the Indian Navy and Indian Air Force.

The mission mode approach has resulted in the development and production of a complete range of missiles in the country since 1980. The first two decades, i.e. 1960 to 1970 and 1970 to 1980, were used for the development of basic technologies. It is only in 1980 when a push was given to IGMDP with the vision of making our own missiles and making India as a missile agency. That has resulted in what you see today as the wide range of missile technology systems. In future, these missiles may be used for multiple land/sea/space targets. We will have multiple platforms to carry Multiple Independently Targetable Reentry Vehicles (MIRVs) – these will have higher pillowed factures and new technologies. You will also see missiles become smarter so that they can handle Ballistic Missile Defence (BMD) kind of threats. And they will have higher accuracy, better sensors and guidance systems, all finally leading to performance levels matching international technology standards. This is the kind of roadmap in which technology growth is going to take place, keeping in view the basic requirements of having technical and strategic missiles for the country.

The emerging scenario is for the development of supersonic missiles where you a fly a high-end supersonic missile at Mach number 6 to 8 to reduce time and also reduce the engagement scenario. Very critical technologies, like scramjets, high-temperature materials, need to be developed for this. And in the future, we will also see light wing autonomous missiles because non-contact warfare is going to be the order of the day. You have to wait for these to emerge. You should continuously be on the scan and that would require loitering missiles with onboard seekers, acquisition of homing systems, data links, remote control variables and seekers, which send the images through data link for giving you the advantage in decision making, and so on.

Development efforts are on in all these technology areas today. The contentious issue is whether or not India should have LAC missile defense? We have argued this out many times. With 'no first use' as our basic doctrine, obviously impregnable defenses against nuclear missiles become imperative. And that's why India went ahead and developed the BMD technologies that are the two interceptors: exo-atmospheric and endo-atmospheric interceptions. These have been realised, giving us capabilities to track ballistic missiles, long-range tracking radars, multiple function radars, data links, supersonics and hypersonic aerodynamics, seeker systems to engage a target at high altitudes at high speeds, and so forth. All this is possible today with indigenous technologies. Yet there are weaknesses in certain areas that need to be overcome. Our programme is two-phased: one is up to 2000 kilometers, which is ready, and the other up to 5000 kilometers, which is under development. So that would see the capability of BMD for us.

In the area of land warfare, we now have Main Battle Tank (MBT) Arjun – a longish programme that went on for almost about 25 years. Today, it is a reality. This is an indigenous tank being produced by our Ordnance Factories. Almost two regiments of these have already been manufactured and delivered. Mark II version is also indigenously developed except the engine, which comes from overseas. The rest of the equipment are being produced in the country, including gun control, stabilisation, armour, hydro-pneumatic suspension and so on. Having developed the capability, we have now taken up the pilot programme of the future MBT. This is already on the drawing board.

In the electronics area, which is essential for all tactical and strategic warfare, tremendous amount of work has been done in our country in Electronic Warfare (EW) systems, radar systems, communication systems, command control, surveillance intelligence systems and information secrecy and electro-optic systems and many of the components that are essential for this. On the delivery front, *Samyukta* has been given to the Army; *Sangraha* EW systems, which are already being produced in large number by our Ordnance Factories and Bharat Electronics, have been developed indigenously.

Solar system has brought in a tremendous change. Gone are the days of constraint faced even during the Kargil War; today we have phase ready radars that can track missiles up to 500 to 600 kilometers, even 1200-kilometers range, and we are also developing radars that can track satellites and even cross-section areas. In radar technology, the country has made tremendous progress and this is visible. Our Akash Phase Array Radar is fully indigenously produced with all elements done within the country. Our BMD Radars have been developed in collaboration with Israel and are being manufactured in the country. And technologically, from mechanical scan to electronic scan to digital beam forming, multiple target handling capabilities and radars for the tracking of long-range missiles for our intelligence agencies are also being developed today in hubs.

New technology is driving the warfare and that is where Net-Centric Warfare (NCW) has come in a big way. The NCW is nothing but the information wing being taken advantage of for shared awareness, shared knowledge of command, set synchronisation, speed control – all this information sharing is a new source of power and that is what is being done.

So, from the early days of the 1970s, we have made rapid strides and now have systems; we have global information grid working on net-centric operations and warfare, basically because of the information, communication, computing – all three put together provide critical synergy. The basic things are the sensors, the shooters, the weapons – all these are integrated into the grid of information that connects these together and act to great advantage in terms of speed of operation and command and control. This would not have been possible unless we have a very good military wireless scenario. So we have today our own satellite communication systems, our data links, our fixed Local Area Network (LAN) systems and we have mobile LAN systems. These will enable tomorrow's unmanned ground vehicles, unmanned aerial vehicles and all this will be further facilitated by software-defined radios and later on, the cognitive radios that are under development today.

These technologies would give a complete spectrum for theatre ballistic missile, national command to theatre defence, joint forces authority, which is now what the armed forces are looking for. In the Indian scenario, this picture is emerging, both for planning, engagement of target and also command control and authorisation. This is majorly because we have data linkages, communication network, computers, sensors and the software intensive teams available for doing this integration.

Asymmetric warfare is emerging as a major track today and we have to look at what is that because today we have enabled NCW that is treated as an end in itself. But my view is that NCW should be treated as an enabler. If you wait in the line, you are vulnerable, and that vulnerability comes from the strategic cyber warfare that is emerging. We have to have a strategy: people call it Revolution in Military Affairs with a strategic effect. Cyber defence is a major requirement in an NCW scenario, which could be credible for our deterrence capability. For the nuclear scenario also, a similar thing has to emerge. And in this, the targets of course are the defence communication network, global positioning systems, the law enforcement networks and the critical national infrastructure. All these targets are actually operated through different layers. We have government targets, military targets and economic targets. This trinity has to be safeguarded in a cyber warfare scenario. This can happen if only we have deterrence that is demonstrated. Merely having deterrence, which is not demonstrated, is not useful. That's why occasionally, all nations, whether they accept it or not, are trying hands on cyber warfare in offensive mode. Loosely connected network of cyber military are involving patriotic hackers, regular defence and civilian assets and isolated conglomerate of air gap networks situated across the friendly nations as part of cooperative defence. This is the kind of tie-up we have to evolve if we have to go in for cyber warfare tomorrow and that is the way technology of the future will take us. If we continue to remain passive in this segment, we will have a large gap tomorrow. This is my vision.

Low-Intensity Conflict (LIC) is another area that is very important for our nation. We have seen many attacks that have resulted in loss of life and property. The technology for LIC is a derivative from military technology but with some differences. The differences are very clear: conventional, which are organised advanced technologies; logistic dependent; national dependent; doctrine acquirant etc. Then we have all kinds of conventions that control it. The LIC is irregular; they use whatever technology they have in their hands – logistics independent, local directive, ad hoc doctrines – and of course there are no laws governing this particular thing today.

We did a lot of work in DRDO basically to convert military technologies for LIC purpose. Many of the products given to the Army were modified. Today we have UAVs given to paramilitary forces: fixed mini-UAVs, foliage-penetrating radar to check the movement of terrorists and impose surveillance. Similarly, we have night vision devices, quasi-passive devices, laser range finders, Global Positioning System (GPS)–assisted devices, explosives detection and diffusion kits that basically use sensors for stand-off detection of explosives, incapacitation devices like the chilly grenades and so on. And since these are biochemical agents, this is another area that is very important. We are developing some specific weapons like the corner short pistol and so on. While their import from external sources is permitted, there is a requirement for going very innovative as far as these kinds of weapons are concerned.

Communication is yet another important area. While static communication is very good, mobile communication even today – unless we use the cell phone technology – has issues. So directly, from the next generation of satellites that are being developed, white band systems, which are being used for giving satellite communication to the armed forces or to the paramilitary forces, and driving technologies are being given today. These are all under development.

Space is going to be the next theatre of war. Having seen what China has done to demonstrate its anti-satellite capability, America too has done that. Given our growing dependence on space with navigation, communication, GPS and everything, the denial of space is eminent. And this would impact our communication, intelligence, navigation, space awareness, space superiority and even economy. What are going to be the constraints? There will be limited availability of space orbits, and radio frequency spectrum is also going to be controlled. Technology readiness levels are also important here and low-cost satellites will have to be replaced and replenished. In the event of a war, if our satellites are denied space, if we are going to take 6 months to launch a satellite, that is not going to be helpful. So we need to develop technologies that will enable us to launch a satellite in the shortest possible time at low cost, low life as replenishment satellites. Then of course, weapons will come: space-based lasers, space-based interceptors and maneuvering satellites. Negation could be through electronic means, it could be a direct attack, and so on.

Now many of the technologies that we developed in BMD will be very useful in this particular scenario, because, with their uses, we can detect, track, classify, identify and act. It is a question of deciding whether we take electronic counter measures or an active measure for denial. And this is possible for a typical satellite trajectory, even with a ground wave radar, to intercept a satellite because satellite trajectory is well defined as compared to the ballistic missile that is maneuverable. So it is possible – you should only have the energy and sensing capability.

Future warfare is going to be non-contact war as I mentioned earlier. It would require surveillance capabilities, unmanned aircraft systems, unmanned ground vehicles, unmanned water vehicles and unmanned aerial vehicles as far as the future is concerned.

There is requirement to now go for the 'Soldier as a System' concept that has already evolved because a soldier is no more having just a gun and a few maps with him. Today, a soldier is having communication, he or she has protection, got GPS for navigation, a computer for giving him information about what he sees and data links to his troops and fellows. So, today's Soldier as a System, all put together, will ultimately require artificial intelligence and expert systems. Technology is driving in that direction. We have already seen what has been happening in Afghanistan where the drones were doing most of the damage. Ultimately, it is going to be land based, under water and the UAV systems that will be doing all this.

Weapons of tomorrow, yet to be developed, will be energy weapons; there will be no bullets. We will have to work on laser-based systems. Development of these laser-based systems is already on where laser operation can destroy something at 1 kilometer. But much work is required to be done in this area. Electro-magnetic pulse systems and high-powered microwave are the future weapons that would be needed. Now e-bomb that can be delivered through an aircraft or a missile would be the requirement of the future. But we have to first develop technologies like explosive-driven flex compression devices, detractors and so on. These are some of the new areas that are going to be developed for meeting the future requirements.

Well you have seen the country making progress in many areas. Similar progress is being made in other areas as well like aircrafts, missiles, tanks or EW, radars etc. There still is a perception that we have not done enough. We should look at why we have not done enough. That's more important because development of demonstrable technology and production leading to availability of the system throughout the life cycle to the armed forces at a globally competitive cost are two important aspects. The cost factor is becoming important. We have to learn from history. While I am specifically talking of aerospace, it is generally applicable for all defence systems as well. It is about licensed production route that we have followed since 1950s till today. And while it has given us the capability to manufacture certain aircraft, certain tanks, certain guns, certain explosives and so on, it has led to full benefits only when we have indigenously produced them. But the indigenous content is limited and we do not know how to derive more through this route.

Just as programmes like the development of technologies in Space – SLV-3, PSLV – were very important, in DRDO it was IGMDP. These were positive aspects that resulted in certain amount of self-reliance. The systems for these programmes, with all the bugs that were there earlier, had to be handled. So when IGMDP and things like that were done, there was concurrent development and production. It was achieved through the involvement of production agency in the development and involvement of R&D in the setting up of production infrastructure. DRDO and Space invested at that point in time, even before the design was completed. The country took a decision to invest in production. Infrastructure such as Hindustan Aeronautics Limited (HAL) aerospace divisions were set up. Such decisions were taken and all the issues were discussed and impediments removed. The issues related to likely cost control methodology, cost planned development, redundancy management. All these were identified right at the sanction stage of any programme, leading to success in terms of realisation of the project and upgradation of the infrastructure. With these, finally, the country has technologies for air frames, rocket motors, warheads and engines – Russian aviation systems. The country has today migrated from the old machinery technologies to modern machining centers and we have learned the capability to handle the latest materials.

These are some of the important lessons for us to take a direct focused approach to development and production in a synchronised manner. You have chances of better success, greater self-reliance, despite the fact that there was a missile technology control regime creating severe problems. What then are the key restraining factors responsible for many of the products that do not succeed and what needs to be done? Some of these are as follows:

- Systems are technology intensive and involve high development risk and call for high investment;
- Assured minimum quantity is not available. This should be made mandatory for all projects under development;
- Selection of industry partner at the very beginning of the project based on technical capabilities and not just on lowest tender basis;
- For development projects, competition should be on technical issues and not on low cost. Achieving success is of paramount importance;
- Level playing field for private sector industries to be ensured;
- Participation of private industry has remained only at the level of seminars and conferences. Actually, if one looks at the impact on the private sector, it is to be analysed by those who have been talking about it.

In this scenario, I think India is being rightly seen as growing. The country has talent in all segments; it has R&D, engineering design capability, manufacturing base, assembly system and civil aviation facilities. One of the fastest growing aerospace markets is mostly due to the defence planning. In fact, if you took all programmes that have been sanctioned – military aircrafts, missile programmes, UAV programmes, all put together – today India has approvals for the next 15 years, more than Rs. 1,40,000 crores worth of projects and programmes. And if these are to be done in 15 years, certainly the existing infrastructure, R&D and the academic institutions are not adequate. These need a great push. This is the most opportune time for us with the presence of multinationals in our country; Honeywell, Bharat Aerodynamics Limited (BAL) are there, United Technologies is there, all willing to participate in our R&D and production effort. This is the kind of scenario that is emerging.

As I mentioned earlier, we already have civil aviation, we have ports, communication, radar facilities, satellite launch vehicles. All put together, we have intensive technology growth, we have industries that have matured today despite the fact that we did not give the private sector as much impetus as was required. Compared to the 1970s when we were really only fabricators, today we have fabrication and testing. There are agencies that can do sub-system design, fabrication and testing, and we are looking at many of the industries who can even become lead integrators for the future weapons and equipment. In fact, in the production of Akash that is going on today at BAL, to meet the requirement of the users, apart from BAL, we are going to Bharat Electronics. And we are looking at companies that are willing to set up production lines for Akash. That is the kind of minimum block we have to overcome to promote the industry like this. We can certainly improve on that.

Now what was the basic problem? Problem was that we were all talking of 'know-how', but not 'know-why'. As a result, every design, whether it was in HAL or Bharat Electronics or BDL or in many of the other private institutions, had to be only for manufacturing. But today, in all our systems, programmes, the DRDO is getting into joint ventures – there is know-how and know-why. That's more important and that would give us technology and that has been the world trend. So we have to start looking at the new development models that we can take from here: joint development, joint ventures, exchange of scientists for getting technology and collaborative research programmes in universities – these could be the models that have to be applied.

R&D has to play a major role. In fact, this has been a major contention between us and the Department of Defence Production. When you go for technology tie-ups, if you do a tie-up only on production, you lack the technology assimilation that is most important. You have to bring in the technology and assimilate through R&D. Special R&D projects should involve the industry in different models with system integration and choices based upon capability and capacity. We need to create higher-ending industry joint ventures to form concurrent technology transfers, R&D, and for investment in production infrastructure. In fact, DRDO invested in HAL Aerospace Division, in Bharat Aero Dynamics and BAL that resulted in augmentation of their production infrastructure. This led to *Prithvi* and PSLV production in the country. But after that, over the last 20 years, we have not invested even 10 percent of what we did at that time. How do you expect LCA to be produced, a fourth-generation aircraft with two-and-a-half generation manufacturing capability in HAL which is available today? Obviously, investment in production technology also has to be done and that can come only if we are investing in upgradation of infrastructure through R&D.

There are gaps in technology and those have to be sealed. Cauvery engine did not see that kind of progress mainly because of the propulsion system (whether it is aircraft propulsion or automotive propulsion, or UAV propulsion). The country lacks capability of designing propulsion systems. Many of us are very happy that the automotive industry is everyday giving a new model, but all of you should know that the engines that are being used today initially come from Italy or Spain or wherever, and then we started indigenous production. So propulsion is one area – in rockets we have good technology, gas turbines, alternate propulsion – in which we need to build separate design houses. Similarly, in the fields of long-range radars, approach systems and advanced materials, actions need to be taken along with creation of additional capacity for production of aerospace equipment in selective areas.

Royalty models also; people are not participating today because they feel that there is a problem of volume. Many technologies, like navigation systems and control actuation systems, are required only for specific uses; here volumes are very small. So money has to be spent and infrastructure has to be created only by the government. The private industries won't do it due to low volume of requirement. Can the 'Offset' mode be used in acquisition of critical technology, to make such items available to Indian industry? Industries associated with R&D could be given tax benefits to encourage greater participation. We have to certainly take care of that. In fact, today if you look at many of the tax policies we have, if a person is doing built-to-build or built-to-development as part of offset, he sends the equipment and when the equipment comes again, it is taxed. So actually you are getting into double taxation which will have to be rationalized. Similarly, taxation aspect for joint ventures, collaboration and also R&D products, which are under development, needs to be looked into. If royalty is not paid, the market will not open up and then who will do the risk sharing? So these are some of the suggestions that we should examine to smoothen all these aspects.

In many cases, the Government Owned Corporate Operated (GOCO) model has worked very well, particularly where initial investments are required and private industry won't do that because of volumes and assured market. We have done that in the case of windless and gyros; we have done that in the case of actuators where we set up the production facility and made the industry to run it. It has paid rich dividends. In fact, it has also let them learn a particular technology and they are now in a position to go from Product A to Product B. So that certainly helps.

In many instances, private agencies have the technology but their capacity is limited. In such cases, we have to do micro-financing to meet the defence needs. We did this in some cases and it paid huge dividends. So, micro-financing policy needs to be taken recourse to.

Indisputably, there is a requirement to invest on technology. Nobody can say that you can remain in a static mode on technology. Today, while programmes are being funded and they are related to the delivery of the systems, the investment on technology in all sectors, whether it is space or DRDO or nuclear energy, is limited and that needs to be augmented to something like Rs. 100 crores to 200 crores per year, or maybe, even in the range of 300 to 500 crores per year. In some of these technologies, we need investment to be done either by way of R&D programmes or infrastructure development. They are listed and they need to be taken up. Now technology development cannot be done in today's scenario. Today, if you see the R&D policy of the government, the actors, services, the production agencies, industries and also the academia, you have the government which is in firm control. We have to change this to facilitate investment. Similarly, we have to de-risk the industry, anchorage the academia and make the customer a partner in the process. For enhancing self-reliance, defence industry has to be supported along with production. These are some of the factors that we have to change in our current system of controlling the defence R&D and production.

Now there's a new engagement model emerging because of the presence of three very clear actors, namely the university, the R&D and the production agency. The user, of course, will remain an important player. What we are looking at is that research technology innovation should be done through the R&D community of experts; regional institutions should form part of the research team. Similarly, when you talk of industry, development, and production process, innovation should be their forte and they should work with various industries – small, medium, public sector, large-scale industries and so on. And production, product upgrade and lifestyle support with synergy should become their responsibility. Same should be applicable to R&D running large programmes with focus on programmes, concepts and specifications, system integration, HR development and international collaboration, whatever be the case. So this new model has to be taken for the future growth in R&D. There are gaps in manufacturing everywhere. We do not have today any agency that is manufacturing the machines. There's no national composite center; there's no national technology manufacturing center and such centers have to be set up because we have to cope with the emerging technologies in these areas.

There are also problems of programme management and programme planning that have resulted, in the past, in failures. So when we are looking at the example of next-generation aircraft, we need integrated design and manufacturing, ultra–low-cost storing, and reconfigurable and adaptable developments because we can't be globally competitive unless we follow these requirements. Through live digital engineering, the ICT has become so intense today that old methods of manufacturing, planning of manufacture will not be valid. With 3D printing, hands-up machining, the complete structure realisation, fiction stabilising, the entire scenario of manufacturing technology has changed whereas what we have today in our private and government sectors is technology of the 1980s and 1990s. So if we have to make the next-generation aircraft, if we have to make civil aircraft that the country is talking of – 90- or 70-seater – it cannot be done with what we had done in 1970s, 1980s and 1990s. So we have to follow this cycle and that needs to be supported.

Now how do we do this? Obviously not with some kind of a magic wand. Technology acquisition by leveraging provisions of the offset route is very important. If you try to do it all by yourself, the process will be time consuming, costly, and the gap will keep widening. So we should leverage offset in a big way. But offset, as we have seen today, is not bringing in the necessary input. Offsets are to be negotiated before finalisation of contract. Currently, we are finalising offset only after the contract has been signed. That means that we lose the leverage in capability. We cannot continue with this method. People who have used offset – Japan, Spain which have been architects of offsets – utilised it effectively because of the best methods of offset management.

Institutional collaboration with friendly countries for technology development, as we have done with Israel, can be done with many countries. Brahmos is a fine example. Acquisition of technology from various countries is one thing our industry can do. If TATA and Reliance can go and buy a steel industry or coal industry, why can't we go and buy an aerospace industry or a defence industry that is today on the downturn? It is possible. That will give you tacit knowledge of technology and infrastructure, and facilitate Indian industry to set up a strong R&D base for technology development in collaboration with R&D centers and academia.

I would also like to say that we have to change our education pattern because there is an acute dearth of human resource availability. In many areas, we are wasting our investment on creating high-value production test and infrastructure – because certification becomes very important – and creating an institution to develop next generation of machines. Machines are denied items by the way. If you want to ask about machining or if we want the machines for the 3D printing, these will not be made easily available to us. So obviously, we have to get the manufacturing, design and development of machines at one of the major centers.

After Hindustan Machine Tools was closed, we have the Central Manufacturing Technology Institute (CMTI) that is the only design center available in this country. We don't design machines anymore. So that is the scenario I am talking of. We have to go back and start this institution.

And finally, to create this kind of an eco-system and give directions, there has to be an integrated approach from the top downwards. That is what I have been at. I want a National Aerospace and Defence Commission, to coordinate, review, prioritise and take investment decisions, include exports and give directions to aerospace production. This will help improve the country's level of self-reliance, GDP and find the right place as a developed nation in the aerospace sector, defence sector that can hold its own against global competition. The Indian Space Research Organisation (ISRO) and Department of the Atomic Energy have functioned well, because of the two commissions that were responsible for maintaining certain amount of coherence and guidance. However, in the defence sector, that has been missing all along. Aerospace has been like the proverbial *Trishanku* – its neither in defence, nor in aeronautics. People in the past used to talk of an aeronautics commission but that never happened. On the one hand civil aviation would like to have it; on the other, defence would like to have it. So, let's call it Defence and Aerospace Commission and make sure that all technologies that are required for these two segments are properly controlled and guided through this kind of a focused approach.

Thank you very much gentlemen.

(This lecture was delivered by Dr Saraswat at the VIF on November 11, 2013)

*

11

An Overview of Failures, Lapses and Opportunities in Jammu & Kashmir

Dr Sudhir Bloeria

A very good evening, ladies and gentlemen, General Vij and distinguished guests.

Right in the beginning, I would like to say that my job has been made doubly difficult by two developments. One, friends present yesterday in the roundtable discussion will find my presentation a bit repetitive. Second, General Vij has already very elaborately summed up what I was about to say. That makes it so much more difficult for me. Also, I am missing the presence of General Sinha, who, if he was here this evening, would have mentioned something that not many people would know of. His association with Jammu and Kashmir (J&K) started with the first airlift of troops in 1947, and he was a Staff Officer to Lt. Gen. Sir Dudley Russell who was GOC-in-C of the East Punjab Command based in the Red Fort. From that day onwards, he has been involved in J&K, and as you know, his last assignment there was as Governor of the State.

Anyway, my presentation this evening would be in five parts. The first part will deal broadly with the background of the problem we have in J&K from 1947-48, followed by a brief overview of the militancy years, and then we take on the failures and lapses. Then we come to what is the current situation, and last, before I conclude we discuss the opportunities that are available and the general sense of direction that, in my opinion, we should follow in J&K.

First, on the background. Given this learned audience, I would not like to spend too much time on describing the background of the J&K problem. Most of you are very well versed with it. I would only invite your attention to two statistics. One, that the area of Jammu & Kashmir on 15 August 1947 was 2,22,870 sq. kms, going beyond Skardu, Gilgit, Chitral and right up to the Karakoram. Of this, today we have only 46 percent with us; 54 percent is not with us, of which 37 percent is occupied by Pakistan and 17 percent by China. Pakistan has handed over roughly 2 percent of their 37 percent to China, for the Karakoram Highway. What we have today is less than half of what we had in 1947!

The second statistic is that of the losses the security forces have suffered during the militancy over the last 25 years. These have exceeded 5,500. I will compare these losses with the regular war with Pakistan in 1947-48, which lasted for 14 months. The total casualties of the Indian Army, including that of the J&K state forces, were not more than 2,400. When you compare 2,400 from the 14-month war with the militancy years of 5,500, you see that the latter is more than double. That is the kind of problem that we have in J&K. The question arises, why does this happen? This happens because Pakistan has consistently depended on the predictability of Indian responses. That predictability has risen from the lessons they learned in 1947-48, their first engagement with India. In my opinion, they learned four important lessons. The first was that belligerence pays. The second was that a mix of covert and open aggression is cost effective and gainful. They have carried out this mix throughout, in 1947-48, in 1965, partly attempted in 1971, though not in J&K but more so from 1989 onwards, including in the 1999 Kargil War. The third lesson they got was that high-pitched propaganda, manipulation of the UN systems and very influential friends are a very potent mix. Then they realised once the whole case went to the United Nations, how the diplomatic games were played in the UN was absolutely against the ground reality that existed in J&K at the time.

These games started with British interest in this area, which they quietly and deftly handed over to the Americans. These have been very well recorded, not by Allen Campbell Johnson, who was Press Attaché to Lord Mountbatten, but by two Indian Ambassadors, Mr. C.T. Dasgupta and Mr. Narinder Singh Sarila. These two Ambassadors have documented the British and American press. They helped Pakistan. The fourth lesson they learnt was that India would tackle the aggression defensively and localise the area of conflict. If you see right through the militancy years 1947-1999, this assumption has been borne out. That is what makes Pakistan so confident of what they are doing. They became all the more confident after 1998, and they now feel they are operating under a nuclear overhang. Almost as if they are taunting us to pull something off, and then they would have the option of first nuclear strike. What happens after that, is not talked about by either them or us. We have also been very magnanimous in our victories; at times, we have been irrationally magnanimous in our victories. This is a point we must accept.

Having spoken about the background, we can now come to the militancy years. I will quickly go over these. They roughly corresponded to four phases. Phase I, I would like to term as the building of the storm, or the gathering storm. It lasted for two years from 1988 to 1989, when those who could perceive deeply could feel something was wrong. The second was the blow-up, 1990 to 1991, which again lasted for 2 years. The whole thing literally blew up in our faces in the Valley, and then quickly spread to south of the Pir Panjal as well. Practically all the important institutions of the State as well as the Centre folded up, right from intelligence agencies down to the post offices. Even the judiciary and state police were affected. The third was the containment phase, where after literally hitting the ground, slowly the buildup started. This lasted for 3 years, 1992-1994. During this period, the security grid was put in place, more forces were inducted, and the Rashtriya Rifles were raised. The last phase marked the turnaround. This was the time when the security forces manifestly got the upper hand on the militants.

The State was then able to conduct two important elections, first the Parliamentary elections in May 1996, and second, the State Assembly elections in September 1996. These brought back an elected government. It was a shift from Governor's Rule that had been instated since January 1990, back to an elected government in October 1996, more than six and a half years later. This did not mean that militancy had ended. It had another ascendancy curve following the Kargil conflict. In fact, statistically, the peak of the militancy was 2001. However, in 1995-96 there was a lot of bloodshed in J&K, particularly in the Valley. Although, as I said, the peak was reached in 2001-02. I will discuss more about how militancy has continued later on.

To make matters worse, over the last more than 60 years, there have been a lot of failures and lapses, both by the State government and the Government of India. I will just flag certain issues, because in a short span of 40-50 minutes, it is not possible to discuss these in detail. I will leave the rest for the question-and-answer session.

The first mistake that we made as a country was dithering on the question of accession of the State. For precious long months, the Government of India was uncertain on this aspect. There was no need for Standstill Agreements and all that followed. The second was the management of the war with Pakistan in 1947-48. A lot of the guests sitting here know more about the actual operations of 1947-48, but I would like to mention, just at the time it suited Pakistan to cease the conflict, we agreed to stop it. In fact, in the second half of 1948, it was more suitable for India to carry on operations to their logical end, till we were in enemy territory. We were in absolutely good and comfortable positions, from military and political points of view. We had established a link with Ladakh. The enemy was pushed back from the Valley, the siege of Poonch had been broken, and to make matters worse for Pakistan, they had not only suffered defeat on most fronts, but Mr. Jinnah had also died. There was a lot of political upheaval in Pakistan at the time. That is also exactly when we decided to stop operations and accept the ceasefire. This was the second thing.

The third is the issue of perception, particularly in the Valley, that the governments and leaders of J&K, more so between 1947 and 1987, have been propped up by Delhi and have been brought down when they didn't suit Delhi. We can keep on arguing about the truth or lack thereof in this, but this is unfortunately the perception of the local population. This perception has held on. Nobody has made efforts to clear these doubts, once and for all from the peoples' minds. Therefore, this remains a major concern.

The early response of the Central Government during the initial days of militancy was completely ill-advised. It was a knee-jerk reaction, inadequate and lacked focus, especially in the first two years. People like me, who were there in the State, felt that at the decision-making level, we did not know what was happening and therefore did not know how to respond to the crisis that was building.

The next lapse, I would say, was that there were no tangible or concerted efforts to mainstream the Kashmiri population, in physical and psychological terms. Please remember that the Valley has been historically and geographically a region that has been cut off from its surrounding areas. I remember as a child, once the winter started and the Pir Panjal passes closed – much like Ladakh these days – for 6 months the region was absolutely unapproachable. You had to dry your vegetables if you wanted to survive, store rations, and that is why you will find that the road that is the National Highway to the Valley when is open, everything is alright. If that road gets closed even for a day, there is noise everywhere, "*Mar gaye! Kerosene, meat, oil, ration khatam ho gaya...mitti ka tel khatam ho gaya.*" Now this doesn't happen overnight. This is because of the psychological effect; people in the Valley have to fend for themselves for 6 months in a year. The moment they find that the supply line is closed, even when they have stored victuals and can carry on for a month or two, they will still create an uproar. For them, stocks for a month or two are not enough; it is ingrained in their DNA that they require at least 6 months' stocks. If not in their homes, then at least in their godowns. If the road gets closed, everyone gets worried.

I belong to Jammu, and General Sahab will bear with me. The train came to Jammu in 1972. This in itself is a big failure that it took 25 years for a train to come from Pathankot to Jammu – there is no excuse for this. However, till 1972, I used to feel that Delhi is in another country. That is the psychological impact of getting connected. No such effort has been made to connect the people of the Valley. In that connection, I have to mention that irrespective of the national highway, rail connectivity, power projects – of course, I will talk more about these later – and employment opportunities, most importantly, understanding the local psyche and behaving in that particular manner is much required. Now in every crisis situation, there are people here who understand much better than me; in similar situations, people in one part of the country would react in one way while those in another part will react entirely differently. Each part of this country has to be dealt with accordingly; therefore, you have to understand the local psyche, local sensitivities and deal with them accordingly. Not many people who are from outside understand the local psyche. This has been one of our biggest mistakes.

The next failure has been of the political establishment of India to build and nurture credible political leadership across the three regions of the State. This does not apply to the Valley only; it applies even to Ladakh and Jammu. I am talking about mainstream, national political parties, not regional political parties.

Lastly, there is inability at the national level across the political spectrum to build a national policy on J&K. We have this interesting scenario of a party at the centre going from power to the opposition and criticising the same act of the new government, which they were pursuing themselves earlier. There is no declared policy that could be called the national policy on J&K. I think that has been one of the biggest failures of the Indian State as such.

Before I go on to the opportunities that we have, I must mention that in J&K all that has happened over these years is not negative. There have been some positive developments as well. I would like to point out four positive developments during the militancy years. The first one happened in 1991-92. The structure of the State, particularly the intelligence gathering machinery was put in place, and I think that was a huge effort. Most of it, as it happens with intelligence-backed operations, will never be brought into the public domain. It was a very huge effort, and its success must be accepted.

The second was the creation of the Unified Headquarters in May 1993. That became a focal point for much better utilisation of all resources, whether armed forces, civil administration, or intelligence-gathering agencies that we had. All of these worked in tandem for the first time. The third was the revival of the political process in J&K from 1996 onwards. The fourth, for which credit goes to General Vij, was the creation of border fencing – LC fencing of which 750 km was completed in a span of one and a half years. Those who have been in J&K or have served there know that it is mountainous terrain, snowbound in winter and absolutely treacherous. No agency, no construction agency, not only from India but, I think I can say, even from across the world as well, could have achieved this feat in one and a half years. This is a commendable achievement. If you look at the figures of infiltration and losses on the terrorists' side, the numbers up to 2002 of people crossing the border were more than the number of terrorists neutralised. It is only from 2003 onwards that this ratio gets reversed. Year after year for the last 12 years, the ratio has been reversed. Less people have been able to enter from across the border and more people have been neutralised within the State of J&K. While it may not be the sole reason, the border fencing is definitely one of the reasons for this. This is the fourth positive development that has taken place over these years.

Now, one would like to say that the situation in J&K has improved. It has improved, as we now have the fourth elected government in place in J&K. The security situation is certainly much better, but traces of militancy still remain. As General Vij was mentioning, this new phenomena of radicalisation of the local youth is a matter of concern. Therefore, there is a need to take measures with a view to removing even the last traces of militancy from the State – similar to what we were able to manage in Punjab. The same methods may not be used, but the end result has to be the same. The last traces of militancy have to be removed from J&K, before we say that we have succeeded.

Talking about the opportunities, I would like to divide them into two parts. One is good governance. The second is making efforts for greater integration.

Good governance, as I was mentioning yesterday, in several places we see makes a lot of difference. The opposite is equally true. I would like to give an example of how the British dealt with the Sikh population in Punjab, after the two Anglo-Sikh wars. In the first, they totally decimated the power of the Khalsa and turned the situation around to make them one of their mainstays in 1857. We found in J&K, particularly in the Valley during the 1996 elections, of the six Deputy Commissioners in the Valley, five were non-Muslim for the entire duration of almost 2 years. The sixth one who was a local person was specially picked up. During this entire period, there was not even a single representation by anyone against any of the Deputy Commissioners saying that the people had been wronged because of the denomination to which the Deputy Commissioner belonged. Not a single grievance!

They were able to provide good administration. That is the efficacy of an administrative setup. If you are able to provide good administration, I think a lot of problems get solved. Look at J&K; in 1947-48 who supported the Indian Army? In 1965, who supported the Indian Army? We had inherited a very friendly population. But we achieved the reverse of the British example I had given. We managed to turn a friendly population against ourselves. Now I think it is time to undo the vicious circle. This can only be achieved through good governance. As I mentioned, this has a few connotations of which rail connectivity is one. All weather connectivity with the Valley is the key, whether through four laning of the national highway or otherwise. Today there are two major blocks: one is Patni Top and the second is Pir Panjal, or the Banihal Tunnel as we call it. The Patni Top issue will be sorted out by next summer. There is a 9-km tunnel between Chenani and Nashri, which will be thrown open to traffic by next summer. The second, for which the work is on for an 11-km tunnel just below the adjacent 2-km tunnel, which is called the Jawahar Tunnel, will soon be complete as well. If these two are completed, the road widening can be carried out in time; at least with these two, connectivity with the Valley will be maintained throughout the year irrespective of snowfall. With these two tunnels completed, the road may at maximum be closed only for a few days in the entire year. Once the four laning is completed, then the journey between Jammu and Srinagar will be reduced to a 6-hour road trip. This will be very important.

Power shortages too have been an issue. There was a great debate that took place yesterday as well, that there is no power shortage in the country. However, J&K has a peculiar problem because of the Indus Water Treaty. Because of this, there are storage capacity restrictions imposed on all the dams in J&K – all dams including those on the Jhelum or Chenab, partly Ravi as well, the water of which is meant for Pakistan under the Treaty; therefore, India can only have 'run-of-the-river' schemes on these for things such as hydel power generation. 'Run-of-the-river' schemes go down to 10-15 percent during winter. That gap then has to be covered. This can only be covered by massive import of electricity from the rest of country that is very costly and the transmission distribution losses are too high. The only alternative then is to have a power mix in J&K. Now a power mix in the Valley cannot be solar, wind or thermal because of environmental factors. The only option is nuclear or atomic energy, tucked into the mountains.

I would like to reiterate that this is not my original idea. This idea was floated, when I joined the State in 1974, by the then Power Commissioner of J&K, Mr. R.S. Gill. He was the father of Mr. K.P.S. Gill. The State government had requested the Punjab Government to lend his services. In his lecture to young probationers at the time, he had mentioned this phrase 'power mix'. He said that the only power mix possible in J&K is hydel based on the Indus Water Treaty and the gap in this to be covered by atomic power stations. If you have surplus power during summer, use it for lift irrigation to irrigate Karewas in the Valley. During winters, the power gap can be met. If there is still surplus power, in every village there should be a building that can be centrally heated only meant for the artisans of J&K. It would therefore be useful to have centrally heated, village craft centres during the day and for domestic power consumption at night. Attract capital flow from the rest of the country. This may not be from individuals but more so from industrial houses. It is important to attract them, particularly to the Valley.

The next point is that the effectiveness of the income tax department and Enforcement Directorate in J&K needs to be improved. They are practically sleeping in the Valley.

There should be greater delegation of regulatory authority to the panchayats. One example, in my opinion, is that teachers' salaries at the village level should be distributed through the panchayats. They should be authorised to release only that much salary to teachers that corresponds to the number of days they have been present in and taught at the village school. If you do even this much, I think it will provide a huge sense of relief to the local population. The amount required is known. It can be transferred at the beginning of the financial year to the panchayat's account, and let them deal with it. It is worth taking the risk. A question that can be flung at me is what was I doing when I was Chief Secretary?

The answer to that is that I tried and failed. I still do hope that somebody else will succeed where I failed. The idea, however, remains sound. I personally believe that it is an idea worth trying, as its time will come very soon.

Penultimate, it is a controversial point I am making. There is an Autonomous Hill Development Council, elected by the people in Kargil as well as in Leh. Leh has already seen the fourth round of elections for this Council. Kargil has had three elections. My proposition is that there should be a similar Council for all districts of the State. Unless you give more power to a greater number of people, their participation in the process of governance will not increase. If their participation increases, the accountability of the people on the ground increases as well. We find the difference in ground-level administration in Leh and Kargil. It is much better than the rest of the State only because of this. They are responsible to locally elected Hill Development Councils. We can have different names for these Councils; it need not be the same as the others and can be elected District Councils. The empowerment of panchayats as well as of district elected councils or urban local bodies will go a long way in integrating the people of the State. Elections took place in 2005 for urban local bodies, municipalities and notified areas after three decades. The next election was due in 2010, but has not taken place till now. Now we are told that they are slated for April next year. Let us hope this happens. Local body elections, district elected councils and greater powers to panchayats can all be clubbed under one point as greater decentralisation efforts.

The last point is not just restricted to J&K, but is for all other troubled areas of the country, such as the North Eastern States or Naxal areas. There has to be a system by which you pick up the best officers and place them on a short-term deputation to the State governments. For a few years after 1947, we had what was known as the Indian Frontiers Administrative Service, particularly in the North East or NEFA areas. Some of those celebrated officers are still remembered by those people. This may be unconventional, but this is an idea that we need to explore and move towards.

These are a few things I wanted to highlight that entail a good governance system. Now I will move on to the efforts for greater integration, the first of which is giving jobs to the local Muslims, particularly from the Valley rather than the rest of the country. There have been two unintended benefits of militancy: Traders from the Valley have gone out for the first time after 1989 and students from the Valley have gone out for higher education after the same year. Prior to that, the entire Valley including traders and students, were insular communities.

As I mentioned before, this was initially due to historical and geographical reasons, but it is only after 1989 that they started going out.

Today there is no place, big city or small town, where you don't find a Kashmiri trader or you don't find a Kashmiri student. This has not happened because of government. My point is, let the government lend a helping hand in both these activities. On the student front, the Army started very well. That has been picked up by BSF and CRPF also; Army's Bharat Darshan Tours are still ongoing. The State and Central Governments' efforts in this case are very minimal, almost non-existent. That is where they have to pick up and it has to be two-way traffic. Not only is it important for the young boys and girls from J&K to see what is there in the rest of the country, but equally important for boys and girls from other States to come and see what is happening in J&K. It is time that such reverse traffic also begins moving.

The third is strict and effective action against people who have sympathies with militants and their activities, especially if they are in government service, universities and in legal practice. This action should be strictly legal, and nothing draconian like the Public Security Act, nothing of that kind. It merely requires enforcement of normal public laws in an effective manner.

After all, we have the celebrated, so-called separatist leaders who have on television channels accepted their involvement in murders. We've still not initiated proceedings against them. That does not require enforcement of draconian security laws; what I am referring to are normal legal procedures. If we are able to expedite normal legal processes, I think a lot of problems would get sorted out. Then there is this very sensitive issue of media management. Media cannot be controlled, neither should it be. However, perception management is possible through both print and electronic media. This perception management has to be very deliberate, responsible and carried out at a high level. No efforts have been made in this regard. This is a very sensitive issue and I will leave it at this. I have only flagged it here for your consideration.

Then there is a need to meet regional aspirations. J&K, as you all know, includes Jammu, Kashmir and Ladakh. Some people call it an artificial State. The fact is that it is a State that has no parallel in the rest of the country. It is a State that also represents the very idea of India. The kind of diversity in terms of mix of population, customs, weather conditions (where you have sub-tropical, temperate and also sub-Arctic conditions), religions and ethnicities cannot be found anywhere else in the country. They have their own aspirations. Today there are both interregional and intra-regional problems in J&K. Intra-regional problems exist in Ladakh and in the Jammu region. If these are not yet manifested now, they might take place soon in the Valley as well. The integration within the State and integration of the State with the rest of the country, on both these tracks simultaneous progress must be achieved with attention from the highest levels. Lastly, as I mentioned earlier, there is need for a clear-cut national policy on J&K, which is backed by major political parties across the political spectrum. This has not happened so far, and this is something important for us to undertake in the interest of both short-term and long-term national goals.

Before I close, I would like to present two caveats. First, while dealing with J&K one has to very clearly differentiate between integration and assimilation. There is a very forceful case for greater integration, but there is an equally forceful case not to attempt assimilation. The second caveat is what a few months ago some leaders in the Leh Autonomous Hill Development Council elections had promised: that they will give Union Territory status to Ladakh. This has a lot of Constitutional issues involved in the process. This must, therefore, be carefully thought over.

In the end, before I close, two things stand out clearly. Mischief from Pakistan continues and is unlikely to abate. A broad overview of the situation prevailing in different parts of the country clearly establishes that Pakistan's designs are not limited to J&K alone, but target the entire country. Pakistan's involvement in the affairs of India has serious implications not only for national security and territorial integrity of India, but also hits at the very core of Indian nationhood that is based on pluralism, secularism and liberal democratic values. The conflict is not just for an area or a section of population; it is much more fundamental. Therefore, India must garner all national resources; moving beyond just military power to decisively defeat Pakistani designs and make an effort to determine how to turn the corner should be best begun in J&K, where the Pakistan mischief started in 1947.

Thank you, ladies and gentlemen, for your very kind attention.

(This talk was delivered by Dr Bloeria at the VIF on December 23, 2015)

*

IV. Diplomacy and External Relations

12

Climate Change Negotiations: The Challenge for Indian Diplomacy

Ambassador Shyam Saran

Shri Ajit Doval, Director of the Vivekananda International Foundation, Ambassador Satish Chandra, very distinguished guests, ladies and gentlemen,

I am honoured that the Foundation has invited me to speak at its monthly lecture and given me an opportunity to interact with a very distinguished audience. Let me also congratulate the Foundation on the initiative it has taken to promote a broad-ranging and informed civil society discourse, on a range of issues that have an impact on India's national interests.

An intellectually aware and vigilant public opinion is the best safeguard in so far that India's vital interests, whether they relate to security, economy or foreign relations, are based on the best possible assessment and advice available. I must also convey my sense of satisfaction in speaking at a venue that bears the name of one of India's greatest sages and the finest of minds – Swami Vivekananda. One of my favourite poems is the few lines he wrote on the Spirit of Liberty, that which the 4th of July represented not just for the United States of America but for the people all over the world still in bondage to others of their kind. But he has composed it in the form of a poem to the Sun God, who dispels darkness and spreads light as he travels through the heavens, and the poem is:

> *Move on, O Lord, in the resistless path*
> *Till the high noon overspreads the world*

Till every land reflects thy light
Till men and women with uplifted head
Behold their shackles broken
And know in springtime joy, their life renewed.

He wrote these lines in 1898, but now let's get down to more earthly matters. Today I intend to focus on certain key issues relating to the ongoing multilateral negotiations on Climate Change under the UN Framework Convention on Climate Change, which is better known as the UNFCCC. And of course, subsequently the Convention had a protocol known as the Kyoto Protocol. I will not go into a narrative of the negotiations themselves, or very specific items on the negotiating agenda, since these are more readily available. What I will try to do is to try and focus on a broad perspective linking climate change diplomacy to the overall national interest.

Let me begin by pointing out that climate change negotiations as they have unfolded in the past two years have become less and less about climate change and progressively more about the overall economic and political interests of the major countries involved. While the rhetoric continues to be that countries of the world are confronted with a global cross-cutting challenge, which demands a collaborative response, the reality is quite different. The negotiations so far have been conducted instead in a competitive spirit, where each country or group of countries seeks to concede as little as possible and extract as much as it can from others. This is so because action on climate change entails a change in energy access and energy use by countries. A shift away from growth patterns that are based on fossil fuel use requires massive resources, both financial as well as technological. The more rapid the shift, the greater the scale of resources required. Therefore, the crucial question is, who will pay?

Often in our country, the debate on climate change is based on a faulty perspective. Some people think that India is taking an obstinate and unreasonable stand in the negotiations by insisting that it should not have to take on international, legally binding commitments to reduce its own greenhouse gas emissions. The criticism is that limiting or reducing such emissions is in our own interest and that it is countries like India, as Mr. Satish Chandra pointed out, who will be most impacted by climate change. It is certainly not my contention that India should not do anything to reduce its emissions or to embrace a strategic shift from our current reliance on fossil fuels, to a pattern of growth, which is based on renewable sources of energy such as solar and clean sources of energy such as nuclear. Quite the contrary, we must do everything we can within the limitation of our resources (and that is the key phrase) to accelerate such a shift. I have often pointed out that even if there was no climate change argument, even if climate change was not taking place, India will still need to undertake this shift for reasons of energy security.

In a world of rapidly depleting fossil fuel resources, there is no way that this country can maintain a high rate of growth while continuing its dependence on conventional energy, most of which are being sourced from abroad. And to be fair, this is what we have been engaged in, whether through the National Action Plan on Climate Change, which was adopted in June 2008, or through the Civil Nuclear Agreement (contentious as it was when it was being negotiated) that became a reality in September 2008 with the Nuclear Suppliers' Group (NSG) re-engaging India in civil nuclear commerce.

The argument about the multilateral negotiations is about something quite different. The issue is about burden-sharing, relating to a global issue that is subject to both, what is known in theory as positive and negative external economies. Let me try and explain this a little further. India today has emissions that constitute about 4 percent of the global total. Of course, there are countries like the United States of America and China who are responsible for 20 percent or more of the global emissions. So we are very far behind. But supposing if we were by some miracle able to reduce even this 4 percent to zero, unless other countries (in particular those responsible for much higher levels of emissions) such as the US and China are able to achieve much more drastic reductions, the threat to India from climate change would remain undiminished. Our glaciers would still melt, there would still be frequent droughts or unseasonal rain. Our low-lying coastal plains would still get submerged due to sea-level rise. Here is a classic external economy dilemma. What I invest cannot be directly related to the outcome. It is equally possible that I benefit from what others invest in, since I stand to enjoy a global public good that is being created. Therefore, in dealing with cross-cutting global issues such as climate change, it becomes necessary to align the external economies being generated with a burden-sharing arrangement that makes economic sense to the countries participating in the multilateral regime.

Now it should be quite obvious that for any given outcome, say the figure that was put forward at Copenhagen, a 50 percent reduction in global emissions by the year 2050 (with 1990 as the base year), the distribution of reductions among countries could place the burden more on some and less on others, and therefore our argument was, you can't talk about 50 percent reduction unless you talk about how the burden is going to be shared amongst various countries. This goes to the heart of the negotiations.

What is a fair and equitable burden-sharing arrangement? As well, in this regard, what is the stand taken by India and most developing countries on this issue? Our stand is that the basis for such burden sharing has already been agreed to by consensus in the UNFCCC or Rio Convention. In that Convention, there is an explicit acknowledgement that climate change is taking place not due to current emissions but due to the greenhouse gas emissions that have accumulated in the atmosphere, since carbon-based industrial activity began over two centuries ago. There is therefore a historical responsibility that developed, industrialised countries have to take a lead in reducing their current emissions and in supporting mitigation and adaptation actions in developing countries with both financial and technological resources. This is the well-accepted principle known perhaps to people here as 'common but differentiated responsibilities and respective capabilities.' This is a very key principle in the Framework Convention.

So what does this principle do? It recognises the principle of non-reciprocity and differential treatment of developed and developing countries respectively. What is now under attack in the multilateral negotiations is precisely this principle. The United States, the European Union and other developed countries' objective is to eviscerate, if not to abandon, the UNFCC altogether and to push through a new template for global action, where the burden of adjustment will fall mainly on developing countries. Currently, in the Framework Convention, climate change action by developing countries is conditional upon enabling support from developed countries. If this conditionality is removed, then the burden of adjustment will have to borne largely by us, developing countries. Now will this, or will this not constrain our growth prospects?

We have heard the argument that India has been foolish in not working together with China on climate issues, since the latter is in a different league as far as its levels of emissions are concerned. I myself mentioned that they are responsible today already for 20 percent of the global total. It is even suggested that we should de-link ourselves from China and get a better deal for ourselves. This implies that a better deal is in fact on offer, but actually it is quite the contrary. In the two years that I have had the privilege of representing India in the climate negotiations, I have found a deliberate and systematic diplomatic offensive to put India on the defensive, to characterise it consistently as a nay-sayer and as *The Economist* magazine once said, 'acquire the reputation of being obstinate and recalcitrant'. China on the other hand despite being a much larger emitter was regularly praised as being flexible, forward-looking and willing to work together with the likes of the United States. Never mind that in the negotiating room itself, China took positions that were on occasion much more hard line than India.

For example, while India committed itself never to exceeding the per capita emissions of developed countries at any stage during our growth trajectory and thereby diluting somewhat the principle of historical responsibility, China was not willing to relent on this. This state of affairs remained right up to the Copenhagen conference. Nothing that China said or did at Copenhagen represented any noteworthy change in its stand on climate issues and yet, from then on, it was projected as the villain that stood in the way of a meaningful outcome. Why was this the case? Again, in my view, this had less to do with climate change and much more to do with disappointed expectations of the United States and the European Union that China would be forthcoming, for example, on yuan exchange rate adjustment, or sanctioning Iran, or being more helpful in dealing with North Korea's nuclear ambitions, among several other things.

India stood together with China both before and at Copenhagen, precisely because our interests were aligned in terms of the burden-sharing issue that I referred to. There was no willingness on the part of the developed countries to differentiate India's situation from China's nor offer either technological or financial resources to enable India to scale up its own ambitious efforts to deal with climate change. If we were in any case being tarred with the same brush as China was, does it not make sense for us to work with China? The issue here is not that we are being branded as nay-sayers. As a negotiator, one's brief is not to win a popularity contest but to safeguard India's interests. Certainly we should be flexible, we should be open to compromise and negotiate constructively. However, it is also important to appreciate that in branding India as obdurate or as a nay-sayer, there was psychological pressure being brought upon us.

It is for experienced diplomacy to uncover and to resist such pressure and to educate our own public opinion about it. That is, our public opinion should not be influenced by this heavy-duty offensive to paint us as nay-sayers, so that our public thinks what is wrong and why do we have no friends? Why is it that nobody supports us? I think it is important to understand, what is behind this. So what did we manage to achieve in Copenhagen and where do go from here? Several months before Copenhagen, it was already clear that the multilateral negotiations would not deliver on the mandate agreed to, again by consensus at

Bali in December 2007. That was the point in time when the Bali Action Plan was adopted.

The incoming Chairman of the 15th Conference of Parties at Copenhagen, which is Denmark, few months before the Conference already declared that only a political agreement would be possible, which would not entail legally binding obligations. While developing countries including India continue to press for a substantive outcome, it was obvious that we could bring the horse to the spring, but we could not make it drink. After all it was the developed countries who had to sign on to significant emission reduction targets, both for the medium and for the long term. It is they who had to deliver on legal commitments that they had undertaken to provide finance and technology to enable climate change action among developing countries. If they were unable or unwilling to do so, there was very little that the developing world could do.

Confronted with this reality, our objective became essentially a holding operation, that is, to ensure that the multilateral negotiating process continued post-Copenhagen, without diluting the consensus mandate agreed to in Bali. This was achieved, and the only two decisions that were adopted by the 15th Conference of Parties were to re-establish the Ad Hoc Working Group on Long Term Cooperative Action, which is the Bali Action Plan, and to continue with the work of the Ad Hoc Working Group on Kyoto Protocol, under which developed countries must fulfil their legal obligation to assume emission reduction targets for the second commitment period that would commence in 2013. I think this was a significant achievement on the part of developing countries, because there was relentless pressure to denigrate the UN process: to overturn the UNFCC by insisting on a new legally binding agreement and to abandon the Kyoto Protocol altogether.

This was possible only because of the very close coordination among what are today known as BaSIC countries, namely Brazil, South Africa, India and China, and the lead that they were able to give in this respect to G77, a much larger grouping of developing countries. Therefore, we lived to fight another day. But what about the Copenhagen Accord? Before we make any judgements about India's role in the deliberations leading up to the Accord, it is important for us to appreciate the setting and the environment in which this so-called political agreement was born.

This was the first time in the history of multilateral negotiations that a limited group of heads of state and government participated actively and directly in the actual drafting of an outcome document. This is usually the work of lesser beings like us, the negotiators. The Western countries came well prepared since Denmark as Chairman was more than willing to oblige and advance their agenda. It was quite obvious that the Chairman's text, which became the basis of the Accord, had already been the subject of very careful and detailed consideration by the Western Industrialised Countries (WICs). Their leaders were familiar with the formulations, nuances and above all on what they actually wanted to achieve.

Developing country leaders who attended were therefore at a disadvantage, and it was only the professional negotiators from the BaSIC countries, as we had made it known before that since we do not consider the work of our leaders to do drafting, our leaders were not attending. That is why China was not there and the Indian Prime Minister was not there, and most of the time it was either the South African or the Brazilian President. What did we try to do? We tried to work together and offer some corrective as well as resist the more damaging contents of the proposed Accord. Our work was complicated by the fact that several African leaders and leaders of the least developed countries (LDCs), small island developing states (SIDS), who were not familiar with the negotiating process or with the issues being deliberated upon fell in line with formulations and vigorously fell upon the assembly, sometimes with a very unusual aggressiveness. I recall that when BaSIC opposed a particular formulation, both Obama and Gordon Brown looked directly at Sheikh Hasina of Bangladesh and said that because of the stand taken by some countries, LDCs like Bangladesh would be unable to access the financial resources they desperately need to deal with climate change.

Such attempts to divide developing countries were sometimes quite oppressive. We objected to the paltry figure of USD 100 billion that was mentioned as the target for finance by the year 2020. We also objected to this being raised from so-called multiple sources, including private capital flows. You don't need a treaty in order to encourage private flows, but we had to back down because the coordinator for the African group accepted the formulation at President Obama's persuasive urging. Therefore, compromises had to be made. What we did achieve was the careful insertion of principles from the UNFCCC including the key principle, which I mentioned earlier, of common but differentiated responsibilities. We were able to include a global target that would implicitly demand absolute emission reductions by developing countries as well. We were able to forestall the US attempt to apply the same so-called review and verification procedure to our own voluntary mitigation actions as would apply to the binding emission reductions of developed countries. The idea was to do away with the distinction between developed countries on the one hand and developing countries on the other.

We were able to stand our ground on the legal nature of the agreed outcome at the 16th Conference of the Parties (COP) that would now be held at the end of that year in Mexico. Why did we do this? We did not wish to dilute in any way, the continuing legal validity of the UNFCCC and the Kyoto Protocol. The Copenhagen Accord is a compromise, but it does not by itself represent a dilution of our position on key issues. It would if it were to be operationalised as it stands, which is what the US is insisting upon. Our stand is that the Copenhagen Accord should become an input into the multilateral negotiating process, but cannot become the predetermined outcome of the 16th COP. I think we will need to stand firm on this count. Fortunately, the BaSIC group and the G-77 have a common position as yet on this.

There were attempts to marginalise the multilateral process and to seek to operationalise the Copenhagen Accord through a limited agreement among, in this context, a coalition of the willing. We must resist this and uphold the consensus principle. There may be other important global issues, where we may find ourselves under pressure or even in a minority. The consensus principle is a useful safeguard for us and any departure from it should be considered very carefully, lest it become a precedent that comes to haunt us in the future.

Let me conclude on a somewhat different note. It is one's dharma as a negotiator to try and get the best deal for one's country and to engage in the cut and thrust of complex negotiations. It is, however, also necessary to be mindful of the larger picture that looms in the background, which is the threat to humanity that comes from the consequences of predatory and extractive economic progress. We have a responsibility that transcends national and regional boundaries and speaks to our membership of a larger collectivity.

We have the unique opportunity in this country to tread a different path, to embrace a concept of development that does not rely on ravaging nature and robbing future generations of their means of nurture and livelihood. Scientists have spoken of the inevitability of man colonising other planets, since Mother Earth will eventually be ravaged beyond redemption. The former Governor of West Bengal, Gopal Gandhi referred to this in one of his speeches, and I thought to myself, 'Poor Mars! What has it done to deserve humans?' Our own traditional culture from most ancient times has treated Nature as a mother, as a source of nurture. Through centuries of accumulated wisdom we inherited a value system which ensured that what we extracted from Nature never exceeded its power of regeneration. This was the value system that Swami Vivekananda so eloquently articulated and disseminated. This is what we need to deal with as the defining challenge of our times.

I thank you for your attention.

(This lecture was delivered by Amb Saran at the VIF on March 19, 2010)

*

13

Transition in America and China: Implications for India

Ambassador Prabhat P. Shukla

Thank you, Ajit, that was a very inspiring introduction. I hope I am able to live up to the billing, and of course dear friends, pleasure to see all of you. Some I am meeting after a very long time and that makes this evening all the more special.

The topic being 'Transition in America and China: Implications for India', with a great deal of exercise of my intellect, I have broken up the presentation into three parts – one is transition in America, one is transition in China and the last part is implications for India. There are some quick points I'll make on the US transition.

The voter turnout has actually dropped this time by something like 5 percent and this has happened in the face of an increase of about eight million in the size of the electorate. On the Republican side, this has caused a fair amount of heartburn because the suspicion is that they were not able to motivate their supporters to come out in large numbers and vote, and of course, as we go along we will see how much reality there is in this fear or assessment on the Republican side. There were more women than male voters that is actually not that unusual, and one of the most remarkable things that we have seen, of President Obama in particular, is that he has a very strong constituency among single women and that has been proven again this time partly because of his position on social issues, and also because of his position and the Democratic position on the kind of role that the state can play in providing social security to the less advantaged segments of society.

Some of the campaign statements made by the Republican candidates, not at the presidential level, but by the Senatorial candidates, there were some bizarre ones about things like legitimate rape, and that you should never allow abortion no matter whether it is a result of incest or rape, and this really turned off a lot of people. That was the seat of Richard Lugar, a real establishment figure in the Republican Party, but the person who unseated him in the Primaries made these kinds of remarks and the Republicans lost what was presumed to be a safe seat. We'll see how it affected the Senate result later on.

Race obviously played an important part. This is something that has been extensively commented upon. Among the Whites, obviously, Romney carried the vast majority, and among the Blacks, 96 percent voted for Obama; these are as per the latest figures that are now being reaffirmed. The big fight was over the Hispanic vote and that went decisively in favour of Obama. More than 60 percent voted for Obama. Here obviously the main issue was immigration and I think this is one place where we are going to see some kind of change within the Republican Party's positions on this issue because going into it, they have taken very tough stances on the question of immigration. Of course when we do talk about race and demography and all that, it is nonetheless important thing for us to remember that this same demographic in 2010 delivered a real hammering to the Democratic Party. So it's not something that is inbuilt into the demographics that gives the Democrats a lock on victory in all future elections. If the performance of the government is not up to the mark, they are going to be defeated. And in fact, after the 2010 results, Obama himself called it a "Shellacking".

Now a few quick words about the Electoral College because it has been touched upon and is being criticised on the grounds that this is not truly a directly elected president. Had that been the case, that is, if there were no Electoral College, the national vote was much closer than the actual outcome is going to be in the Electoral College. The Electoral College is really nothing but a collection of people who are elected in different states to meet in Washington DC in December and vote for the president. The convention is that these electors are bound to vote as they have been instructed to as they have been voted for by the electorate, but there have been electors who have gone rogue on almost every time, including in 2008. There is the odd vote in favour of some other candidate who is not even on the slate. So the Electoral College has its own occasionally funny ways of operating but it doesn't really make a difference because by and large, the discipline is maintained.

The general rule is that the winner gets all the seats available from a state. Now the number of seats in a state is the sum of the numbers in the House plus the two Senators; every state has two Senators. So since there are 435 members in the House and 100 Senators, you get a total college of 535. Three more are added to represent Washington DC, since it has no representation in Congress. That's how you get 538 seats in the Electoral College; hence 270 is the magic number, the majority. In some states, two are Maine and Nebraska, where they don't follow the winner-take-all system. There they follow the Districts of the House of Representatives; each one of them elects an independent elector, and therefore you can have a situation in Maine and Nebraska where it isn't a winner-take-all situation. After they have voted, they remit their vote to the House of Representatives in its first sitting in January of the following year, which is going to be 3 January 2013 this time, who then formally declare the president elected. That is the full process of the election of the president.

Now some features about this particular campaign. The campaign contributors – the largest contributor for Barack Obama this time and last time was the University of California; I haven't seen any clear indication whether it is Berkley or LA, or any of the other campuses; perhaps it's a lot of them together because I think one million dollars for any one university will be a bit steep. So I suppose it's University of California Berkeley, University of California Los Angeles and some of the other campuses together that contributed one million dollars. The next largest contributor was Microsoft and then Google. The funny thing is that for Mitt Romney this time, the largest contributor was Goldman Sachs and what's funny about it is that in 2008, Goldman Sachs was the second largest contributor to the Barack Obama campaign. That time again the University of California was number one and Goldman Sachs was number two. For Barack Obama this time, they switched sides. All of the investment banks actually switched sides. They all backed Romney. It was a bit of puzzle why they should do this and I figure that the largest part of the reason would be what's called the Dodd Frank Act under which a large number of restrictions were placed on the functioning of investment banks. To that then they added the Volcker Rule that prohibited what is called proprietary trading. The result was that the investment banks were unhappy with these kinds of restrictions and some of them actually went openly negative on Obama. I remember seeing an interview with one of them and the interviewer asked him, "Sir what would you want Obama to do?", and he replied, "I'd advise him to drop out of the race", which was a very strong statement to make given that there was every chance that he was going to be re-elected. But they really broke cover on this one and they were very aggressive in their campaigning against Obama.

Election Campaign Contributors

Barack Obama		*Mitt Romney*	
University of California	$ 1,092,906	Goldman Sachs	$ 994,139
Microsoft Corp	$ 761,343	Bank of America	$ 921,839
Google Inc	$ 737,055	Morgan Stanley JP Morgan	$ 827,255
US Government	$ 627,628	Chase & Co	$ 792,147
Harvard University	$ 602,992	Credit Suisse Group	$ 618,941

Now of course the flip side is that the IT and software companies backed Obama and in a way that's something we can leverage. The US system runs on IOUs and the fact that these companies have contributed so significantly to the Obama campaign means some of the issues on outsourcing at least we may be able to leverage into softer positions.

The other thing that struck me was that the oddity about the way the campaign went. The person who was receiving large contributions from the IT companies, which were very keen on outsourcing, was the one who was hammering away against outsourcing – that's Obama of course, and Romney, who was getting a lot of money from the investment banks, kept banging Obama for having bailed out the banks and for having given them very privileged treatment. On the Dodd Frank Act, he said, "you have defined these as too big to fail, you are committed to saving them even in future", so the conclusion I drew was hypocrisy is a universal feature of politicians around the world.

However, now we come to the pattern of second terms for US presidents. What's remarkable is that every president who wins a second term wins with an enhanced vote in the Electoral College. This I'm starting from Eisenhower because before him there was the four-term presidency of Franklin Roosevelt, so one doesn't know how to compare that, but post-War these are the presidents who have won second terms, Truman being ruled out in 1952, so we start with Eisenhower. We find that the only person whose Electoral College vote fell second time round is Obama. All the others increased their vote, including you'll see here Ronald Reagan. You would think 489 out of 538 would be hard to improve upon, but he got 525 in the 1984 election. So we have to conclude I guess that the endorsement of Obama is less wholehearted than it has generally been in the past when a president has been re-elected; of course some have not been re-elected. That's a different story.

Second Terms of the US Presidents

Name	*Year: Electoral Votes won for the 1st Term*	*Year: Electoral Votes won for the 2nd Term*
Dwight D. Eisenhower	1952: 442 Votes	1956: 457 Votes
Richard M. Nixon	1968: 301 Votes	1972: 520 Votes
Ronald Reagan	1980: 489 Votes	1984: 525 Votes
William J. Clinton	1992: 370 Votes	1996: 379 Votes
George W. Bush	2000: 271 Votes	2004: 286 Votes
Barrack H. Obama	2008: 365 Votes	2012: 332 Votes

There is one other feature about second terms. Most of the second terms have run into various problems fairly early after the re-election. Go back to Nixon, the Watergate Burglary started actually in 1972 during the campaign itself; next second term president Reagan, ran into problems with Iran Contra; Clinton, the Lewinsky affair. Each of them within the first two years of their second term ran into these huge problems that in a way put a question-mark on their legitimacy, and certainly put a question-mark on their ability to deliver their agenda for the second term and that becomes very important because everybody is saying Obama will now be working for his legacy and he is going to have to handle two very big challenges – the war in Afghanistan and the fiscal cliff – which we will come to presently.

A little bit on the election to the Senate and the House. I am giving here the figures for 2008 and the mid-term elections in 2010, and then the current round. And you see the big change has happened between 2010 and 2008, whether you take the Senate or the House. In fact in the House, some of you would certainly remember this, the swing towards the Republicans in 2010 was the largest since 1928. I think they won some 66 net seats, which went to the Republicans in 2010, which actually illustrates what I began by saying that demographics isn't everything. There comes a time when people say well look these guys are not performing well enough and what you see in 2012 is really nothing but a re-endorsement of the outcome of 2010. Of course this is also the time when we will be having the first Hindu in the House of Representatives – it's a lady called Tulsi Gabbard from Hawaii and I was watching one of her TV interviews and she was saying that she was going to take the oath on the *Bhagwad Gita*. So that's something that we will be seeing for the first time on the floor of the House.

Senate and House of Representatives: A Comparison

SENATE	*2008 Elections*	*2010 Mid-Term Elections*	*2012 Elections*
Democrats	57+2*=59 *Independent	51+2*=53 *Independent	53+2*=55 *Independent
Republicans	41	47	45
HOUSE OF REPRESENTATIVES	2008 Elections	2010 Mid-Term Elections	2012 Elections
Democrats	255	193	201
Republicans	175	242	234

Is Obama stronger? The short answer is yes, but there are caveats. As I said, the margin of victory is not very convincing, especially if you set it against patterns of previous presidents who have won a second term. Of course on one issue he is clearly in a stronger position. He had very clearly argued in his campaign that he was going to reverse the Bush Era tax cuts for those people who earn over $250,000 per annum. So in that sense the argument is now going on, on how to balance the budget. He certainly has the endorsement of the people; that much is undeniable, but of course there is another catch, which is that there is a deficit ceiling beyond which even Congress cannot vote funds and that ceiling is about to be hit. The current national debt is just under 16 trillion and the ceiling is 16.39 trillion dollars. So the Republicans have this other card in their hands, if you will, that if they just don't agree on anything, then the fiscal ceiling will be hit and there will be very serious consequences for the spending programmes that Obama is committed to.

With this, we can move on to the Chinese side. Just some numbers. The number of delegates to the 18th Congress was 2270. They selected/elected 205 full members of the Central Committee and 170, actually 171, so the total number is 376. There is one Tibetan in the Central Committee and that is Padma Choling who is the equivalent of the Chief Minister in the Indian system, Premier of the Tibet Autonomous Region, and also the Chairman of the People's Congress. And there is one Uyghur in the Central Committee and his name is Nur Bekri and he is similarly the equivalent of the chief minister of Xinjiang. Otherwise, there aren't too many ethnic minorities in the Central Committee and that conforms to the pattern that we have seen pretty much from the very beginning of the foundation of the party.

The Central Committee appoints 25 full members of the Politburo and seven members of the Standing Committee of the Politburo. I have got their names and their faces in these slides. One gets to see Xi Jinping's face all the time, but some of the others you will be seeing less frequently. The important point to note about Xi Jinping is, of course you have all heard, that he is a princeling; his father was a very senior party member and one of the more liberal ones. In fact, Zhao Ziyand records in his memoirs that when he was facing the flak, when Tiananmen was going up in flames, the only senior party member, one of the elders who spoke for Zhao Ziyang was Xi Jinping's father Xi Zhongxun.

To what extent the son will follow the father's legacy is one of the very big questions that all of us will be watching out for. Xi Jinping also served in the Central Military Commission and this is something that you often don't find in his biography. For three years, he was the aide to Geng Biao, who was the Defence Minister, and in those days the defence minister was also the secretary general or the secretary, if you like, of the Central Military Commission. So Xi Jinping actually worked very closely with the CMC and the PLA for three years. Thereafter he spent a lot of time in Fujian Province right opposite Taiwan, so he understands the economic importance and the strategic importance of the Taiwan question, and I think this is going to be one of his early and firm priorities. The party chief in Shanghai was caught in a corruption scandal, sacked in 2006, and that opened the way for Xi Jinping to take over as the party secretary in Shanghai and that brought him into closer contact with Jiang Zemin. Jiang Zemin, as everybody now notices in the present Congress, played a very important role in the proceedings and personnel selections, and this is a role that the party elders have continued to play right from the days of Mao Zedong and especially after his death.

Number two in the Politburo Standing Committee is Li Keqiang. Li Keqiang is obviously going to be the next Premier of the State Council, that is, the Prime Minister. His career graph is very closely linked with that of outgoing party Chief Hu Jintao. So he has got his man in at number two in the Politburo Standing Committee and this is noteworthy because his predecessor Wen Jiabao was number three in the Standing Committee, so this reflects in part the kind of compromises that the leaderships, past and present, make in placing their favourites in key positions.

Zhang Dejiang replaced Bo Xilai, the famous Bo Xilai, who was bounced from Chongqing and I suppose in a way this is also a message to Bo Xilai that had he not confronted the party establishment, he would have been in the Politburo Standing Committee. Zhang Dejiang is now positioned at number three. Now my guess is he will be the new chairman of the National People's Congress, which is the parliament. Please note he has been awarded the Hilal-e-Pakistan by President Zardari. Then you have the first ranked person Yu Zhengsheng and my guess is he would be the chairperson of Chinese People's Political Consultative Conference (CPPCC) that is the sort of equivalent of the Upper House in that it allows membership of non-party members and gives a greater weight to the ethnic and other minorities in the country.

Liu Yunshan is the ideologue; so he retains his number five position but what he will actually be doing we don't know yet because the total strength of the PBFC has shrunk from nine to seven and the two people who have been dropped were the people who were doing ideology and national security. These two posts have been relegated, if you like, to the Politburo rather than the Standing Committee.

Wang Qishan will be probably be the First Deputy Prime Minister, and Zhang Gaoli is the other candidate for the job of First Vice-Premier, but we'll have to see what they will do. But the thing to note is that with these seven, you have the pattern that is very clear. You have the General Secretary, Prime Minister, Chairman of the National People's Congress, and Chairman of the CPPCC. So these four are automatically members of the Standing Committee. Two more – they are the ones who are going to make way in 2017 or the two new leaders – number 5 and number 7 are the people who will make way because of their age and the people who fill their positions are going to be China's next leadership – the sixth generation: the person who comes in as number five will be the next secretary general and the person who comes in at number seven will be the next premier. That's how it's going to be played out.

Hu Jintao – there has been a lot of speculation about what happened to his candidates, how he performed. The general assessment is that five out of the seven Standing Committee members owe their allegiance to Jiang Zemin and only two to Hu Jintao. But he has played his cards rather well, given that he had a very serious challenger, or a very serious, powerful person to contend with in Jiang Zemin and the kind of applause that Jiang Zemin got at the Congress made it very clear that he was indeed very popular in the party. One of his closest aides was Ling Jihua, who was the head of the General Department. This is the department that does the secretarial work for the Congress and so his removal on the eve of the Congress was really quite an unprecedented event. He was caught in a scandal; his son crashed while driving a Ferrari, he was drunk, he had two female companions, and the scandal was suppressed for quite a long time. This happened in March, but around September, the story broke and Ling Jihua had to be sacked. Interestingly, Hu Jintao placed him in the United Front Work Department, which is the department that deals with Tibet. Tibet is very important for Hu Jintao – he made his career in Tibet, he went there as party secretary in 1988, and 1989 was the 30th anniversary of the uprising after which His Holiness, the Dalai Lama fled Tibet. Hu Jintao imposed martial law in Tibet, which was the first time in the history of the People's Republic of China (PRC) that martial law was declared. The upside was that the Beijing leadership took rather well to Hu Jintao especially after the Tiananmen massacre and that marked him out in Deng Xiaoping's eyes as the leader of the future.

So at a very young age of 49, Hu Jintao was made a Polítiburo Standing Committee member, which is really quite unusual. Thus, Deng selected the leaders for the next 20 years – Jinag Zemin, followed by Hu Jintao. The other noteworthy point is that he has succeeded in promoting another Hu who is not related to him – Hu Chunhua – as a Politburo member. He is 49 years old, the youngest member in the Politburo and served with him in Tibet, where the younger Hu worked from the mid-1980s to the mid-1990. Clearly Hu Jintao, as he is stepping aside, is concerned about the situation in Tibet in particular and the minority regions as a whole. I suspect that the assessment in the top levels of the Chinese Communist Party is that they are going to face serious challenges going forward, which is why he has brought in Hu Chunhua. My guess is that unless he does something wrong or if Hu Jintao begins to lose power after becoming a party elder, Sun Zhengcai and Hu Chunhua will become members of the new Standing Committee when it is elected in 2017.

Just a quick word on the Work Report that was delivered by Hu Jintao, which was the Work Report on the work of the previous, outgoing Congress. We are all familiar about what he said about corruption, but it's worth repeating because there are very stark words that he has used, to wit, that it could lead to the collapse of the party and the fall of the state. I can't remember hearing this kind of stark warning for a long, long time, especially since the stabilisation after the Cultural Revolution. This kind of warning is really a wake-up call to the party.

Hu Jintao's Work Report

- Corruption Remarks: "If we fail to handle this issue well, it could prove fatal to the Party, and even cause the collapse of the Party and the fall of the state."
- Need to restructure the economy – current model "unbalanced, uncoordinated and unsustainable." China must find an alternative model, more dependent on domestic demand, specially consumer demand.
- Need to be able to "Win a Local War in an Information Age." Probable reference is to Taiwan.
- Important reference to consultative democracy, first such reference in such a major document. The experiment took place in Zhejiang Province when Xi Jinping was Party chief there.

The other thing that is very striking, and this I will dwell on later, is the need to change the economic model. The terms he used for it are "unbalanced, uncoordinated and unsustainable". This unsustainable bit is a conclusion we had ourselves reached in the VIF some months ago because it was very clear that the kind of model on which they were depending, with high investment and rapid export growth, could not be carried on the way they were working it. There is a reference, I think an indirect one, to Taiwan, though the direct references to Taiwan are very mild but the stronger reference was on the ability to win a local war in an Information Age. I guess he is referring to Taiwan and there is one last bit that is about consultative democracy. This is a new thought that has not been much in evidence in Chinese statements, especially by their top leaders, because in consultative democracy while it is an experiment undertaken in a province where Xi Jinping was a party leader, nevertheless, it does imply that the people have the right to reject a party-appointed leader, which is something that is going to be fought over – that's my guess.

To sum up, these are the core interests that they have identified – Taiwan, Tibet, South China Sea and Xinjiang. Sometime last year, late last year, they added their own domestic system as one of the other core issues for the party and as you can see there have been a very large number of social disturbances – 180,000 is the official figure. Social disturbances means any disturbance involving 15 or more people. Many of them perhaps would not be serious, but some of them certainly were, particularly in the village of Wukan in southern China, where they actually reversed the party decision on certain industrial programmes.

I have touched upon the role of party elders, but I think it's worth bearing in mind that now there are going to be two party elders mainly – Jiang Zemin and

Hu Jintao. Jiang Zemin is now 86 years old, hasn't been in very good health, so my own assessment is if Hu Jintao is willing to give way (a) because Jiang Zemin is the more popular leader, and (b) also I think he is biding his time, because he knows that time is on his side; he is much younger and in pretty good health.

I don't know how we are doing for time, but now we come to the implications for India. Our Director mentioned in his introduction that economics is going to be really the driver between all the major players in the Asia-Pacific region and I am going to try and elaborate on that a little bit. I will begin with an extract from an article that was written by Giscard d'Estaing, I suppose you all know him, a former president of France, former finance minister of France, and a man who understands international economics quite well. The important thing is what he says here: "Traditionally a US recovery has fuelled exports of developing countries, increasing their orders of equipment goods from countries such as Japan, Germany and France, and the interdependence between European countries has led to a diffusion in Europe of these expansionary forces."

In short, it is very important to understand how the current global economy is structured. People say China is going to drive future growth. No way, the way the world economy is structured; you can produce all you want, but if there is no effective demand for it, if there is no consumer for it, it's not going to get you anywhere. It's not going to get you profits, it's not going to get you high rates of GDP growth, and in this world today, the two main consumption areas are America and to a lesser extent the European Union. This is what Giscard is actually saying that when America increases its demands for consumer goods, those countries that are producing it – it used to be the Europeans themselves in the 1950s and 1960s, then it shifted to Japan and the Asian Tigers in the 1980s, and then it shifted finally to China, especially after the Asian Financial Crisis – none of them can rise on their own. You see the proof of it once American consumption demands shifted to production coming out of Japan, Europe began to stagnate in the 1980s. It was called "Eurosclerosis". Once they shifted away from Japan to China, you see what happened to Japan. They call them the "Lost Decades" – 20 years of virtually stagnant growth for Japan. This is the key to how the world economy is structured and the key really to the power of the United States and the US dollar.

Now, let's have a look at some of the figures, first about Foreign Direct Investment (FDI). We are all familiar about what China enjoyed; we all are in awe of what the Chinese managed to achieve. But a sampling of what I have taken from the Asian Development Bank shows where the People's Republic was in

1990, and the huge spurt in 1995 – the reason is that in 1994, China devalued its currency by 40 per cent. The Yuan was devalued by 40 percent on the first of January 1994 and immediately FDI started to shoot up. There is marginal drop in 1997-98 – this is the period of the Asian Financial Crisis. Then as China entered the WTO in 2001, there was no further doubt or hesitation about whether America would allow them Most Favoured Nation (MFN) treatment, because earlier if you remember, it used to be on a year-by-year basis. And it ends up in 2007 with record FDI. On that account, India does relatively well, but look at Malaysia; it collapses from 1998 onwards and becomes negative in 2007. Look at Japan; it is negative all the way through. And these are the numbers that really tell you what is happening in the world of economics.

As a result, Chinese exports to Asia declined in importance to their overall export basket from 67 percent to 40 percent. To Europe, it is the reverse. They grow from 14 percent to 23 percent; to America, mainly north and central, from 10 percent to 22 percent. Now this is a pattern to say that declining exports to Asia and significant increases, something like 100 percent, in the exports to Europe and America is unique to China. You will not see it in any of the other countries, whether you are talking about India, or Malaysia, Japan, anywhere – in these countries you see the sharp decline in exports to Europe. This is what really the US-China relationship has meant. Deep down, this the basis on which the very special relationship between these two countries has been sustained. And the remarkable thing is that it has carried on regardless of what the president of the day says, and regardless of the colour of the presidency – Democrat, Republican, makes no difference – this is a standard pattern that continues until we come to the financial crisis of 2008.

Now in a way this is something we need to imbibe, internalise, because India particularly has been one of the focus areas for American thinking in the Asia-Pacific region. Increasingly, we have been told that in this rebalancing, this pivot, whatever you want to call it, India is the lynchpin in the American thinking. People like me have always felt that there is something missing in this strategy because while on the security side we are hearing all the right things, on the economic side, the reverse was happening. Now for the first time you could say the alignments are coming into order.

What do I mean by that? I think you would have heard this thing that the "US is tied to China, and the US is too dependent on China to be able to do anything about confronting, containing, balancing, re-balancing, whatever". Now, this is what I found when I actually looked at the numbers.

US-China Relations in the Global Economy

- Dichotomy: While the Security aspects between the US and China seem to be putting relations under strain, their economic equations have strengthened over the last two decades.
- The common notion that "the US is dependent on China economically" must be questioned.
- In 2011, Chinese investment in US Treasurys was $1.3 trillion. It has now dropped to $1.1 trillion. Meanwhile, the share of investment by Japan, the UK, the Persian Gulf oil exporters and India, has increased.
- $1.1 trillion investment is a big number, but for a US$ 16 trillion economy, it comes to just 6.85% of the US GDP, and the same for its national debt. The US is not dependent on Chinese money, and the trend of Chinese holdings is declining.

In 2011, Chinese investments in US Treasurys were $1.3 trillion; it has now dropped. The last figure is available for I think August 2012; it has dropped to $1.1 trillion. In short, a disinvestment of $200 billion has taken place – 6.85 of the American GDP of 16 trillion dollars – which is also approximately the American national debt. So the total exposure of America today is less than 7 percent. So the notion that America is dependent on Chinese money, Chinese loans, China buying their Treasurys, no longer holds. The two largest holders of American debt are still China and Japan, and you see how significantly Japan has increased its holding. I have put India not because it's a major buyer, but just to clarify that India has also made its small, and growing, contribution to buying US debt. Now I'll quickly run through some of the priorities for America. Obviously, the economy comes number one – the fiscal cliff. The fiscal cliff, personally, in my opinion, there is less to it than meets the eye. What's going to happen is that they are going to revert to the Clinton Era tax rates, and they did very well under Clinton, so it is not as if it is going to be the end of the US economy. It'll also force cuts across the board in their spending, which is no bad thing because America needs to do that anyway. If they can't decide it politically, let it be done administratively. Nevertheless, what is worth noting is that the talks are going on right now and both sides are showing flexibility. The Democrats are saying that they are willing to cut some of the entitlements and the Republicans are saying that they are willing to look at revenue raising options. They began by saying that they only wanted loopholes to be plugged, but lately I am seeing some of the Senators especially are beginning to say that even tax rates need to be re-examined.

US-China Relations

Foreign Holdings of US National Debt (US $ billion)

Country	*Jan 2011*	*July 2011*	*Jan 2012*	*Aug 2012*
PR China	1154	1314	1161	1153
Japan	886	885	1082	1153
Persian Gulf Oil Exporters	215	244	267	263
India	40	40	42	52

Source: US Treasury

The other foreign policy concerns are China and the Asia-Pacific region, Afghanistan and Pakistan and the broader Middle East; Iran would obviously be a top priority. The Euro zone continues to be an area of concern, but they seem to be muddling along for now. The pivot to Asia I have already touched upon.

Now, priorities for China. The economy is obviously going to be their main concern and I do want to emphasize this that the economy is in bad shape; the model that Hu Jintao refers to was heavily reliant on FDI. In fact, there is another UNCTAD study that shows that Chinese exports, or rather 60 percent of Chinese exports were from economic entities that had foreign direct investment. So 60 percent of this export machine was reliant on foreign investments. And we have already seen Hu Jintao saying that the model is unsustainable; the Chinese know it, so they are looking for an alternative, which will be driven by domestic demand. Can they get there? The experiences of the Euro Zone, of Japan, of Korea, all suggest that it is going to be very hard. Korea has run up consumer debt that is of the order of 30 percent of their own GDP, and yet the economy is just about doing 4 percent, which is not bad for an economy that size, but 4 percent isn't what they were doing.

Corruption has been mentioned. Now, foreign policy – you know, this is another thing we need to focus on. From Beijing, they have suffered a number of setbacks ever since they started flexing their muscles around 2007, which is the period when Hu Jintao comes into his own.

The Asia-Pacific region, they've drawn a blank. They are having serious polemics with Japan, Philippines, Vietnam and Singapore. Only Cambodia within that region seems to be comfortable with China, nobody else. Myanmar is changing very rapidly, and the notion that the US president would visit would be unthinkable even a year ago. And of course the Chinese in spite of their demurrals are concerned about it. North Korea, last but not the least the young Kim, is showing interesting signs of wanting to break out of the limitations that he has inherited. To my mind, it seems that China's relations with India have also not done well, and in our last few joint documents, we have stopped referring to 'One China'; we have stopped referring to Tibet as being a part of China. So the hard line that China has adopted in the last five years has been really been counter-productive across the board. The bright spot that I think they can see is in the AfPak region and I suspect that we are going to see some serious frictions as the American draw-down comes closer.

On India, there is very little for me to say to an audience like you. The only point I want to make is we are responding positively to both America and China as we should, and we are looking very seriously at the kind of role that people want us to play in the South China Sea and the broader Indo-Pacific region – all to the good. The only thing is that I think we are either not stressing our concerns openly enough or these are not being responded to in adequate measure. But the fact is that we have our set of problems with both Pakistan and China, and it's important to understand when we make our commitments to the maritime strategy, what is it that we can expect from our partners to be. Normally, when we ask them what we can expect, they say, "This is not an international issue; freedom of navigation at sea is an international issue, but what you are concerned of are not international". To this, I think, we need to evolve some answers. For me, there are two, issues – Tibet and Kashmir – on which, I think, we can express our requirement.

On Tibet, there are three issues that can attract international attention. One is the human rights situation; the other is the water diversion and the damming of the rivers, which affects not just India but a number of other countries in South Asia and South East Asia, and the third of course is that there is a UN General Assembly Resolution of 1961 calling for self-determination for Tibet. Now of course the purist will tell you that a UN General Assembly resolution is not like a UN Security Council resolution, which is true. But we should also remember that the State of Israel came into being as a result of a UNGA vote, not a Security Council vote. So it is not as if a vote in the UN General Assembly is of no value.

On the Kashmir front, I think what is very important is that we should persuade our Western partners and our partners in the Asia-Pacific. I don't know how many of you have noticed this, but since the 1970s, the Line of Control in Kashmir, which used to stop at a point called NJ 9842, has been extended to the Karakoram Pass in a North Easterly direction. Now there's no basis for this; legally the agreement of 1949 says that the Line goes "North to the Glaciers", and on the ground we are exactly on that line. So why has this been drawn? I have never got a clear answer to this, but I think this is something on which we can certainly negotiate with our partners to be, that this is the least that we can expect in return for whatever we want to do together in the maritime space, or the maritime dimension.

Afghanistan, as I have already hinted, is the next, and continuing, hotspot. I think it is important for us to understand that China has somehow managed to keep a very low profile. But increasingly now people are beginning to comment on the approach of China to this region, and that it is not necessarily as negative towards the Taliban and the Islamic forces as many people presume. They presume that because of the problem in Xijiang, the Chinese will be negative, but the fact is that when the Taliban were in power in Kabul, the Chinese did pretty good business with them. And, of course, they are confident that with Pakistan onside, they can contain the negative fallout. In short, China is roughly where the United States was in the 1980s, backing the Mujahideen. These are difficult partners to work with, but these are serving a larger purpose. In the American case, it was to destroy the Soviet Union, in China's case, to embarrass and worse for the United States.

Now China has also signed a Treaty of Friendship with Afghanistan and with Pakistan. In both cases, the text has never been published, so we don't really know what it says, but Pakistani press comments suggest that in the treaty with Pakistan they have committed to uphold the country's territorial integrity. The Americans have also made pretty strong commitments; I think there is a general sense that they are going to just cut and run. It's possible, but I wanted to read this excerpt from their strategic partnership agreement. It says that in the event of any security danger, "the parties shall hold consultations on an urgent basis to develop and implement an appropriate response, including as may be mutually determined, political, diplomatic, economic, or military measures in accordance with the respective constitutional procedures." This is actually stronger than Clause Nine of the Indo-Soviet Treaty of 1971.

I am now coming to the last part, which is the Indian foreign policy choices. We are seeing the emergence, the glimmerings of a strategic realignment, a downturn, between America and China to begin with and this will have its implications for the entire region. America has been very open about the growing weight they attach to India in their policy calculus, and for China, India is of course important in one negative sense, which is, they don't want India to help in any way, aggravating or destabilising the situation in Tibet.

Nevertheless, India is becoming an important partner for both the countries, especially China. Their trade surplus has shrunk to 155 billion in 2011 out of which India contributed 40 billion – 25 percent of the surplus, because China actually runs a deficit with the rest of the world, barring the US, the EU, and India among the main partners. But there are a few countries that are providing surpluses – India is one of them. So economically too, India is important – and I'm mentioning here the role of Walmart. This is an aspect that needs a little more attention because Walmart is the largest private sector of Chinese goods – 30 billion dollars in 2011, whereas all of India bought 50 billion dollars worth of Chinese goods. So wherever Walmart goes, Chinese goods follow. This is something we need to bear in mind as we work our way through the FDI question.

Finally, I want to say that there is this issue going on about non-alignment being the right response. A number of people both in India and abroad are telling us that the best thing to do is to be non-aligned in the face of this increasing stand-off between America and China. Personally, I find that hard to accept. One country is sitting in occupation of our territory, and not only sitting in occupation, it is even refusing to find a solution, even to try. Since 1988, we have been talking, and they haven't even given us their maps; they haven't even indicated where they think the boundary or the Line of Actual Control should run. So I think to be non-aligned in this situation is to be non-aligned with our own vital interests. It is also important for us to maintain very good ties with some of the other major powers and I can straight away think of Russia, France and Israel. Of course, Iran is a challenge, but we need Iran, and I think we are going to have to do some tightrope walking, if you like, because this whole area is going to be unstable for the foreseeable future – you see what's happening in Egypt. So we are going to need to be prepared to be agile and intelligent in our responses.

On some of the gaps in power, I just briefly mention this because people very frequently mention to us, "oh look here, we are one fourth the size of China, you know what dreams you are dreaming?" The fact is that we are not one fourth, we are one third, which is bad enough, but if the rupee were to strengthen, we would be a 2 trillion dollar economy; at 55 rupees we are not, but at 50 rupees to a dollar we are. I wish we would stop talking down the Rupee.

But equally important, look at the gap between India and Pakistan for instance. We are ten times their size – do you ever hear anyone, even in India, pointing this out, so that Pakistan should not tangle with us? No, you don't. Likewise China is half, or less than half of the US GDP – no one tells the Chinese don't tangle with the Americans. So I think we need to stop paralyzing ourselves. What we really need is a little political will and a little better organization. And that brings me to the last part, which is really organising for our defence.

Our economy is good; our structures are extremely good, far, far better than any of the other major economies – and you can see the result just today. The Sensex has climbed 300 points today and Shanghai has fallen to the level of 2009, which was the lowest point in the Chinese economy. So this whole thing about China being in an inexorable steady rise is not true; India is doing economically very well. It's on the security side that we have a problem. We have neglected our defences for the last 20 years or more and it's time to fix that. Once that is done – and we don't need a huge lot of spending – the immediate requirement is to bring up our serviceability, ammunition, spare parts, but get this right so that in the long run you are ready to defend yourself against any contingency.

Last point is I think that with all our major partners we need a new platform for cooperation. I think we have come as far as we could with our Western partners and with China and with Russia. It's time now to review the entire platform and see how we take the relationships forward.

Thank you.

(This talk was delivered by Amb Shukla at the VIF on November 27, 2012)

*

14

CONFLICT ALONG INDIA-CHINA BORDER: MYTH AND REALITY

Shri R.N. Ravi

Director VIF Shri Dovalji and eminent participants,

I thank Mr. Doval for giving me this opportunity to share my perspective on an issue that is crucial. We are talking about the India-China border issue, an issue that is the fulcrum of our relation with China, an issue that has defied solution for the last 60 years.

At the outset, I would like to mention that any public discourse over the India-China border is severely handicapped primarily on account of insufficient, crucial facts that are not in the public domain, facts that are withheld by the governments. This withholding of facts is not a recent phenomenon; it is a legacy.

I would only recall a letter of Prime Minister Nehru, on 26th of September, 1959, which he wrote to Zhou Enlai. By the time much water had flown down the Indus, things had taken a very ugly turn. The letter makes for an interesting, yet sad reading. It carries the flavour of a jilted lover. In that he wrote,

> ...from 1954 till today, you have done a lot of things. You have built over 100 miles of road in Aksai Chin. You killed our soldiers at Longju, detained our patrol for long in Aksai Chin and we didn't tell our people. We didn't even tell our countrymen, hoping that we might be able to settle it among ourselves.

This characteristic of withholding crucial facts about the country is a legacy of those days.

When you read the pieces coming in either the journals or dailies, written by respected and mature analysts, very often one realises that these are essentially based on occasional statements made by our leaders – those in positions of authority. Even statements made by Chinese leaders, publications in Chinese journals, write-ups in our papers or maybe even in third-world countries are referred to. However, all these are written in a manner of interpretation of semantics. For example, I recently read a paper, which has been quoted in some other papers as well, not exactly the same paper, but the same narrative. The narrative was what the Chinese President, Xi Jinping said before the BRICS Summit and what he said on its sidelines. What he said a week before the Summit was that the problem was a legacy of the past and will take time to resolve. What he said on the sidelines of the Summit was that he expected the Special Representatives to strive for a fair, rational and mutually acceptable framework, as soon as possible. So the interpretation is that perhaps there was urgency on China's part to settle the issue.

If the interpretation is on the semantics and devoid of substance, it can be ludicrously absurd. China is not in a hurry to solve this issue. Many a times I feel that the analysts are akin to a character from an anecdote. A man after having a convivial evening comes out to leave for home, walks to his parked car and drops his key at some point, and for the whole night searches for the key under the nearest street lamp. Not because the key was there, but that is where the light was. You pick up a statement given by our leaders, the Chinese or here and there, and use it, while the basic facts have been withheld and not shared with the people at large. Therefore, many a times, the interpretation of the situation is misleading. Now, with this caveat, we will progress the talk for the day.

I will now try to give a short cruise through the history channel, primarily to give the issue the right context. Then we will come to the contemporary myths and realities of our conflict along the border. One of the myths that the Chinese have created, and have been bought by us and our strategic analysts and citizens, is that we have an undefined border with China. Nothing could be farther from the truth. This was written first by Zhou Enlai in his letter to Prime Minister Nehru in January, 1959. Of course, before that he had made some utterances but through this, he made it very specific. Did he mean to say that India and the areas, like Tibet, which were there at that point in time in the past, had no border? By a defined border, if we mean that the border is settled, or delimited, using modern cartographic tools and techniques, satellite imagery, then yes, there was no such border. However, borders in the past were defined customarily by the contours of mountains and course of rivers. Traders knew when they crossed a pass, who they owed a levy to. Those who came by the rivers knew at their landing points, which jurisdiction they paid the levy to, and likewise for pilgrims and other travellers. Borders were defined by customs and traditions, and we had such borders.

When it comes to our Western border with China, we have the treaty of 1842: the Treaty between Maharaja of Jammu, Gulab Singh and the Emperor of China, which is so specific and clear; so clear that four years later when the British set up a boundary commission and set up a cooperation with the Chinese, the Chinese questioned why? We had a clearly settled border and there is no need to revisit that. We'll come to the Eastern sector later. The Gazetteer of Kashmir, of 1891, has a dotted line that shows the external boundary's route. It has clearly marked locations of Aksai Chin and Lingsdan. These were all part of Jammu and Kashmir and were once part of the kingdom of the Maharaja of Jammu. This map was handed over by the Chinese to the British in 1893, when the Russians were moving towards Central Asia and had taken much of it. There was a concern among the British rulers, whether they would come close. The boundary of Ladakh with China was marked in red.

In fact, these were photocopies, so they would not be very clear. For the sake of authenticity, let me state clearly that I have not manipulated these images in any way.

The fact is that the rifts are in the Karakoram range. The boundary in Karakoram Pass is marked and goes beyond this. As I said, this map was given by the Chinese.

After that, in 1908 the Imperial Atlas exactly defines this as well as in the Eastern sector, which shows a boundary running very close to the McMahon line. A postal map of China issued in 1970 also gives the boundary outline, including the Aksai Chin. This was a postal map of China officially issued by them and they had given the outline of the Chinese empire. These positions were very proximate to what we have as the McMahon line. They have carried on with this map; it is not that they changed it.

The mischief began in 1935-36 when they issued, what is called the Sin Pao Atlas in Shanghai. There they started showing Aksai Chin and some bit of our Eastern frontier as part of China. That was the map that they had drawn. As far as we are concerned, the maps had already been settled prior to that for the Western and Eastern sectors. The Chinese maps themselves showed the area that belonged to India. The McMahon line, drawn after the Simla Convention in 1914, confirmed the position, delineating the boundary of Tibet with China, and with India. This had a dark line: what is called Outer Tibet. The space between the red and the black lines is what is called Inner Tibet. The British accepted that the Chinese had sovereignty or a much greater say. As far as Outer Tibet is concerned, it was only suzerainty. The Chinese had a very limited say in the affairs of Tibet. This was signed or initialled by the British, Chinese representative Ivan Chen and Tibetan representative Lochen Shatra. All of them signed the map; however, the Convention was not signed. That was initialled by Ivan Chen, but later he received instructions from Beijing not to sign it. As far as maps are concerned, there was a map that delineated our border with China. If anyone says we have an undefined border with China, they are propagating a Chinese myth. Nothing more than that.

What happened after Independence is very interesting and that is what changed the course of events. Two months after Independence, on 16th of October, 1947, a letter arrived from the Tibetan administration. The present Dalai Lama was very young then, under 14 years of age. One of his ministers dashed off a letter to Prime Minister Nehru asking for the return of the five fingers to the palm. The five fingers were Tawang, Bhutan, Sikkim, Darjeeling and Ladakh. They said these were all parts of Tibet and the imperialist power, the British, had taken over them. Now that they had left, they should be returned to Tibet.

At that time, the Government of India did not pay much attention to it and did not respond to that letter. Later Zhou Enlai quoted this letter, saying they had made a demand. The fact is that this letter warranted a response at that point in time, but perhaps it was thought that Tibetans writing to India should only be met with indifference.

In 1950, after the Chinese PLA moved into Tibet, things started heating up. In 1954, we had an agreement that is known more for its pompous preamble than for its content. This was the *Panchsheel.* I have been at a loss over the last 23 years of my study of this border, in trying to fathom what India gained out of this agreement. Why did we go forward with it? I have talked to people who are much wiser and better informed seeking the answer to this question. There is no rational reason for it. That particular agreement was a total sell-out, which China wanted and needed as they were far more vulnerable then.

India had a special political interest, specifically mentioned in the Simla Convention. Under that, by virtue of being a neighbour, India had placed a telegraph office, trade office and a component of armed detachment to provide protection to these establishments. India even had a treaty marking an independent relationship with Tibet.

China, which had moved into Tibet and was very uncomfortable in dealing with this new territory, wanted to divorce India, which had a history of a special relationship, from Tibet. It is an agreement between the People's Republic of China and Republic of India for trade and cultural interaction between the Tibet region of China and India. The Tibet region of China, without specifically mentioning the autonomy aspect of it and accepting the sovereignty of China and territorial integrity of Tibet in the first part of the preamble, was something they wanted. They needed a commitment from India that China had sovereignty over Tibet and that India should acknowledge this. One of those five preambles was being touted as *Panchsheel*, which we were told as students at the time that '*Chacha*' had given the legacy of this great doctrine as an example of international diplomacy.

The first legacy was the recognition of Tibet's territorial integrity and China's sovereignty over it. The second was non-aggression. The Chinese were very apprehensive since the British used to send military missions. They didn't want us to do that. Third related to no meddling in internal affairs. You shall not interfere no matter what happens in Tibet. Of course, the fourth one was mutual benefit and the fifth one was peaceful co-existence.

The preamble of the agreement and India's acknowledgement of Tibet as a region of China, with China having sovereignty over it, was something they wanted and they got it. We didn't get anything. What was the trade between us at that time? Some salt, some sugar, some yak tails and yak hair, not enough volumes of trade to have an agreement.

Panchsheel was essentially a projection of the then Prime Minister Nehru as the leader of an emerging new world. When the colonies were being liberated, one after another, they had formed a league against imperialism. Many people say, he was far more British than the British themselves. He was carried away and influenced by the rhetoric of anti-imperialism. It was also to prove that we did not have any imperialistic ambitions and that we did not subscribe to the British way of doing things. In so doing, great damage was done. The Simla Convention was undermined. How can you recognise the integrity of a convention when a signatory party to that is not a sovereign power? Therefore, this did a lot of damage.

That was in 1954. By 1958, a lot of other things had happened. Then came

1959, when on 20th of October at Konga Pass, one of our police patrols was disarmed and detained by the Chinese. They had already reached up to that point. The next day, when a larger party went up, they were ambushed and attacked and we suffered heavy casualties. Look at what happened thereafter. On 22nd October, the Chinese wrote a very strong, stinging letter to India, accusing us of provocative and unacceptable behaviour. We responded on 23rd October to the letter and not the event.

We kept quiet. At the time, I don't know what the intention was, whether it was merely lethargy or whether it was intended not to make known this fact to the people of India. However, we only responded after the Chinese letter was received on the 22nd of October.

Till 1958, our patrols used to go up to the outer perimeter of Aksai Chin. In his 1956 letter, Zhou Enlai claimed that this dark line was their position. Their claim was that China had jurisdiction up to that line. By 1960, they had changed this to another dotted line and kept trying to push it forward. We all know what happened in 1962. After that, we went into a cringe mode and retreated. In a map issued by the Government of India in 1960 by the Ministry of External Affairs, the Western sector, the middle sector and the Eastern sector were shown. This map clearly reflects the tradition and custom regarding the boundary that we have had all through.

After that, we had a very volatile situation in 1987. In 1986 when North Eastern Frontier Agency (NEFA) became Arunachal Pradesh as a state, the Chinese reacted strongly. We had our own defences and in 1987 we had a showdown at Namkachu in Arunachal. Thereafter, the Chinese continued maintaining the fiction of Line of Actual Control (LAC) and kept the concept of LAC dynamic, without freezing it in any location. The existence of the LAC is another myth, which has been told to us by our government from time to time. Recently in April when there was a situation in Depsang in the Western sector, the government said it was only a perception of violation of LAC. The Line of Actual Control is a myth and we do not exactly know for sure where this line is drawn. Ask the troops at the border; they are confused about this specific aspect.

We have created another concept called LOP or Line of Patrol. This is far behind the supposed LAC, which is perceived based on who is there at a location to defend it. We have a Line of Patrol further behind, with instructions to our troops not to cross this LOP and not to go near the LAC. We have been restraining our troops, not allowing them to go or even be present at the LAC to consolidate and ensure that the LAC, as we perceive it, should be defended.

Often in writings we also hear about disputed pockets. Again, these are a myth. What is a disputed pocket? The entire border is disputed. Whenever they create a situation, we say it is disputed. It is a dispute that has been created by the Chinese. Wherever they show aggression, we mark those areas as disputed pockets.

Except for the Sikkim border that was settled through the Treaty of 1890, the rest of the border remains unsettled, unresolved. I do not subscribe to the notion that we have disputed pockets. Many people believe that 9 pockets or 10 pockets are disputed. However, when an entire border is disputed, where does the concept of disputed pockets come from?

There are certain contemporary realities that we should be aware of. These realities are that there has been a spurt in intrusions, more so after 2008-09. On an average, since 2009, there have been over 400 intrusions. These intrusions were not merely minor detachments or a small patrol straying into our area. These were aggressive intrusions. Here 'aggressive' means intrusion by troops in larger strength, rarely less than a platoon in strength. In fact, it was often more than a platoon commanded by officers. These were not small detachments led by their NCOs coming and walking in. They were more aggressive in their behaviour, aggressive in terms of manpower, ordnance and even in terms of the rank of officers commanding them.

For the last couple of years, 2009 onwards, there have been more frequent air intrusions too. We find more helicopters, aircraft and unarmed vehicles making forays into our areas. In 2011, there were 30 such air intrusions.

These are not random pinprick tactics. Recently, when there was an incident in Depsang, our Prime Minister said it was a localised issue, as if it was some kind of skirmish. That was not the case. These were strategically focused in certain areas they consider crucial to them. What happened in April in the Western sector is an example. This incident got leaked to the media. They somehow got to know about it and subsequently became a topic of discussion. Many people however, don't know that in 2009, the Chinese had built a 15-km road that came close to our Trig Heights junction. In 2010, they had completed about 23 km of the road. This is not one of the accurate maps; there is a Jeevan Naala below Burshe. This axis, that we have here, the Karakoram, Daulat Beg Oldie, Tri-junction and Burshe, has posts along it. Moving up to Trig Heights, they have the capability to deny us access to maintaining Daulat Beg Oldie post. By striking us at Jeevan Naala, they are developing the capability to block our movement beyond Burshe. Not that they have acquired the capability yet, but they are nonetheless increasing our vulnerability. This has been going on for the last many years. The country, however, is not completely aware of it.

Of the 400 odd intrusions taking place on average, around 250 are in the Western sector and the remaining 100-odd in a pocket of the Eastern sector. In the Western sector, mostly you will find that the Pangong Lake is the gateway to the entire North sub-sector. Over 100 intrusions take place here by boat and by road, sending their troops along. Of course, inside they are building roads and other infrastructure that are coming up very close to our supply lines. It is focused, and I will come to the reasons for that very shortly.

So why is it that all this has picked up after 2009? What happened in 2008 or 2009 that prompted the Chinese to be aggressive? In 2008, we got the news of the Tibet uprisings again. A lot of things happened in Tibet during 2008 in the run-up to the Olympics. It was in that year that Xinjiang, the adjoining province erupted. There was a massive riot in which over 200 people were killed. You must have read in the newspapers two days back that 27 people have been killed in Xinjiang again. In April, there were 21 killed. This too was all over the media.

Xinjiang is boiling. There the unrest is unlike what the Tibetans do; they self-immolate. Here they were killing and were also getting killed. Xinjiang is in turmoil. Tibet is not yet pacified, and is unlikely to be pacified in the foreseeable future.

Meanwhile, under the 1963 agreement, an area of about 5,100 sq. km. in Pakistan occupied Kashmir (PoK) was ceded by Pakistan to China. On the map, this can be seen along Xinjiang. The tri-junction that we had with Afghanistan and Xinjiang has now shifted. Our northern frontier had three ranges – Hindu Kush, Mustaad and the Karakoram. Of these, two ranges have been virtually pushed back from our frontier and the de-facto tri-junction now lies somewhere where the Karakoram Pass and the small Siyog Valley area that is ours. Of course, one can say that there is a big mountain between Nubra and Shyok; it would be difficult to cross. But then, nothing is impossible in this age of technology.

The point is that there is a very small corridor and the Chinese are denying us the capability in this corridor, thereby distancing us from Xinjiang. They believe that a troubled Xinjiang in the vicinity of India is not good for them. They are doing this with a purpose and I would link it to the 2009 disturbances that became apparent in Xinjiang province.

Coming to the Eastern sector, among the 400 intrusions, nearly 250 are in the area of Ladakh, Pangong and above. Over 100 intrusions are taking place in the eastern sector at a point where Lohit enters from Tibet into India in the Anjao district of Arunachal Pradesh. That is the point where they are pushing forward. They had an agreement with Burma in 1960 by which they shifted the tri-junction 8 kms down to a place called Diphu Pass. There is a mountain range there that is the source of the Dichu River. It flows down and becomes a tributary of Lohit. They have shifted the tri-junction to that point. The Indian patrols cross there and move along the Dichu River. They are thus denying us the ability to cross and come near the tri-junction.

What is the ground situation? These intrusions started again in 2009 and have been increasing in numbers each year since. At the point where the McMahon Line goes over what is known as Madan Ridge and forks into two (Northern and Southern), from this point on in all terms, it is the Northern Ridge that should have been considered as the Line. Somehow, we have pulled ourselves back to the Southern Ridge. What the Chinese have done is to have built the road in the passage that comes between the two rivers. They are working on building this road right up to the Southern Ridge. This is very close to the point where Dichu meets Lohit, the point from where our patrol goes to the tri-junction. As a result, this entire area is now vulnerable and likely to fall to Chinese control. When this falls, it doesn't mean that we will be up to that point. Beyond this Ridge, the next point is close to Walong. If you are pushed further from Walong, you come up to a point that is close to the Lohit and then the plains of Assam.

These are the aggressive designs, both on the Eastern and Western extremities. In between at Shipki and Korik in Himachal, and Barahoti in Uttarakhand, they have created problems by sending troops further inland. All the passes that lead to Tibet except from Sikkim – where the border is well fortified by them and us – they are blocking them, thereby blocking any access to Tibet or Xinjiang. On the Eastern extremity, they are pushing us down to points of higher vulnerability.

Meanwhile, what are we doing in this process? We remain in a state of self-denial. Every time something happens, we try to play it down as if nothing big has happened. Our Foreign Ministry record calls what happened in Depsang, an acne. By playing it down, we are playing into the hands of our adversary, making it seem as if nothing has happened. By publicly playing it down and restraining our troops from confrontation, the face-offs are seen as fewer in numbers. It is often said that there is an exponential increase in intrusions; the natural corollary of that should be greater number of confrontations. How, then, is it that the number of face-offs keep declining? There are hardly 6-8 confrontations being reported in a year. This is only because our troops have been restrained as a matter of policy.

What happens thereafter is very interesting. Whenever there is a face-off, the Chinese carry a placard that says "Indians go back". Indian side will say "Chinese go back". Along with these, there will be another banner that will say, "*Hindi Chini bhai bhai*". We carry two sets of placards. This is not the way to secure a frontier. In fact, we are doing a great disservice to the country.

What should then be done? As a student of this border for so many years, the first thing that occurs to me is that unless we get out of this self-denial mode, there will be no answers. We need to accept that there is a serious problem here and that it needs to be resolved. Not all problems need be sorted out through war. There are alternative tools. We need to take recourse to these. However, when we deny the existence of a problem, how do we even address it? We must set right our strategic coordinates. What are our interests? Nobody has seen tomorrow. No one had predicted that the USSR would disintegrate the way it did. There is nothing to say China will not disintegrate tomorrow.

Xinjiang opens up our access to all the Central Asian Republics. We are being denied access to that whole region. Are these losses acceptable to us or do we need to ensure that we do not suffer them anymore? After taking a clear, strategic view of it, what we need to do is not to treat these as localised incidents or mere skirmishes. Having a broader, strategic perspective, we need to augment our border infrastructure. This is badly needed and everybody knows it.

Geography apart, we are in a terribly asymmetric situation when it comes to infrastructure along the border with China. We have been very slow at pursuing this. There is also a need to review whether we need to keep our troops occupied in a sector that is not of high relative priority. Let us take the case of IV Corps. They are supposed to help us defend against the Chinese in the Eastern sector. However, two entire Divisions of the Corps are involved in counterinsurgency operations. Can we give this further thought? We need to take our border with China more seriously.

At the end, I will say that the government needs to share certain crucial facts with the people and believe in the collective wisdom of the country. A handful of people in the government alone are not patriotic. Nobody can say that one person is more patriotic than the other. We are all Indians, and we are proud of our country. We have as much stake as anyone in the government. Therefore, take advantage of the collective wisdom.

I have not gone into the Chinese defence preparations, but only discussed what we have on our side. Essentially, my attempt has been to highlight the increasing vulnerabilities, and how in self-denial, we have been retreating in the face of Chinese aggressive tactics, that the Chinese have been strategically aggressive in a focused manner, in certain chosen sectors, and we have not been able to defend our positions.

Thank you so much.

(This lecture was delivered by Shri Ravi at the VIF on June 28, 2013. The slides and illustrative maps shown during the presentation are unfortunately not available at VIF)

*

15

Rise of Islamism as a Direct Consequence of the Creation of Pakistan

MrTarek Fatah

Thank you for inviting me. I want to give my perspective on why I think in Pakistan lies both the problem and the answer: the question and the answer to why the rest of the world, why human civilisation involved in what I would call the fourth World War, the third being the Cold War that was, you know, only cold for Europe. It was pretty hot, as M J Akbar mentioned, in Ethiopia or Congo or Vietnam or Cambodia or a whole lot of places where proxy wars between the Warsaw Pact and North Atlantic Treaty Organisation (NATO) were fought. India was in a security pact with the Soviet Union and Pakistan was part of Central Treaty Organisation (CENTO, earlier on with what was called the Baghdad Pact) and South East Asia Treaty Organization (SEATO).

But let me go back to the end of the Second World War where you will find the birth of Pakistan taking place. On May 5 (1945), fighting had died down in Berlin and the West was trying to weasel out a deal with the Nazis on the Baltic side and on areas north west of Denmark to create a government there, and a separate peace talk of surrender to the United States and Britain was going on. Berlin had already fallen to the Red Army by May 7; all fighting had died down, and the war was over.

On 5th of May 1945, Churchill in his wisdom was less worried about Europe than he was about India, for what he called British interests in the Indian Ocean region. On that day, he asked the cabinet to come back to him, or his Cabinet

Secretary to come back to him within 15 days as to the impact of the Soviet Union and the Red Army winning the war against the Nazis and its impact on British India and the British interests in the Indian Ocean.

Fifteen days later, the report that was presented to him said quite explicitly that the Red Army had already created two states in Iran – one was Mahabad, a few of not surviving republics now, and an Azeri Republic. Both were formed with Kurdish and Azeri Communists. Afghanistan was under a pro-Soviet king, with very close relations with the ruling Indian National Congress. In the Far East, the Quilon Islands had already been taken over by the Red Army. In this geostrategic situation, the West had no armies and the Soviet Union had about 20 million men under arm. It needs to be noted that 30 million Russians had already died. It was a country fully geared for a very long-term war. Churchill asked the Indian National Congress for the right to establish military bases, of primarily Britain as the leading power. United States at that time was secondary. In North West India, which today means what is Pakistan, they had in mind some of the princely states that were Swat, Gilgit and all these areas.

The Indian National Congress, as expected, said a flat "No" – that post-independence, the Republic of India will have absolutely no place for foreign military bases. That is when the idea of Pakistan was first floated – I'm talking of 1945. You have to see that in the 1939 election, the Muslim League had been wiped out. And then 1946 elections were prepared for, and for the first time with active British help, to enable the Muslim League to create the buffer state that was absolutely necessary to stop the Red Army from reaching literally up to the Arabian Sea, which the Chinese, by the way, are now doing quite effectively. So, with the 1946 elections, in fact, even before that, Mr. Jinnah was quite content to have Pakistan and what was later to become East Pakistan. Punjab didn't have a Muslim League government, the NWFP had a Congress government, in Sindh, Allah Baksh Sumroo was pro-Congress, and Balochistan, by the way, became an independent country three days before India, and Pakistan became independent. So the state of Kalat had direct relations to West Hall and not to Delhi. It was in this framework that the Islamic state of Pakistan was created. A lot of effort was put together in the elections of 1946. The only place where the Muslim League formed a government was Bengal with H S Suhrawardy as the Prime Minister. Punjab did not have a Muslim League ministry.

If you look at it from that point of view, then the Islamic state was nurtured for the Third World War, which was the Cold War, to use the forces of Islamism to fight against the infidel atheism – that was coming out from the teachings of Karl Marx and Engels and implemented by Stalin and later by Mao Tse Tung (Mao Zedong) in China. And this is why, if you do not understand the significance of Pakistan, as to why we have an Islamist movement around the world today, your analysis or outcome will fall flat. If you want to visualise an India that was undivided, I can assure you there would be no Islamic state in Syria and Iraq. The concept of an Islamic state was absolutely foreign to the Arabs, to the Iranians, to Turks, to Indonesians and to Indians to a large extent, till the turn of the 20th century.

You will have to understand that Iqbal's *Qorana* only became a *Militarana* after Tagore got the Nobel Prize, which is another big division that occurred. I wish they had given it to Iqbal; a lot of problems of ego would have been settled. But imagine the points where these turns take place. There was no poet in Iran in the last 500 years who talks about an Islamic state. There was no Arab that wanted it. The entire political movement of the 18th-19th centuries talked of the nation state. In fact in Islam, if it had a golden period, it was from 1850 to 1950. It is the only time where after comprehensive defeats, people came to recognise that the printing press was superior to writing the Quran by hand. It was not something holy; it could be done by a printing press. By the way, the last handwritten newspaper in Pakistan got printed in the late seventies. Jung was still being hand-written all these days. So supreme was the thought that writing with a pen on paper was holy, and printing on a press was unholy. If you recall, when the Portuguese brought the printing press to a Mughal emperor, he asked what was the Caliph saying; they said that Caliph in Istanbul was saying this was 'haram'. Then the Mughal emperor said, 'let the Christians of India use it as much as they want and the Muslims will stay back'.

Between the era of 1850 and 1950, you find people critiquing, questioning Iqbal's *Shikwah* and *Jawab-e-Shikwah*, but the man who takes pride in India and mocks God, within 10 years, has surrendered himself to the power of the Islamists and becomes a pan-Islamist. By the way, he wrote to the foreign minister of Iran saying, "Don't you know that Tagore is a Hindu, who's a Bengali and you are inviting him, not understanding that he is working against the interests of Muslims of India?" I wish he were alive and had heard that the Bangladeshis honour him as the national poet. Such are the people who made Pakistan. So is the case if you look at the Islamic Republic of Iran, the Kingdom of Saudi Arabia, the Islamic State of Boko Haram, Taliban, Al Qaeda, Lashkar-e-this and that, Jhangvis, and all these Pakistan Army irregulars who in one form or the other follow the essence of what came about in Militarana of Iqbal first printed in 1924 in Lahore.

They say, Iqbal wrote these after he came back from Europe, and is based on the false notion that the nation state can only be formed on the basis of religion. So, a failed construct was launched by a man who didn't know what Islam was! Secondly, both Iqbal and Jinnah had the heritage of a very close Hindu past. It was their grandfathers who were Hindus; it's not people who were 8th-generation Muslims who had forgotten where they came from. All of this epitomized in the Islamic Republic of Pakistan and my suggestion to you is that till the Islamic Republic of Pakistan exists, as long as it stays, India will not have peace because its very essence, its existence, is based on hatred of its heritage. It's not just a hatred of the Hindus, but a hatred of itself that says that I am not a Punjabi, I'm some Kazakh who came and invaded and raped Lahore, and therefore, my missile will be called Abdali!

It is so bizarre that when no other human history, no other people in human history could be accused of celebrating the rapist, the people who raped Lahore are celebrated! And what is even more interesting is that the victims of these marauders were often fellow Muslims, that the Pakistanis only celebrate Babar, not Lodi. They have no clue who is Lodi. And Babar could say that 'this was absolute rubbish country'; what sort of people were they? Look at the colour of their skin; the admiration was for that white person from north Central Asia. He was a purer Muslim. And if you think that a bit of education would do you good, then you should ask why educated Indians and Muslims educated in the UK are heading towards the Islamic Sate of Iraq and Syria (ISIS)? Why the Indian peasant who is not very educated in Patna or Hyderabad is not going there? That falls flat on the argument that the real problem is enlightenment. Unless you destroy the notion of Islamism and Jihad, and Sharia, you cannot have enlightenment. And for all my Indian Muslim friends who stay shy in taking on this beast that is out to destroy Indian civilisation, I think it is time for you to stake responsibility because Shah Waliullah came from you.

The first pan-Islamist and the first pan-Islamism predate the movement for Pakistan. It even predates Iqbal's *Militarana*; it goes back to Shah Waliullah and Abdal Wahab who met in the 'enlightened' Kingdom of Saudi Arabia where in the 1750s everyone believed that the world was flat. Both Abdal Wahab and Shah Waliullah believed that the world was flat. And when the Muslim Ummah is to take the inspiration from these two people who caused immense harm to the Muslims of India, in the end, the victims of Islamism are often Indian Muslims who are dark skinned, who are not even allowed to fight next to ISIS guerrillas, and are only employed as cooks, cleaners and sanitation workers in the Islamic State of Iraq and Syria, or whatever they call it.

So look at how far back it is going without the presence of Islamism. And by the way, Shah Waliullah and Abdal Wahab did not come in a vacuum. They entered the field at the worst part of Indian Islamic history. Which is what you guys celebrate on your streets – Aurangzeb. No other people would name a street after someone so brutal, someone so murderous, someone so hateful of Hindus and Shias and Zoroastrians, his own father, his brother, his son, his sister. He was culpable in three murders – even Dara Shikoh doesn't have a street named after him in Delhi, but Aurangzeb has. Some of Pakistan has rubbed onto you and it's done pretty bad. So we cannot get this through our heads that meeting Pakistanis and allowing them to run circles around us is good, because it is so good to feel that we met our enemy! '*Dost se sabhi gale milte hai, koi dushman se mile, toh baat alag haina*'. So, '*ye ego satisfy karne ke liye ham Pakistanis se gale milke aaye, Lahore mein kisi ne hamse bill nahi liya!* Did you ask them about how you feel about the two-nation theory? '*Nahi nahi, us tak baat hi nahi hui, Nihari muft mein khaa li, sahib ghar mein bula liya, chaat pe*'. I'm so sick and tired of guilt-ridden Hindus feeling good about Lahore and Karachi, but I can't get my head over it. '*Bhai did you ask, will your daughter be allowed to marry a Hindu? No no, us tak baat hi nahi aayee sahib, Itna naashta khilaya*'. For goodness sake, does the guy believe in two-nation theory? If he does, he is a hatemonger, he is a Fascist, and he should be rejected. If he believes in his Indian heritage, he is free to be a Christian, or a Muslim, or a Hindu, Buddhist? I mean if a '*Baba*' created a whole new movement, nobody told him that he has left India; he is as Indian as Guru Nanak, isn't he?

This is a place that flourished religions – the gentleman comes and lives in Ajmer where there are no Muslims, and most of his followers are non-Muslims. The first mosque in India is near Kochi, about 100 miles north of it. Many found that partition '*ho gaya, sir mujhe zameen chahiye masjid ke liye*'. The local residents said, 'that's okay, you want a mosque, we will build it for you.' Now look at it that way – not a single Indian Muslim considers that to be the arrival of Islam in India. No, we like it to come on horseback – like that Mohammed bin Qasim. The invasion of this land is celebrated in Old Delhi, in Urdu books authored by Nasim Ijazi and he sold it for 30 rupees each. But it's written in Urdu that nobody in India now reads. So, you go to Srinagar and it is written in Urdu, '*America Murdabad and Ayatollah Khomenei Zindabad*'. Nobody knows '*ke kya keh rahe hain*'? In Balochistan, by the way, there is a mountain on which it is written, '*Ab*

Ki Baar Modi Sarkar,' and every Indian thinks it is written '*Allah ho Akbar*'. How would you know that? I can't read Gujarati. If in Gujarati it's written, ''*bakery*' and somebody tells me it is 'no parking', I'll take it as 'no parking'.

Some Indians will have to die to fight this Jihad. And they will have to be Muslims. The responsibility is on us; we have found refuge in Hindustan. Do you know that the prophet's family sought refuge in Raja Dahir of Sindh when no place on earth allowed them? Do you know that Mohammed bin Qasim came here to take the prophet's family and hang them in Baghdad and Damascus? *Pata hi nahi kisi ko*. Ghazi Sheikh-e-Mazar – people who have been to Karachi will see it right on the coast, in Clifton – is one of the descendants of the prophet killed by Mohammed bin Qasim. And who is the hero for Muslims, Mohammed bin Qasim, and who is followed, Prophet Mohammed, '*Sal Allahu Alayhi Wa-Sallam*'. Are you crazy? I mean how much sense does one have to make mathematically, physically, historically, sociologically, archaeologically to say, 'For goodness sake, *kabhi toh bête ka naam Ashok rakh lo. Kab tak Arabo ka naam rakkhoge?*'

Islam doesn't mean that you have to have Arab names, because Arabs could be atheists, Christians, Jews. *Woh to apne naam nahi badal rahe hain! Irani kyun nahi rak rahein hai Arab naam, Turk bhi nahin rakh rahein hain, Indonesian bhi nahi rakh rahe hain. Unki Islamic University pe likha hua hai 'Greeish Temple'. Kya humne thekha liya hai ki har naam Arab ka ho?* How can I be Tarek Fatah? Seriously,I don't know what my parents were thinking – was I going to conquer Spain? My brother, by the way, is named Mehmood. So they named two sons after two generals. Now they are not political people but imagine Tarek Ali's mother who recently died, from the Communist Party of India, named her own son as an Islamic general.

In India, we have a serious problem: not identifying yourself primarily as Indian and then as a Muslim, or a Jew, or whatever, or an atheist, or whatever you wish to be. You can wear whatever you want. You can come in a lungi, you can come in a suit, you can wear a bow tie, you can do anything. Flexible piece of art! If the entire universe died and India was left, there would be nothing dead. Five hundred years ago there were a billion people; we'll start again with a billion people. Every religion, every colour, *gore se leke kala, sab hamare pass hain, French bhi hai.* Wajahat the author, was writing about the *Veda. Batayen, jahan Dara Shikoh paida ho ke mar gaya, jahan French writer hai, jahan meri Dadi, who was French, uski qabar hai Bombay mein, where the* only thing is respect for the other – *unhe thorah sa shukriya karne ki adat dalo ki bhaiya Mohammad ke family ko panah di thi.* Thank you so much. *Taimur ne pahar banae Hindu skulls ke, galti ho gaee, maaf kar do, yehi toh humne suna hai kitna zulm nahi kiya hamne, panch sau tees saal tak kiya.*

What is wrong in having a frank discussion about the sanctity of believing in your religion and making sure that this curse called the Islamic Republic of Pakistan that is planted in our souls is facilitated to disintegrate, because it will; so the sooner, the better. Once painlessly it is done, less people will suffer. But for that you cannot have the drama that you enact at the Wagah border. That is the single biggest accomplishment of Pakistan to show that they and India are equal. You don't even understand who we are dealing with. Facing you are people who want to die and I am not exaggerating. If we believe that earth is a transit lounge and here you are to take a connecting flight to paradise, then why would you be just looking at the time on the departure flights – *yaar kab hai flight, yeh kab, delay ho gaya hai, jitni jaldi jaaye utna zyaada phaida.* One side wants to die, the other wants to live. We have to deny them death. And you can deny them death by winning the ideological war. And the ideological war can only be won if there is not a single anti-Muslim rhetoric even from the far-right Hindu nationalists.

We started with the thesis that the fight/war against Islamism cannot be won as long as there's an Islamic state of Pakistan, as along there's Saudi Arabia that feeds it, as long as India caters to Saudi money and as long as India caters to Iranian petroleum ventures. You are in a fix; you want to win and retain your country as a liberal democracy – poor or rich, it shouldn't matter. If you want dignity and respect, don't talk about economic progress, talk about the moral progress, but you are not able to retake your moral high ground of your 5000-year-old civilisation. You cannot tell your children *that 'Sindh to chala gaya, Punjab aur Sindh joh aapke national anthem mein hai', aur aapke bachcho ko pata hi nahi ki* Lahore is the city of Ram's son. People don't know that Mahabharata was fought in Punjab, not in some area which they would like you to believe. It's all in the Indus Valley, and you lost it. In fact, you do not even have a sense of what you lost. Can you imagine a Muslim saying *Mecca chala gaya, theek hai yaar.* It's not possible; it's impossible. So you have to ask your Muslim intelligentsia to rise – the M J Akbars, or General Ata, but these voices are not being heard. *Nikalen Dara Shikoh, Upanishads ko translate karen, aur samjaye inko ki* this is it, *jannat yahin hai. Jannat Pakistan ya America nahi hai. Maine toh sir aapke yahan apply bhi kiya thaa citizenship ke liye, lekin Pakistani koh pehle baar aap citizenship nahi denge.*

Tell your intelligence, professors, academics, generals, writers to stop this

'*Aman ki Aasha*'. We don't need talks; the only thing that Pakistan can offer is international terrorism, and we don't want it. There is no need to attend any Pakistan Day events – it is a slap on your face when Indian stooges of Pakistan proudly come on TV and say, 'We are not Indian'. – it's infuriating. Where did the fellow come to? He came to the Pakistan High Commission in India; where do you think he was going to – Baghdad. And if he doesn't like India, why didn't people tell him to go away? And you must realise that Pakistan comprises just two communities of people – Muslim Punjabis and Urdu-speaking UPites that you sent to destroy Sindh. And Sindhis will not forgive you for that, *but who baad ki baat hai*. Other than that, we cannot see a Pakistani flag flying in Baluchistan. *Jin pahaaro pe 'Abki Baar Modi Sarkar' likha hai, wahan jitney bhi fauj bhej dein, Bangladesh banega wahan pe.*

Another thing that I am begging you folks to tell your politicians and friends is that you have to, at some stage, seriously think of calling the Kashmir bluff. Yesterday, I asked about 200 students, and not a single one of them had read the UN Security Council Resolutions. Chances are most Indians in the academia have not read it. I am stunned at the position that India takes that it is a bilateral issue. I mean nobody even understands what is bilateral – where is Shimla, who is Indira Gandhi, who is Zulfiqar Ali Bhutto? Simple reason is that the first point of that old UN Security Council Resolution is that Pakistan Army and every civilian has to withdraw from areas that it has occupied after 1947, right? Who else is there – 50,000 Chinese troops? *Arey inka bluff kaat ke to dekho*, you will not hear them come back because you will tell the *Chinese*, who have taken 25-30 billion dollar from you, '*kya apke fauj Baltistan occupy kiya hai*' and you have to now move out.

I've been enough times to the UN, and the UN Rights Commission in Geneva and see Indian diplomats on the back foot. You have to listen to what Haqqani said. I think he is the only Pakistan diplomat who is anti-Pakistan, and he says, 'I would feel so awkward that my points are getting across while the Indian side is not making the right argument'. It's ridiculous. The guy is on your side; the guy becomes Pakistan's Ambassador to the United States of America and one magazine says India needs 50 diplomats to deal with that sharp fellow who's actually from Delhi. Second, whether you agree with me or not, but think about calling the Kashmir bluff; the air will go out of their bags. You think two million Pakistanis living there will say, 'okay', – in Mirpur, where construction of Mangla Dam has pushed two million Pakistanis to the United Kingdom, they are Mirpuris, Punjabi settlers in Jammu and Kashmir, but no one knows that they are not Kashmiris and they don't speak Kashmiri. By the way, Lord Nazir is not a Kashmiri.

India still has the right to retain military control of the Valley and Srinagar. This is in the UN Security Council resolutions. Everything in the resolutions favours India. There's nothing that favours Pakistan. *Plebiscite tak toh baat hi nahi aaygee, who aur baat hai ki* legally Pakistan is bound not to raise the subject. However, you have NGOs to raise those issues. Why can't your Foundation call the bluff?

In today's day and age, you can affect public policy by non-state actors who don't use AK-47s but Twitter and Facebook, and you can effect change in policy. It has been done. We banned Sharia in Canada totally with just ten people and social media. And General Zia-ul-Haq's Minister of Religious Affairs who implemented Sharia in Pakistan got Canadian citizenship and was implementing it in Ontario as its launch base for all of the United States. And we decimated them. Sharia was banned in Canada. And the effect? There's no anti-Muslim feeling in Canada. You would never hear of an anti-Muslim incident there because non-Muslim Canadians know that there are enough Canadian Muslims to take care of these lunatics. Where there is no one speaking out against the Jihadis, or Muslims saying that Jihad is a foreign construct – like in the United States and Britain – you will always encourage anti-Muslim appetite that is not fulfilled.

Do these few things and I can tell you it will put Pakistan on the back foot. Finally, you have to understand that in 1948, March 27, the Pakistan Army invaded the independent state of Kalat and occupied it. It has since had six or seven civil wars. Eighteen thousand young men from villages are missing, 50,000 are dead and no Indian knows about this. (Member from the audience says, 'Even Nawab Bugti was killed'; Fatah replies, 'Well he was gassed, not killed, they are using chemical weapons that sucks away oxygen, and you die out of being choked'.) The places where the Baloch have fought are mountain alleys in which only one person can go and come. The Marri areas where this war is being conducted, or in the south, there are no 'sardars'. There are doctors and engineers and ordinary workers who are dying. They begged from the Khwaja, with his brother in Balochi, '*aap toh jaa rahe hain Hindustan, unko bolna ki khana hi drop kar dein hamare liye, kapde, khambal daal dein, aur bamboo kyon nahi daal sakte in par. Yaan iitne bade mulk pe kabza hua hai, yeh jo Kalat State India ka Taluk thaa*'. Bizenjo was a poster friend of Jawahar Lal Nehru. He was a member of the Central Committee of the Communist Party, moved around with all those people, played in Aligarh in a football field there. And you abandon these people.

Bada mulk hoga, toh responsibility bhi lenee padegi. Aap Bhutan nahi hai, India hain. And the world looks at India as the only country that can offer a civilisation *jisme rang, nasl, mazhab, nationality ka jhagra hai hi nahi. Ab Manipur se Kashmir tak aur Keral se Kashmir gaayen us Iqbal ka 'Sare Jahan Se Achcha". Lekin aapko doosron ka kyal rakhen, yeh zimmedari aap pe aati hai*. You have to look out for Tamils of Sri Lanka; nobody else will. They have been defeated but there are still problems there. Who's going to talk about the Baloch? Why should Bangladesh be abandoned in such a way that Pakistan has a more infiltration in Bangladesh through the ISIS than India has? How is that ISIS people from Iraq and Syria are meeting in Chittagong? Even today a report in Dhaka Tribune said so. You know what I would do; I would just tweet that Pakistan's nukes are no threat to us because all the Pakistani officers there are on our payroll. *Kal se harek ki* checking! *Kam se kam chhe mahine ke liye satyanas hoga* – I overheard three serving generals say, 'satyanas ho jayega sab ka'. Be like the Pakistanis who cheat; I mean you can't win by straight methods.

These are very devious people. They are not bad; they just don't know who they are. Have you ever heard Pakistan television guys debate in Urdu? And in the Punjab National Assembly, you are not allowed to speak in Punjabi; that creates for dysfunctional people who need to be corrected. The day *Pakistan* dies, Punjab will be a landlocked country which will wake up to see "*yaar saade naal ki hoeya?*" Are there any people in the world who are 100 percent illiterate in their own mother tongue?

And all of this can be done by India with minimal expenditure by just showing the high moral ground and say Baloch are our brothers; they have been. You know, if you look at the genetic code of most of India, the Baloch have, I think, 40 percent of our strain. Our DNA is coming from the Baloch; we don't know, we think it is just some Saraswati River that just disappeared somewhere. It is a reality; Balochistan is as big as France, and it is the most pro-India place on earth that the Indians don't know about.

Thank you so much for bearing with me. I think that some of what I said did not suit the academia level that so many official Indians expect all the time, so please be critical of me. I'll be more than happy to answer your questions.

Thank you.

(This lecture was delivered by Mr Fatah at the VIF on March 25, 2015)

*

Index